SURVIVING THE STREET

ABOUT THE AUTHOR

Gerald W. Garner, a 28-year veteran of law enforcement, is a captain with the Lakewood, Colorado Police Department. The holder of a Master's Degree in Administration of Justice, he has served as a guest lecturer for the FBI National Academy, the International Association of Chiefs of Police and various colleges, law enforcement academies and police specialty schools. Specializing in officer safety topics, Garner has published six books and over 150 magazine articles. His law enforcement assignments include tours as a patrol officer, patrol supervisor, SWAT team member, detective sergeant, watch commander, press relations officer, academy director, internal affairs manager, crimes against persons detectives commander and informational services manager.

SURVIVING THE STREET

Officer Safety and Survival Techniques

By

GERALD W. GARNER

Police Captain
Lakewood Police Department
Lakewood, Colorado

CHARLES C THOMAS • PUBLISHER, LTD.
Springfield • Illinois • U.S.A

Published and Distributed Throughout the World by

CHARLES C THOMAS • PUBLISHER, LTD.
2600 South First Street
Springfield, Illinois 62794-9265

© *1998 by* CHARLES C THOMAS • PUBLISHER, LTD.
ISBN 0-398-06813-5
Library of Congress Catalog Card Number:97-27061

Printed in the United States of America
CR-R-3

Library of Congress Cataloging in Publication Data

Garner, Gerald W.
    Surviving the street : officer safety and survival techniques / by
Gerald W. Garner
        p.   cm.
    Includes bibliographical references and index.
    ISBN 0-398-06813-5 (cloth)
    1. Police patrol–Safety measures.   2. Police–Assaults against.
3. Arrest (Police methods)   4. Self-defense.   I. Title.
HV8080.P2G373   1997
363.2'32–dc21   97-27061
                                                                              CIP

Dedicated to
Those Who Have Gone Before,
And Shown Those of Us Who Follow
How to Survive.

PREFACE

There is really nothing new about how and why law enforcement officers are being murdered in the United States as the country approaches a brand new century. They are most often dying because of the same fatal errors that killed peace officers ever since there has been something called law enforcement. The weapons have changed a bit, but the mortal mistakes have remained unchanged. Officers are dying because they performed a poor search, handcuffed improperly or simply got careless. They are dying because of bad habits. They are dying because the sloppy "routine" they got away with using a thousand (or ten thousand) times before failed them this time when they finally encountered an opportunist who was looking for just such a lapse to allow him to attack a law enforcement officer.

Make no mistake: these officers are not killing themselves. Their personal survival mistakes, no matter how careless, do not cancel out the fact that responsibility for their deaths rests squarely on the loathsome criminals who killed them. These are the individuals who must be punished to the fullest extent of the law. But at the same time we assess criminal responsibility we cannot overlook the truth that too many dead officers helped bring about personal disaster by making themselves vulnerable to their killers. It is that fatal vulnerability that this book is intended to banish.

Today we know precisely how and why officers die. Perhaps more important, we know how to prevent virtually all of those deaths. And that is what this book is about: recognizing and dealing effectively with the very real threats to officer safety and survival that lurk on the busy city streets and quiet country lanes of America. Unfortunately, there is no shortage of real-life examples of these fatal threat scenarios. Each chapter of the text contains true case histories as compiled by the Uniform Crime Reports Section of the Federal Bureau of Investigation of actual murders of police officers. There are lessons to be learned from these tragic deaths, and from the discussion of fatal errors the book shifts to specific, practical, time-proven tactics and techniques for surviving a potentially hazardous profession. This results in a virtual "how to" of street survival for the law enforcers of this century—and the next.

From bikers to bombers, barfighters to "boosters" gone violent, *Surviving The Street* equips the safety-savvy officer with common sense suggestions and advice to mitigate or remove many of the dangers of police work. But it is worth remembering that in many cases there are alternative measures that under certain circumstances may work as well or even better. That is the nature of police work. The survival student is certainly free to improve even further on what is set down here. At the same time, however, the author and publisher accept no responsibility for harm to persons or property resulting from the application of tactics and procedures contained herein.

Reading, absorbing and practicing the advice given in these pages can save your life. That is the sole purpose of the book's existence. Surely there is no more relevant objective for today's hard-pressed law enforcement professional than *Surviving The Street*.

INTRODUCTION

If you are a law enforcement officer today, one of your primary goals can be summarized in very few words: staying alive and healthy to reach retirement in a job that can turn suddenly and violently dangerous. This book is all about helping you reach that goal. The author, a veteran police officer, manager and officer safety instructor, presents numerous practical, common sense guidelines for *Surviving The Street.*

Chapter One utilizes actual case histories and statistics provided by the FBI in illustrating the fatal errors officers make. Chapter Two discusses vital preparations for personal survival, ranging from physical preparations to mental and emotional conditioning. Threat awareness, recognition and response are detailed. Next, Chapter Three identifies specific steps to survival for the safety-conscious officer.

Handling the suspicious person or situation assignment is covered in Chapter Four, while Chapter Five examines the dangers and safety measures involved in all kinds of vehicle contacts, including traffic stops. Chapter Six explores the various facets of safe prisoner handling and is followed by an examination of the perils of "under the influence" persons in Chapter Seven. Chapter Eight tackles the safe handling of frequently-risky crime in progress calls. Chapter Nine lays out the rules for safely defusing disturbance calls and is followed by an indepth discussion of the dangers of domestic violence intervention in Chapter Ten.

Chapter Eleven shows the reader how to search a building or other structure for an offender. Chapter Twelve goes into the proper handling of barricades and hostage-takers. It includes a discussion of negotiation techniques. Chapter Thirteen reveals the danger of high-speed vehicle pursuits and offers some advice for markedly reducing the danger level. Chapter Fourteen offers the "how to's" of safe raids and warrant service, while Chapter Fifteen provides solid guidance for working with emotionally disturbed people. Chapter Sixteen seeks to keep the law enforcement officer safe while he or she is involved in off-duty activities. Chapter Seventeen dissects the very real threats of today's terroristic groups and offers solid tips for dealing in safety with these people. A myriad of threats to survival ranging from accidents to mental health dangers are scrutinized in Chapter Eighteen. The text concludes with Chapter Nineteen's discussion of police management's responsibilities concerning officer safety that should be of special interest to the current or budding supervisor.

Each chapter includes real-life examples of police killings culled from the studies of the FBI's Uniform Crime Reports Section. Every chapter ends with a quick summary and a helpful "Street Survival Checklist" for the law enforcement practitioner. Resources for additional survival reading are listed following the last chapter.

ACKNOWLEDGMENTS

The wisdom and experience of a great many law enforcement professionals is represented in this book. Indeed, so many police practitioners have contributed so much that it would prove unwieldy to name them all. Many are instructors; suffice to say that all are experienced street cops. All have something relevant to say about staying alive on streets that can turn suddenly deadly.

Sadly, other officers referred to in the text were the ultimate casualties of officer safety errors. While they will not be named nor their agencies identified, many have paid the highest price for perhaps a moment's inattention, a missed recognition of a warning sign, a poor decision (or no decision) in the face of danger. They have given their all in service to their respective communities, and we salute them. Their very personal tragedies will be illuminated in these pages in the near-perfect vision of hindsight in hopes that others who come after them might avoid their missteps—and live. To all of those who have gone before, dead or alive, we are grateful.

A special debt of gratitude is tendered the Uniform Crime Reports Section of the Federal Bureau of Investigation. The statistics and anecdotes published by the Section in the annual *Law Enforcement Officers Killed and Assaulted* reports provide much raw material for discussion in this book. In addition, the Anti-Defamation League is thanked for the contribution of up-to-date information on hate groups in this country. Today as always, the dangers posed to law enforcement by armed, extremist haters are all too real.

The editorial staffs of *Police* and *The Police Marksman* also are recognized for their assistance. Editors Randy Resch, Connie Dees and Darlene Hutchinson-Hunter have done a lot for the cause of officer safety education in their respective magazines. In addition, thanks to Bruce Cameron of *Law and Order* as well as David Yaw and Al Menear at *Police and Security News* for supporting the author's interest in officer survival topics.

Finally, a special thanks to Pierce R. Brooks, the retired Los Angeles homicide detective turned author who is sometimes referred to as "the father of officer safety training" in the United States. From this thoughtful and wise teacher the present writer first learned the critical importance of *Surviving The Street.*

G. W. G.

CONTENTS

Contents

SURVIVING THE STREET

Chapter One

WHAT'S DANGEROUS ABOUT THIS JOB?

In the Northeast, a 37-year-old officer was off-duty and out of uniform when he stopped the driver of a vehicle he observed going the wrong way on a one-way street. The driver produced a .380-caliber handgun and shot the officer fatally in the chest. The killer, who was missed by the officer's return fire, reportedly had been involved in a minor traffic accident minutes before and was looking for the other driver when stopped by the officer.

On the East Coast, a 29-year-old patrolman entered a shopping center at approximately 8:45 P.M. and contacted several males. He then returned to his patrol car and was seated in the vehicle when he was shot once in the head and once in the jaw with a .380-caliber weapon. Four young males were subsequently arrested for the officer's murder.

Shortly after midnight in a suburban city in the Midwest, a 39-year old police sergeant was killed after stopping a vehicle driven by a robbery suspect. The sergeant and a backup officer took the driver into custody. The sergeant then went to the rear of the suspect's car and opened the trunk. A second male subject, concealed in the trunk, shot the 14-year veteran in the head and neck with a sawed-off rifle.

Nearly 30 years ago, a uniformed patrol officer responded alone to a disturbance call at a residence. As the officer stepped onto the porch and approached the closed front door, he was killed by bullets fired through the door from inside the house. Last year, another uniformed patrolman approached the front door of a residence while answering a report of a domestic dispute in progress. Before the lone officer could knock at the door, he, too, was slain by rounds fired from inside the residence.

Two American law enforcement officers, dying violently with almost three decades separating their deaths. Beyond courage and a willingness to serve, what did the two officers share in common?

3

Tragically, they both made critical mistakes, fatal errors that allowed a violent criminal opportunist to get the upper hand, with deadly consequences. The errors they made were identical. Both committed without awaiting backup help. They both positioned themselves poorly by remaining in front of a closed door, oblivious to what might be on the other side. They both may have assumed things that they didn't really know for fact. Namely, they apparently assumed that the situation they were facing did not represent a serious threat to them. Both were wrong. And they both perished.

In the "old days" of law enforcement, hardly anyone discussed the mistakes officers made that helped get them killed. Because of the family, because of their peers, because it was "too late," the dead officer was praised for his bravery, buried with full honors and eventually forgotten by all but his loved ones. Perhaps out of "respect for the fallen," the officer's errors generally were not dissected and discussed at all. And so the next week or the next month or the following year another officer went out and made the same mistakes. Then, that officer died, too.

The mistakes that fell peace officers have changed little over the years. The very same safety errors that killed deputy U.S. marshals riding the backcountry of the last century are still being made—with the same dire consequences—by the big city cops and suburban officers of the late twentieth century.

This chapter will not dishonor fallen heroes. What it *will* do is identify these deadly errors and discuss how they happen. Later chapters will detail how to avoid the critical mistakes and keep yourself safe and alive on the job.

Thanks to the long-term information gathering efforts of the Uniform Crime Reports Section of the Federal Bureau of Investigation, we know a great deal about how and why American peace officers are dying on the job today. What those efforts can teach the living is the next topic for discussion.

WHAT THE STATS SAY

Every year the FBI publishes a report entitled *Law Enforcement Officers Killed and Assaulted.* The publication contains a compilation of law enforcement casualties from the preceding year. It also offers a multi-year perspective on past fatalities and injuries. The report sheds considerable light on what happens when an officer dies at the hands of a criminal.

The FBI report for the sample year of 1994 notes that information supplied by 10,626 American law enforcement agencies indicated a total of 76 officers were murdered in the line of duty during that 12-month period. Of the victims, 45 were employed by city police departments, 14 by county police and sheriff's offices and eight by state agencies. Three federal law enforcement agents were slain during the year. Another six police killings were reported in Puerto Rico. The total of 76 dead was up from 1993 when 70 officers were murdered.

Some 73 of the 76 officers killed in 1994 were males. The average age of the victim officers was 36. Eleven of the victims were Black, 64 were White and one was an Asian/Pacific Islander. The peace officers killed in 1994 averaged 10 years of law enforcement experience, although eight had less than a year on the job and 27 had over 10 years of experience. Patrol officers accounted for 50 of the 76 victims. Fourteen were in investigations or other special assignments, while 12 were off-duty but acting officially when killed.

As in most years, making or attempting an arrest killed the most officers in 1994. Some 31 died in arrest situations. Meanwhile, 11 officers were killed while involved with traffic matters, 15 were slain investigating suspicious persons or circumstances, 8 were killed on disturbance calls, 6 were ambushed, 4 were murdered while working with emotionally or mentally disturbed persons and one was killed while on prisoner-handling duties.

In 1994, firearms were used to murder 75 of the 76 victim officers. Over the ten-year period of 1985-1994, 92 percent of the 708 peace officers murdered during that time were killed with firearms. Handguns accounted for the great majority of the deaths. Some 89 officers were killed with their own weapons during the same ten-year period. In 1994 as in recent years, the weapon calibers most often used to kill law enforcement officers were the .38-caliber, .380-caliber and 9mm.

Of the 223 officers murdered while wearing body armor over the last ten years, only 11 died when projectiles penetrated their vests. Head wounds claimed 130 of these vest-clad officers, while rounds entering just above the vest, below it, through arm openings or between side panels killed most of the other victims.

The country's most heavily-populated region, the South, tallied the most officer killings in 1994: 24 of the total. The West reported 18 murders, the Midwest 16, the Northeast 12 and Puerto Rico six.

Of the suspects identified in 1994's police killings, 61 had prior arrests and 41 had at least one prior conviction. Criminal records revealed that 46 had previous arrests for crimes of violence, 26 for drug-related offenses and 41 for weapons violations.

THE FATAL ERRORS

It was L.A.P.D. homicide detective turned officer safety expert Pierce R. Brooks who first spoke convincingly of distinct mortal errors that always seemed to be present–sometimes in profusion–nearly every time an officer died at the hands of a criminal. Based on his many years spent investigating cop killings, Brooks identified a core of dangerous officer mistakes that became the focus of his 1975 book, *OFFICER DOWN, CODE THREE.* (See *Additional Officer Survival Reading.*) That text remains as pertinent to officer safety today as it was when published over 20 years ago.

Since the beginning of modern officer safety eucation in the mid-1970s, other law enforcement safety writers and survival instructors have added, deleted and revised, to one extent or another, the original set of "survival sins" cataloged by Brooks. A library of books, magazine articles and video tape presentations have resulted from this welcome and overdue focus on fatal mistakes and how to avoid them. While the lists vary somewhat from one safety expert or instructor to the next, one or more of the following key errors are generally found in evidence when a law enforcement officer is slain:

1. Missing the danger signs
2. Failing to get needed help
3. Making dangerous assumptions
4. Following poor weapon retention practices
5. Failing to watch their hands
6. Inadequate searching techniques
7. Poor handcuffing practices
8. Being out of shape
9. Poor approach or positioning

10. Failing to maintain proficiency with equipment
11. Relaxing before the threat has passed
12. Being apathetic, preoccupied or careless
13. Being tired or asleep on the job
14. Rushing when the situation does not require speed.

Each of these key errors can result in the injury or death of a law enforcement officer. When more than one is present in a single incident, as is not-infrequently the case, the risks are multiplied. Because of their real potential for bringing on a tragedy, each of these "terminal" errors merits further examination.

Missing the Danger Signs. A careful review of several years' worth of police killings reveals that in almost every case, certain, readily-identifiable warning flags or signals were present that should have told the soon-to-be-victimized officer that danger lurked just ahead. But in each case the officer either missed, misinterpreted or, perhaps worst of all, detected but ignored one or more danger flags and bulldozed ahead anyway. Although every experienced law enforcement professional has his or her own list of warning signals, a roster of the most commonly identified ones is provided in Chapter Three. The important message for you: ignore warning signals only at your own, extreme peril. Missing or disregarding the danger signs results in the violent deaths of many American law enforcement officers every year.

Failing to Get Needed Help. There really is added safety in numbers. The officer who determines to "gut it out" without summoning needed aid is asking for an early and violent death. By harsh experience over a lot of years law enforcement has learned the value of having one or more backups present when an officer must deal with a dicey situation. Going it alone anytime identifiable risk factors are clearly in evidence is another good way for you to earn a spot in the casualty column. The failure to call or wait for needed backup assistance is worse than stupid. It can instantly become just plain deadly. "Daring but dumb" is not something you want as your epitaph.

Making Dangerous Assumptions. Every day law enforcement officers make risky assumptions that the danger they are facing simply is not that great. Sometimes they're right because they're lucky. But

luck is a poor substitute for safety skills. When an officer runs out of
luck while making assumptions, he may be dead. On increasingly violent streets, law enforcement officers like you can never assume as true
anything that they do not know for a certainty. Assuming that a drunk
is "just a drunk" and thereby won't fight you is a classic example of a
dangerous assumption. Intoxicated persons have murdered police officers time and time again. Drunks will murder still more police officers
next year, and the next. Making throwaway assumptions about safety
can get you killed.

Following Poor Weapon Retention Practices. Routinely unsnapping your holster as you approach every call or contact is an excellent
way to lose your weapon, and just possibly your life. So is standing too
close to an individual you are interviewing, with your gun side towards
him. On average, at least a half-dozen law enforcement officers are
killed with their own firearms each year in this country. One cold,
hard statistic based on past experience stands out: an offender who
gains control of an officer's weapon is most likely not simply to run
away, but rather to first kill or attempt to kill the officer with it. Poor
weapon retention practices mean greatly increased chances for your
violent death on the job.

Failing to Watch Their Hands. By neglecting to keep the hands
of a subject or subjects he has contacted constantly under visual observation, a law officer is setting himself up for attack. It is the subject's
hands or what he puts in them that can do you the most damage. By
failing to remain aware of them at all times you are inviting disaster.

Inadequate Searching Techniques. Peace officers are routinely
killed by weapons they never detected during their search of a suspect
or prisoner. Sometimes, careless officers fail to conduct any search at
all when they have legal grounds to do so for self-protection purposes.
Poor (or no) searches result in several law enforcement deaths every
year.

Poor Handcuffing Practices. Like bad searches, poor (or absent)
handcuffing still kills peace officers with appalling regularity.
Sometimes, officers assume a subject presents little or no threat to

them, so they do not handcuff at all. Other times, they apply the cuffs in such a sloppy and careless manner that they may as well have not bothered. Indeed, the improperly handcuffed subject may be more dangerous than the uncuffed one because of the false sense of security for the officer that may accompany this inadequate means of prisoner restraint.

Being Out of Shape. Some officers are overpowered, disarmed and killed because they were not as physically fit as their street opponent. Unfortunately, the tired old image of the donut-gorging, cigarette-smoking, booze-swilling, sedentary and grossly overweight cop is not totally out of date. Some officers still have little or no real upper body strength or aerobic endurance. It is this group of officers who are most at risk for disease, injury or death on the job.

Poor Approach or Positioning. By approaching a call or contact carelessly, or by letting a suspect move himself into a position where he holds the officer at a tactical disadvantage, American peace officers are murdered on a routine basis. There are, of course, all sorts of ways to position yourself in a tactically bad location. Letting an offender get way too close is just one of them. Amazingly, it is also not unusual to see an officer slain while still seated in his patrol car as potential danger approached. On that particular subject, Pierce R. Brooks sums it up best: "Get out of your vehicle if you are going to contact someone. Is it going to be your car or your coffin?"

Failing to Maintain Proficiency with Equipment. The most expensive and potentially the most useful piece of survival gear amounts to little more than a costly paperweight in the hands of an officer untrained or unskilled in its use. This holds true for police vehicles, firearms, impact instruments and restraint devices. The very best handgun will do you no good in a life-threatening gunfight if you cannot hit anything with it. The best-quality handcuffs in the world cannot help you if you are unable to apply them properly. The physical skills you hopefully learned in the academy are perishable ones. They won't continue to serve you unless you continue to practice them for proficiency.

Relaxing Before the Threat Has Passed. "Standing down" too soon can get you killed. The danger is not always over when it seems at first glance to be. The fact that your backup has arrived is important, but it is no guarantee that a belligerent drunk won't attack you anyway. The fact that you have captured a burglar hiding in a building does not mean he doesn't have a still-lurking partner, or several of them. Dropping your guard too soon can invite calamity.

Being Apathetic, Preoccupied or Careless. Take your pick. Any one of these can make you dead. The guy patching holes in the street may be able to have two-thirds of his brain otherwise engaged. You can't. Law enforcement is like that. Tough as it may be, you truly cannot afford to daydream about that upcoming fishing trip or fantasize concerning the date of your dreams while you are wearing that uniform equipped with a big target painted on the front and back. Trying to do a potentially dangerous job with only part of your mind at work is really pretty mindless. It is yet another route to becoming permanently brain dead.

Being Tired or Asleep on the Job. Everyone gets tired. Everybody gets sleepy. The point is that you can ill afford to be either while you are working any law enforcement assignment. Officers who consistently burn the candle at both ends risk not being at their best when danger suddenly arises. That even-slightly dulled edge could make all the difference when it comes time to match wits and skills with an armed adversary who wants you dead. Staying awake seems simple enough. Until, that is, it's 3 A.M. on the quietest night of the year and you haven't even seen a cat for the past five hours. If you succomb, it's not the Sandman who may get you but a very real criminal with a much more malignant purpose.

Rushing When the Situation Does Not Require Speed. Yes, it's possible that you will have to intervene to save a life the instant you arrive on a scene. But it is much more likely that you will have at least *some* time to gather information, plan a course of action and get help, if you need it. There is a place and time for speed, but very many field situations do not require an instantaneous response from you. Slowing things down, taking in the big picture and avoiding ill-advised or rash actions could save lives—yours included. Speed frequently does not make for the very best decisions. Don't rush if you do not have to do it.

BAD HABITS AND SHORTCUTS

For at least the last 20 years, good law enforcement academies and inservice training schools have discussed the fatal errors of officer safety and how to avoid them. By now, most veteran officers *know* what they should do and avoid doing to stay healthy. Why, then, are so many of these same officers still dying from the effects of the same errors that killed cops decades ago?

The answer may be as simple as it is disheartening. Considerable evidence suggests that many times officers are still perishing because on the job they fail to *practice* consistently what they know about survival from the classroom and their own experiences. Because it's raining, or cold, or hot or because it's late in the shift, or because they are simply too lazy, they take shortcuts they *know* at heart not to take. They fail to search properly, or they fail to make a careful approach to a vehicle or pedestrian or they make other, equally dangerous survival errors.

And nothing bad happens. Because the vast majority of citizens have no intention of killing a law enforcement officer, these same careless officers are able repeatedly to get away with risky shortcuts and quick and easy procedures without serious repercussions, until those mistakes become ingrained as habits. The bad habits are compounded one on the other until they can, if left unchecked, make up a careless and potentially deadly routine. By this point, the officer has set himself up for disaster for the day or night when he applies his safety shortcut in the presence of a subject looking for an opportunity to attack. If that opportunity is granted, a dead or maimed law enforcement officer may be the result. That's just how dangerous bad habits and shortcuts can be when it comes to officer survival.

The smart officer critiques his own safety performance on a continuing basis. He looks for beginning bad habits and other safety lapses. The ones he detects he repairs without delay. The safety-sharp law enforcer also seeks the constructive criticism of his peers and supervisors where safety and survival are concerned. He knows that they may

well be able to pick up on a bad habit or unsafe practice he is personally "too close" to see. These he quickly fixes, too.

WHAT THE EXPERTS SAY

Twenty years after *Officer Down, Code Three*, the present author
queried several well-known officer safety experts as to what they saw
as factors still resulting in officer deaths today. Pierce R. Brooks was
asked about what had changed over the years.

"Really, nothing has changed," he emphasizes.

"Cops are still dying because of the same mistakes I wrote about in
the book back then. The mistakes are exactly the same."

Brooks feels the FBI's *Law Enforcement Officers Killed and Assaulted*
reports make excellent safety training tools because they illustrate so
clearly the fatal mistakes cops make on the street. He feels they serve
as first-class survival training tools for the contemporary safety instructor.

Ed Nowicki, a nationally-renowned police instructor and a leader in
the American Society of Law Enforcement Trainers who has personally trained thousands of peace officers, emphasizes the value of well-
organized, professionally conducted survival training programs for all
officers.

"Trainers need to demonstrate how vulnerable officers can be by
using actual case histories and by discussing or even reenacting the
scenarios. This takes away the 'could be' and replaces it with the 'did
happen.' There has to be a direct correlation between what is taking
place in class and what is happening on the street or did happen on
the street," Nowicki says.

The veteran trainer notes that, in order to be most effective, survival
training needs to extend beyond the classroom to patrol roll calls and
other settings where hands-on skills can be honed.

Nowicki has an additional opinion as to why officers sometimes
may be getting hurt on the street.

"During training programs I have seen officers hesitate in using
force where they should not have hesitated. This has got to be happening on the street, as well. You want to respect the constitutional
rights of all individuals, but you also must protect yourself from
harm," he concludes.

Dennis Anderson, a well-known law enforcement survival trainer and a co-founder of the highly-successful Calibre Press Street Survival seminars, books and tapes likewise holds some strong feelings about the state of officer safety today. He worries that some law enforcement academies may be devoting more and more time to "soft" subjects as opposed to emphasizing safety-related instruction. But he also lays the blame for dangerous streets where he believes it properly belongs:

"A factor is the increasing number of violent subjects in our society and their rampant disrespect for authority," he says.

Anderson believes it is vital to point up and reward the good and safe work done by officers, even as we acknowledge our shortcomings:

"Overall, we know the factors that have helped to stabilize the number of officer deaths—increased threat awareness due to officer survival training, the wearing of body armor, use of modern equipment, working more with a backup and planning rather than rushing into a situation. All have helped."

Anderson's philosophy is a positive one. Emphasizing and improving upon what we do *right* may well be the key to working still better and safer in the future. After all, doing *safety* right translates into actual officer survival on the street.

SUMMARY

In the final analysis, there really is nothing new about how and why law enforcement officers are being murdered today. Cops are still making the same critical errors their nineteenth century predecessors made, and in the process they are giving criminal opportunists the openings they are seeking to attack. It happens time and time again. None of this is intended to forgive or lessen the guilt of the criminals who pulled the trigger or thrust the blade. These officers did not, after all, kill themselves. It remains the violent offender who must be held accountable for the deaths of these victims. At the same time, by identifying and examining the safety lapses of the victim officers we can prevent the same mistakes from being made by more officers with the same bloody consequences for the future.

This chapter unveiled the deadly errors. The next will explore some personal preparations you can make to avoid them.

STREET SURVIVAL CHECKLIST FOR AVOIDING
JOB DANGERS

1. Know the errors frequently found present when a law enforcement officer is murdered.

2. Realize that the more critical safety errors you make, the more likely you are to become the victim of a criminal opportunist.

3. Vow never to fall into bad habits or shortcuts where on-the-job safety is concerned.

4. Listen to what the officer safety experts and instructors have to say about the fatal errors you must at all cost avoid. Apply these teachings to your daily street activities.

5. Never stop critiquing yourself and seeking to uncover your own safety errors. Promptly repair any shortcomings you discover.

Chapter Two

PREPARATIONS FOR SURVIVAL

In the Southeast, an off-duty policewoman was killed during an attempted robbery. The 34-year-old officer and a male companion were leaving an apartment around 12:40 A.M. when an armed male approached and announced a robbery. While her companion handed over money and car keys, the officer drew her service weapon and exchanged shots with the robber. The offender was wounded but survived; the 6-year officer was hit several times and died of a chest wound.

In the Southwest, a highway patrolman and his partner responded to a one-car accident shortly after 8:30 P.M. They met a deputy sheriff who had placed the driver, unsecured, into the front seat of his patrol car. The 17-year-old driver stepped out of the vehicle as the trooper approached. While the victim was questioning the subject, the youth suddenly pulled a large caliber revolver and shot the trooper fatally in the head.

Two veteran officers were attending a workshop with other officers in a West Coast hotel conference room when, at about 3:45 P.M., a masked man wearing a protective vest and displaying two handguns entered. The two officers, one a captain and the other a sergeant, moved on the man and were both shot fatally in the chest. Each man died unarmed.

In actuality, preparations for your vital but all-too-often risky job take several different forms. You must be physically conditioned to handle the many challenges of the street. You must master the technical and motor skills required to do the job safely and well. You must be mentally and emotionally capable of standing up to the difficulties posed by danger and frequent conflict. And you must certainly have access to the tools you need to carry out all of your responsibilities. Indeed, you must be prepared many times over.

Law enforcement is not unlike most other fields of endeavor in that before you can go out and do it well, you must prepare thoroughly for the intricacies of the job. This chapter will guide you in making the preparations necessary to ensure your success and survival in a some-times-risky environment.

MENTAL AND EMOTIONAL PREPARATIONS

Particularly if you follow the wise dictates of your own common sense and good judgment applied to the survival advice contained in this book, the likelihood of your being killed or seriously injured on the job is remote. But the possibility exists, nonetheless. You need to give that ample thought before you commence or continue a career in policing. That realization is a part of your honest mental and emotional job preparations.

Most peace officers go through a law enforcement career without having to kill or seriously injure anyone. But the possibility neverthe-less exists that you will have to take a life—or more than one. You need to think about that, too. You need to be as certain as you can be that you can do what you have to do and then live with yourself afterwards, just in case the need to take a life ever arises. Getting all of this straight in your mind should be done now, before the incident occurs. When and if it ever does, there will be no time to ponder the ramifications and engage in an intense internal debate on morality *before* you have to act, perhaps to save your own life.

If, after careful consideration, you determine that you could never resort to deadly force in spite of having the legal and procedural right to do so, you are obligated to take yourself out of law enforcement without delay. The reality is that a situation may one day arise in which you *must* use lethal force to save a life, perhaps your own. If you *know* that you could never do so no matter how compelling the threat, by remaining in law enforcement you constitute a danger to yourself, your fellow officers and the citizens you all serve. You are probably a fine person, but you should not be carrying a gun as a law officer.

To prepare mentally and emotionally for the role of a law enforce-ment officer you also must develop what might be called a "winner's attitude" or mindset. Many officers who have survived a literal battle to the death with an opponent have reported that while the struggle was in progress they experienced a feeling along the lines of "no punk is going to leave me bleeding in the street. I'm the one who's going home from this." They determined to fight to their utmost endurance and somehow win. Their survival can be contrasted with officers who received a relatively minor and survivable wound but laid down to die. In some cases, they *did* die when the offender who wounded them in the first place came over to put a round in their head. Clearly, a personally-developed determination to win and live should be a part of your mental and emotional preparations.

Preparing now to survive "upstairs" should include the realization that you may face emotional and physical trauma including night-mares, sleep disorders, sexual dysfunctions and mood swings as well as other ailments following a critical incident that occurs on the job. Or you may experience nothing at all out of the ordinary following an incident in which, say, a life is taken. Feeling nothing in particular most certainly does not mean you are a heartless, cold fish. Far from it. *Whatever is normal for you is normal.* People differ. That's one of the ways the human mind works. You may or may not want the aid of out-side, professional assistance, such as a police psychologist, at such a time. You may simply need to talk—a lot—with someone you are very comfortable with, like a spouse, a peer or another officer who has gone through a similar experience. In any case, thinking about and accept-ing the possibility of mental and emotional disruptions in the future is part of preparing right now to survive in all ways. You must do it if you are to remain healthy in all aspects of the term.

PHYSICAL PREPARATIONS

Preparing to survive on the street requires you to keep yourself in reasonably good physical condition. You need some sort of a person-al conditioning and exercise program that provides you with enough "wind" to finish a foot chase or a struggle and enough upper body strength to win the battle. That requires both aerobic conditioning that boosts cardiopulmonary capacity and an exercise regimen that bol-sters arm and upper body strength. An obvious means for accom-plishing the latter goal is a personal weightlifting program.

The law enforcement job does not really require that you be either a marathon runner or an award-winning power lifter. It only requires that your program of personal conditioning keeps you from running out of breath and strength during a struggle or a dash up a flight of stairs. Following an exercise routine that increases your heart rate for 30 minutes four or five times a week can, if practiced regularly, help build aerobic strength. Jogging, walking, swimming and biking all can help accomplish this objective. To add arm and upper body strength and flexibility, you might look at the possibilities of a program of exercises that includes some light weightlifting under the tutelage of a qualified fitness counselor or instructor. The idea is not to bulk up with showy muscles but rather to develop strength that you actually can rely on to overcome an arrestee's resistance and help control a violent offender. Naturally, you would be well-advised to seek the counsel of a physician before you launch a brand new exercise program of any kind, particularly if your lifestyle has been sedentary of late. That makes for good survival advice, too. Don't overdo it, hurt yourself and then swear off any kind of exercise for good. Be patient. Good results will come, but not overnight. Work at personal conditioning in a planned, methodical manner.

Whatever route to improved conditioning and fitness you decide to take, avail yourself of some good, professional guidance rather than striking out on your own. There are plenty of good fitness instructors, books and tapes available today. Take advantage of this considerable expertise. Again, however, you will need to remain mindful that your body will take time to reverse the effects of long-term neglect, if that happens to be your situation. You will have to persist on a long-term basis if you want to see long-term results. Personal good health and a high level of physical fitness should be your career-long goals as you work as a law enforcement professional.

SKILLS YOU'LL NEED

To stay safe in policing, you will need to master a number of specific, physical skills, tactics and techniques aimed at assuring your continued safety. These skills and abilities are discussed in detail at several points in this text. Since they all require physical skills and motor responses to one extent or another, you obviously cannot master them simply by reading about them in a book or watching them demonstrated on a videotape. But there are a number of vital points and principles you can learn about them right here. Combined with classroom training and application in the field, on the range or on the exercise mats under the guidance of skilled instructors, these can help you assemble a reliable survival package that will aid you in coming home safely at the end of each shift. View them as yet more tools to reduce and control the hazards of your job. For instance:

Failing to Get Needed Help. Cover is what you will want to be tucked safely behind if someone appears really intent on blowing a hole through you. Cover is what you will need to think about every single time you approach a call or contact. Think: Where can I go quickly if a weapon comes into play? To help you, cover has to be solid enough to stop bullets and close enough to allow you to get there before the shooting starts. At the same time, almost *any* cover is better than standing in the open, shooting it out with a bad guy, particularly if *he* has cover. On the street, hunched behind your vehicle's wheel and tire or behind the engine block may be the best cover options available. Use what you have. But do not overlook other cover possibilities. One officer who had been shot at on a nighttime traffic stop abandoned his patrol car for the cover of a nearby, thick-trunked tree. With his opponent still focusing his attention on the squad car, the officer ended the shootout with return fire directed from good cover.

Whatever cover you select, utilize it properly. Stay behind it completely as much as possible. Do any peeking quick and low, but never from the same spot twice. One eye is all you should quickly edge out from behind cover to look for a threat. As soon as you can see what's going on you should already be pulling yourself totally back behind cover. As they say: Don't expose what you want to keep.

Approach and Positioning. When you are afoot, approaching an address or an individual, be thinking about what kinds of threats could develop—and how you will respond if they do. Keep thinking about cover possibilities. Keep watching people for any obvious threats, like hands not visible or potential weapons in view. Don't get too close, too soon. Consider keeping natural barriers, such as the hood of your patrol car, between you and an individual you are contacting, at least until you can better gauge his attitude and intentions. Do not try to control multiple subjects by yourself, particularly if they are belligerent, intoxicated or unruly. Call for assistance promptly. Try to keep things nonconfrontational until you have enough help on hand to act in safety.

Never approach alone if you believe a subject to be armed. Call help and keep him under surveillance until assistance arrives. When you do issue a verbal challenge and instructions, be sure you are behind cover with your sidearm drawn and ready.

Keep several feet between you and a subject you are contacting, unless and until you decide to take him into custody. (Then you'll place him off-balance and at a disadvantage before you get closer to secure him.) Stay out of his easy arm's reach. Keep your firearm side turned away from him. Watch his hands. Even when you are otherwise occupied, as in using the police radio, use at least your peripheral vision to warn you of any sudden moves by your subject or anyone else in the vicinity. Do not let anyone move in close or maneuver behind you. Don't hesitate to use clear oral instructions to tell one and all exactly where you want them for your continued safety.

One particular type of approach deserves extra attention: Your approach to the apparently "downed" subject. Law enforcement officers have been killed by offenders who had received numerous wounds and were apparently out of action. Do not be in a hurry to approach a downed subject who has shot himself or who has apparently been hit by police gunfire. Stay back behind cover and try issuing verbal commands: "Police! Push the gun away from you! Put your hands on your head!" Or whatever is appropriate for the circumstances.

Hang back awhile and see what develops. The subject may not be as badly hurt as you thought. He may be "playing possum," hoping to sucker you into leaving cover and coming close. Stay put, even if minutes elapse. You can get emergency medical aid on the way while you continue to observe pending its arrival. When you do move in, do so carefully with a backup officer covering you. Keep your firearm on target as you cautiously advance. Be prepared to fire and withdraw if a new threat to your life develops. When you reach your subject, remove any weapons beyond the reach of a still-living subject and secure him right away. Stay alert all the while you give emergency medical aid. It ain't over 'til it's over.

Verbal Commands. The human focus of your attentions–guilty, innocent or somewhere in between–cannot read your mind. You will have to utilize oral instructions that are clear, concise and to the point to let him know exactly what you want him to do and how you expect him to get it done. Keep your words to a minimum—talking distracts you from doing other vital things, but be sure your words are meaningful ones. Say what you mean and mean what you say. You do not need to sound belligerent, macho or unnecessarily threatening—unless, of course, a threat is required by the circumstances. Don't scream, curse or belittle—just say what needs to be communicated to gain compliance and increase the safety margin for all concerned. For example: "Police! Slowly lay the gun down or you will be shot! Do it now!" The instructions are clear, direct and concise. They tell your subject exactly what you require and precisely what will happen if he fails to respond appropriately. The order can be repeated, if necessary.

Give your instructions in a loud, clear, authoritative voice. Do not plead for compliance (please" is not required here). Demand it. Your voice should project that you are in charge and expect obedience. Practice, if you need to. Just go someplace where you won't upset the neighbors!

Arrest and Control Techniques. Much of officer safety requires you to keep a safe distance between yourself and potential threats. You can no longer do that when you move in close to perform a pat-down search or take someone into custody. That's when you must rely upon the hands-on training you have received and practiced on controlling others via physical tactics and techniques.

Obviously you only learn the skills of baton use, chemical spray application, handcuffing, searching and come-along holds on the mats with a partner and under the supervision of a qualified instructor. There is no substitute for this kind of mandatory initial as well as continuing training. At the same time, there are several principles that can be absorbed outside of class. Consider, for example, the following guideposts for protecting yourself:

• Simple really *is* better. Learn the control holds and defense moves that work for you, and practice them regularly. Do not overcomplicate by trying to figure out and keep straight a half-dozen versions of essentially the same tactic. Stick with what works easiest and best for you.

• Realize your limitations and know when hand-to-hand tactics are appropriate. You would not want to go up against an opponent armed with a knife with just your bare hands or a baton, for instance, if you were in possession of your firearm. And no matter how strong you are or how talented you may be in defense and control tactics, it makes absolutely no sense to struggle with someone all by yourself when by delaying the confrontation slightly you can have another pair of hands on scene to help you.

• Do not apply *any* defense or control measure half-heartedly. You are not out to hurt anyone, but neither should you engage in a lengthy wrestling match with a violently resisting opponent. The longer any struggle continues, the more likely it is you will get hurt as your strength starts to ebb from the exertion. Once the struggle starts, you cannot afford to lose. If you are overcome, you weapon is available to an offender. You easily could die if he gets control of it. As a result, you must win the fight as quickly as possible. If you clearly are losing a hand-to-hand struggle, it may be time to move to a defensive aerosol or an impact weapon to establish control. Or you can back-off and call for assistance, if your situation permits you that option. Just don't continue the same tactics without change when you are losing the battle. Either you or your subject getting killed is not the preferred ending for a contact turned violent. Apply all that you have learned about arrest and control. Learn to use all of your officer safety tools properly.

Firearms Use. With the exception of your brain and its accompanying supply of good common sense, your firearm is probably the most important piece of safety equipment you will carry on and off the job. Handled improperly, it could be your downfall. The correct and accurate use of every firearm you carry—sidearm, shotgun and/or rifle—should be mastered in the classroom and on the range under the close supervision of expert instructors. At the outset, you should vow to operate under three unforgiving rules of firearms safety:

All guns are always considered loaded and functional.

Keep your finger away from the trigger until you are ready to shoot.

Don't point a gun at anything you are unwilling to destroy.

Treat all firearms as the serious and deadly tools that they are. Never engage in horseplay with or around them. Do not tolerate such from others. Be certain that any training that involves weapons take-aways and the like is conducted with dummy or nonfunctional weapons. Virtually every year American peace officers are killed accidentally by firearms discharges. You do not want to be one of them.

You also do not want to get shot on purpose by a gun in the hands of a criminal. In preparing to protect yourself, think about the following general guidelines as accompaniments to your on-the-range firearms training. These, too, can help take care of you.

• Be very familiar with your jurisdiction's laws, policies, procedures and rules governing use of deadly force. Be sure that any time your weapon leaves its holster you are in compliance with those guidelines. Job and legal survival go hand in hand with street survival. It's also the *right* thing to do.

• Be sure you remain qualified with all of the firearms you carry. For the benefit of your own skill level and peace of mind you may want to train and qualify more often than your agency requires you to do.

• Ban warning shots from your arsenal of tactics. They seldom slow down or halt a fleeing offender. In some cases, they may be illegal. And they almost always expose you to the risk of hitting someone or something you had never intended as a target. Warning shots are needlessly dangerous, sometimes not to the bad guy.

• Be sure your firearms practice is as relevant as possible to what you may face on the street. Most police-involved shootings take place quickly and at less than six feet, so you should hone your own quick-firing shooting skills for these distances. Do not spend all of your time plugging away at a paper target that never moves. Your range instruction should, where possible, include firing at moving or turning targets, multiple targets, in low-light conditions and in shoot-don't-shoot scenarios. Good, practical firearms range training is often limited only by the imaginations and resources of the trainers and pupils involved.

• Perfect sight pictures and a great stance are wonderful in a perfect world, but chances are if you ever face a live shooting encounter with one or more offenders you'll be a lot more concerned with self-preservation than perfection. Most cop killers are instinct shooters. If *you* are confronted by a short-range shooting situation, instinct shooting may give you the best chance of delivering incapacitating rounds to your target in the shortest time. Point your weapon at your target (as you would point your finger) exactly where you want the bullets to go. Aim for center mass, or the biggest part of the target, as that's what you have the best chance of hitting. (That means the center of the torso or chest area, or course.) Fire until the target ceases to be a deadly threat, whether achieving that goal requires one shot or several. Realize that an offender, even though clearly hit by your fire, may not immediately drop or even cease shooting. If you believe that the offender who is menacing you is wearing body armor, shift the focus of your fire to his head or pelvic area below likely vest coverage.

• Practice reloading your weapon at combat speed. Do so behind cover with your objective being to get back on target as quickly and cleanly as possible. Get in the good habit of never "shooting dry" in the first place.

• Do some thinking in advance about how you would respond to multiple, simultaneous threats on your life. Plan to direct your gunfire against the greatest or most imminent threat first. In other words, you would fire on the guy with the sawed-off shotgun ahead of the subject with the revolver. You would shoot at the guy with the knife who's charging you from ten feet away before the man with the blade who is starting from 20 feet distant, and so on. In your mind, go over your reasoning for why you would choose as you did. It's not bad preparation for the day, if it ever comes, on which you must truthfully lay out your logic and reasoning for your bosses, the D.A. and/or the Grand Jury as to why you took the lethal, self-protective measures that you did.

Communication with Your Helpers. The best officer safety plans involving multiple officers will only work well if everyone knows his or her role. That calls for excellent communication among the participants, whether by radio, in-person voice exchanges or hand signals. For obvious reasons, it is advisable that many of your communications be kept secure from those you are discussing. That is why you and your partners should have in place ahead of time a system of voice or hand signals representing the more important commands or exchanges that you will use. Four fingers held up for "Code 4" or "I'm O.K." is a familiar one. But you should have more. Five fingers held up, for instance, might indicate to your arriving backups that the party or parties at hand are wanted or troublesome. Or your closed fist held over your head might signal that a dangerous situation exists–I need help *pronto*!"

Number codes or signals also can be used to keep your intentions a secret from a subject you are at close quarters with at the moment. "He's a 45" may tell your backup that the subject is mentally disturbed. "I'm going to 25" could tell your helper that you plan an arrest–stand by to cover me.

Virtually any system of codes and signals you want to come up with should work fine. Your primary concern should be that everybody involved who *needs* to know their meaning and required response *does* know. That's communicating in safety!

EQUIPMENT CONCERNS

A highly-skilled carpenter or mechanic would not dream of approaching his work without a set of the best and most appropriate tools he could afford to make his job as easy as possible. You cannot afford to do less when it comes to assembling your own tool chest for accomplishing an even more difficult (and certainly more hazardous) job. For you, the goal of getting the task done *in safety* must be added to the craftsman's need to get it accomplished with ease.

To do this you will need the very best personal equipment that you and your employer can afford. Your agency owes you the benefit of sound, reliable tools. But in today's atmosphere of tough budgetary constraints claimed by many law enforcement agencies, your department may not be able to purchase *everything* that you would like to have to do your job safely and well. In that case, and assuming your employer will permit it, you would be wise to invest some of your own, hard-earned funds in getting what it takes to bolster your chances of staying safe at work.

Where your survival is concerned, you want only the best. If that means you must fork over a few more bucks, so be it. It's worth giving up a new toy or some beer and pizza if it means avoiding having some new apertures in your body to go with the ones nature put there.

What, exactly, do you need? High-quality body armor, for one thing. You'll need to religiously wear it, too, no matter how hot or humid it may get outside. Survey the available literature on soft body armor (check out the law enforcement magazines), talk to other officers who have purchased the various kinds of armor, try some on and then purchase the best and most comfortable vest you can afford. Although the vest manufacturers have yet to invent truly comfortable body armor, get what feels best to you without sacrificing round-stopping ability. Comfort is vital, because the most ballistically effective vest won't help you if it is so rigid you won't wear it. It can't save you if it rides in your car's trunk. In recognition of the fact that so many officers are shot with their own guns, be sure your vest is rated to at least stop rounds from the weapon you carry. If you work in a lockup facility, purchase the kind of armor especially designed to protect you from stabbing or slashing attacks.

You should carry only top-quality handcuffs. You also should carry more than one pair, since many times offenders don't come solo. The newer, hinged variety cuffs are nice in that your cuffed subject has less wrist flexibility. The cuff openings also are bigger to help you secure monster-size wrists—or regular-size ankles, if need be.

Impact instruments generally translate to some sort of baton, as slappers, blackjacks, beaver tails and the like really belong to an earlier era of law enforcement. Carry what your department officially blesses, and know how to use it well.

Flashlights carried on duty should be the 20,000 to 30,000 candlepower rechargeable models, even if you must forego another supply of beer and pizza. Any flashlight can put out some illumination, but when your life literally could depend on you lighting up a hidden or distant opponent as brightly as possible, you don't want to be holding a cut-rate special in your off-hand. Pay for it yourself, if you have to, but get the best light you can.

You should have at your disposal as many less-than-lethal force options as you are qualified to use and can carry with you. That should include a defensive aerosol product. Experience has shown that the oleoresin capsicum (OC) pepper sprays are about the most effective items out there at the moment, so that's what you should consider carrying. Be sure you are trained and certified in its use. Be equally certain that you follow the manufacturer's instructions and your agency's guidelines for dispensing it and then decontaminating and caring for your sprayed subject. Be careful not to get a big whiff of it yourself. But realize that OC sprays, whatever the type or brand, have limitations, just like your other equipment. They can fail totally or partially in subduing an attacker. That's why you want those other equipment options as well as additional tactics readily available from your bag of tricks.

Then, there are your personal firearms. At a time when the crooks are carrying better and bigger guns and show an increased willingness to use them against you, you need the additional rounds of a high-capacity semiautomatic pistol and a couple of extra magazines carried with you on duty. Fifteen rounds instantly available are better than six; 30 more rounds quickly at hand are better than twelve. It can amount to the mathematics of survival, particularly when you realize that in the stress of a gunfight even the best police marksman often throws rounds off the target. Said another way, the ability to put a great deal of firepower on target quickly could save your life one day.

Once more, you want the best tool for keeping you safe. Many law enforcement officers have their own biases about the "best" make and caliber of personal sidearm to carry, and joining that fray is not the purpose of this discussion. Suffice to say that all of the major manufacturers make good weapons. Let researched and informed personal preference be your guide. Likewise, calibers ranging from 9mm to .40-caliber to .45-caliber are effective for police work. Choose your favorite, based upon what you have been able to learn from your own weapons research, which most likely has included discussions with peers and veteran firearms trainers and armorers. Your employer may already have chosen for you regarding what kind of round you can carry. If the choice is left to you, you probably will want one that spreads and expends its energy within its primary target rather than continuing clear through whatever it hits. That most likely calls for a semi-jacketed, hollow-point bullet.

It goes almost without saying that you absolutely must be well-versed in the proper use of all the equipment your job demands, most especially the tools that are safety-related in any way whatsoever. That mandates that you must practice for proficiency well beyond what happens in a recruit academy setting. Your work to maintain proficiency with equipment must continue throughout your law enforcement career.

Likewise, you must properly maintain all of the equipment you use on your job. You inspect it regularly and you follow the manufacturer's instructions as well as your agency's guidelines for keeping your top of the line stuff clean and functional. It's all part of preparing for the equipment concerns of modern law enforcement.

SUMMARY

The best way to succeed and survive at your difficult job is to prepare well for it. Physical preparations for your various tasks will run from personal physical conditioning to learning and practicing the hands-on skills of the job, including firearms use, arrest and control tactics and verbal commands. Mental and emotional preparations are musts, too, if you are to survive the risks of your challenging profession. The same holds true for the equipment preparations and choices you make to accompany you on your rounds. You must make thoughtful, informed choices.

Good preparations for a tough job help make that job ultimately survivable for its practitioner. By preparing to work safely now you can take the lead in assuring your own survival later.

STREET SURVIVAL CHECKLIST FOR PREPARING TO SURVIVE

1. Keep yourself in good physical condition. Your life may depend on it.

2. Work to maintain a healthy mental and emotional perspective concerning your job. It can help you get through rough spots with mind and body intact.

3. Learn and practice the various physical skillls required in your job, paying special attention to firearms use and arrest and control skills.

4. Choose the best equipment available for your profession. Don't scrimp on pennies where your life is at stake. Then, maintain your equipment properly and stay proficient with it.

5. Stay up to date with all of your preparations for job survival. Threats, tactics, techniques and equipment change over time.

Chapter Three

GUIDELINES FOR STAYING ALIVE

Shortly after 9 A.M. a deputy with an eastern sheriff's department was shot to death by a 15-year-old juvenile. The officer was serving a juvenile petition at the youth's home and allowed him to change clothes. The male juvenile instead loaded a .22-caliber rifle and shot the deputy in the forehead when he looked into the boy's room. The youth then took the downed officer's 9mm handgun and shot him behind the right ear.

At about 1 A.M. in a northern U.S. town, a 33-year-old patrol officer with four years of law enforcement experience pulled over to talk with a suspected drug trafficker outside of a public housing project. The officer got out and had a short conversation with the 23-year-old man. The subject pulled a 9mm handgun from his waist area and began firing from less than five feet away. The officer was hit by several of the 14 rounds fired and died from a bullet in the chest that entered between the side panels of his body armor.

Again in the North, a 28-year-old city patrolman was killed while pursuing a vehicle containing a jail escapee and two female accomplices. At about 9 P.M. the vehicle was pulled over with assistance from other police units and the patrolman approached the driver's side door. The escapee, who was in the back seat, then shot the officer in the pelvic area with a .30-06 rifle. The wound proved fatal.

By now you have heard a lot about what can go wrong to get you hurt or killed. You have seen examples of what officers do wrong (you'll see a lot more) to set themselves up to become murder victims. You have encountered plenty of terminal errors.

Now it's time to turn things around. The point is, you do not *have* to become a victim of anyone or anything. By applying your good judgment and able decision-making to some very practical officer survival guidelines, you can greatly improve your chances for making it to the end of a long and successful law enforcement career with all of your personal equipment still intact and functional. Consider carefully, then, all of the officer safety suggestions for staying alive that follow.

STEPS TO SURVIVAL

Gather Information First. Whether it is from your dispatcher, witnesses on the scene or your own observations, get as much data as you can quickly collect on the situation you are facing *before* you commit yourself to a course of action. What you learn in a very short time should enable you to handle the problem with increased safety and effectiveness.

Stop, Look and Listen—Don't Rush. Yes, there's always a chance you will have to commit yourself to life-saving action the very moment you arrive on-scene. But it is unlikely to happen frequently. More often you can slow down to catch your breath, wait for your backup to arrive and size up what you are confronting. That means taking in everything you can via your senses of sight, hearing and even smell. Train yourself to be as quietly observant as possible. It should pay safety divdends for you.

Get Help. As soon as you have assessed the problem(s) you are facing, call the kind and amount of help you estimate you will need to handle the situation in safety, assuming sufficient help is not already on the way. Wait for your assistance to be in place and briefed on the situation before you get involved, if at all possible. It's much better to call in too much help than not enough. You can always send away unneeded assistance once the situation is clearly under control.

Look for the Danger Signs. The presence of any of these hazard indicators should tell you that the threat level may have just gone up. It's time to alter your tactics and techniques before proceeding further, whether that means you simply increase your level of alertness, call help, go to cover, draw your weapon or all of the above. The roster of danger flags will vary from one officer to the next, based upon training, experience and other factors. But a common list for any veteran peacekeeper could be expected to include at least the following:

Weapons present
Intoxicated or under the influence of alcohol
Emotionally disturbed; irrational

Furtive movements; hiding
Hands not visible
History of violence
Subject escalating; tensing up
Defensive or attack posture
Vacant or distant stare
Subject visually sizing you up
Subject trying to close the distance
Subject states suicidal intent ("suicide by cop")
Suspicious bulges in clothing
Threatening statements ("I'm going to kill you")

Obviously, your detection of one or more of these red flags does not mean that you go on auto pilot, draw your gun and start blasting away. Their detection *does* mean that you should alter some aspects of your approach and handling of the call or contact to increase the safety margin for yourself in a situation that has given indications that it *may* be more hazardous than you initially believed. It is unacceptable to bulldoze ahead with your tactics unchanged, hoping that blind luck will get you through.

Wear Your Body Armor. Armored vests have saved literally thousands of police officers from serious injury or death over the years. Like any other piece of equipment, they are not infallible. But they do save lives on a regular basis. If you do not have a vest already, get one. Wear it without exception. There is no acceptable reason for not doing so.

Maintain a Reactionary Gap. That's the distance of 5-6 feet separating you and the person(s) you are contacting. The distance will be less if your subject is seated inside a vehicle and you are standing outside. The space is intended to give you time and distance to react and defend yourself if someone launches a sudden attack. It also helps protect you against a weapon takeway lunge. Some officers try, where possible, to place added barriers in the gap, such as the hood of the police car or a piece of furniture to give even more protection. The key is to not let the subject you are dealing with get too close for comfort. Issue him verbal instructions to back off and adjust your own position, if necessary, to maintain the gap. A subject who still moves closer after being cautioned not to has just sent you a red flag warning signal. Beware and prepare!

Watch Your Approach and Positioning. Don't set yourself up for an assault by putting yourself in a position of extreme vulnerability. That means you don't stand dead(!) in front of a door you are knocking at, put an unsecured violator in the front seat with you, let a prisoner walk behind you or stand too close or between two subjects. Always be conscious of your own location in respect to potential threats around you.

Always Watch Their Hands. If you cannot see both of their paws at all times, that constitutes a potential threat to you. Instruct them to bring their hands in view and keep them there, but be prepared just in case when their digits become visible they are grasping something (like a weapon, for instance!) that presents a danger to you. Be aware that most folks whose hands you cannot immediately see do not constitute a deadly threat. You can certainly be courteous in your dealings with them. Just remain eternally alert for the hand-held surprise and stay prepared to respond to it promptly and effectively.

Don't Make Dangerous Assumptions. Where your safety is concerned, do not count on anything you don't know for a fact to be true. You cannot afford to assume that a drunk is harmless or a burglarized building is empty of offenders. You can never, ever assume that all alarms are false or that a given suspect won't fight now that you have help on-scene. These are precisely the sort of dangerous, false assumptions that have resulted in the violent ends of countless peace officers. Don't join their ranks. Assume little beyond the reality that *every* call and contact contains at least the potential for life-threatening danger.

Use Cover Properly. Officers have died within a few feet of what would have proven excellent, bullet-stopping cover had they realized in time that they needed to be behind it. Don't forget that there is a big difference between cover and concealment: cover can stop projectiles; concealment only hinders vision. Cover may be an engine block or a brick wall; concealment may amount to a sheet of plywood or a bush. Naturally, you want the best cover you can get to quickly. But also remember: cover is relative. Cover that will stop a round from a Saturday night special may not give pause to a rifle round.

Once you get to good cover, minimize your exposure from behind it. If you must look for an adversary, peek *quick and low*, and never from exactly the same place twice. A bullet may be waiting for you the second time out. The general rule for you: Don't needlessly expose anything you want to keep. *Think cover* on your way in to any call or contact. *Think*: Where could I go in a hurry if this situation goes sour and weapons come into play? Stay prepared to act on this knowledge if the need arises.

Practice Contact and Cover. This very simple tactic saves lives by allowing you to make the best use of your partner or backup. The contact officer carries out the primary business of the contact (making an arrest, writing a summons, searching a vehicle, etc.) while the cover officer does nothing but watch out for the welfare of the contact officer, prepared to instantly intervene with necessary force if the contact is threatened. Contact and cover, which works equally well on a vehicle stop, in a small apartment or elsewhere, dictates specific responsibilities for the players involved. For instance:

IF YOU ARE THE CONTACT OFFICER, YOU MUST:

• Carry out the work of the contact.

• Tell your cover officer what you know and what you want him to do.

• Tell your cover officer where you want him.

• Tell him what you plan to do next.

• Notify him of any hazards that you are aware of, or of any change in the situation ("I've found a gun!")

• Stay out of your cover's line of sight and line of fire.

• Call in as much covering help as you need.

• Make it clear to your cover when you no longer need his or her help.

IF YOU ARE THE COVER OFFICER, YOU MUST:

• Tell the contact officer of any information you have on the situation. (Examples: radio traffic you have heard or observations you have made while en route.)

• Tell him what you are going to do and where you'll be. (You must be clear on each other's plans.)

• Stay behind cover to the extent possible.

• Call more contact or cover help if you think it is needed.

• Cover, watch, protect–and nothing else.

• Don't talk to others present other than to issue directions or shout an alarm to the contact officer.

• Shout a warning to the contact officer the instant you spot danger. ("Knife!")

• Use the appropriate amount of force to defend the contact officer and yourself from an attack from any quarter.

• If there is more than one subject present, do not abandon your covering duties to join a struggle unless the contact officer asks for help or you see he clearly needs it.

Maintain Control of Your Weapons. Be conscious of who is around you at all times, even if you feel you are on "friendly" turf, such as standing in line at the fast-food joint. You just may have an enemy around. On a contact, keep your weapon-side turned away from those you are dealing with. Also consider the following weapon retention tips:

• When others are around, keep your holstered weapon covered by tucking your arm and elbow over it.

• Do not finger your weapon's grips or hammer absent-mindedly, rest your hand on it or otherwise draw attention to your holstered sidearm.

• Don't bend or work your holster until the weapon's butt sticks out at an angle, thereby making it an easy grab for an attacker.

• Check your holster's condition regularly–stitching can become weakened; snaps can break.

• Avoid the "trick" holsters and super fast-draw rigs. You want a safety holster that keeps your sidearm securely snapped in.

• Do not get in the habit of unsnapping your holster when approaching calls or contacts. You're too apt to lose your weapon by doing so.

• Practice your weapon retention moves under the guidance of a competent physical tactics instructor.

• Remember that if you are in a fight for control of your weapon, you are fighting for your life. Any actions you can take quickly to make an adversary concentrate on something else (like how much his shins hurt!) are fair game.

• Protect your other weapons, such as a baton or an aerosol spray, from an opponent's takeaway moves, too.

Never Stop Looking for More. More threats, that is. Once you find one, start searching for the next one. In other words, if you find and remove one weapon while searching a suspect, immediately begin looking for the next one. (Streetwise crooks sometimes carry backups, too!) If you find and secure one burglar during a building search, start seeking his partner or partners. Don't relax too soon.

Expect the Unexpected. Your bad guy may not be reading from the same script you have. Realize that he may not react in the way you might expect in any given confrontation. He may, for instance, respond to your entirely reasonable instructions by fleeing–or drawing a weapon. Be ready for surprises. When one officer engaged in a gunfight with a suspect in a parking lot, it's doubtful she expected him to leave the cover of the car he was hiding behind and advance by running over the hood, top and trunk of the car while firing down at her. She was killed.

Expect the unexpected. Determine to survive.

Have Some Contingency Plans. Make some plans in advance for what you will do when faced with some specific threats, such as losing your weapon, seeing your partner disarmed or coming under attack by a sniper. That way, when and if you ever face a similar situation for real you will have at least some idea of what to do in response. Plan now for what you might do later. It should help make you safer if one day you face that contingency for real.

Don't Be a Cowboy–Or Cowgirl. In other words, do not work at becoming a hero. Do not go in alone or wave off a backup when your safety sense tells you that you should have help. Trying to prove something to someone–particularly yourself–could well earn you a trip to the hospital or the morgue. Fake, tombstone courage is neither needed nor welcome in today's law enforcement agencies. Save your career as well as your life by avoiding it like the plague.

Remain Constantly Alert on the Job. You cannot afford to be hung over, sick, ultra-tired, sleepy or asleep on the law enforcement job. The work is potentially dangerous enough that you need all of your faculties and senses functioning at their full output. Anything less is dangerous. That means that daydreaming and sleepwalking your way through your tasks are out, too. Stay alert and stay alive, instead.

Maintain Proficiency Via Practice. Know how to use well all of the equipment involved in your job, from vehicles to firearms to handcuffs to batons and defensive aerosols. You will not retain proficiency indefinitely on a given piece of equipment just because you learned it in the academy. Regular practice under the supervision of a qualified instructor is the only sure way to maintain skill with the tools of your job. If your training and practice identify a specific weakness, get expert help and work at fixing it. On the street you cannot be *too* good with your equipment. Be sure your stuff is kept clean and properly maintained, too. You don't need a malfunction at crunch time.

Realize That All Equipment Has Limitations. You have limits. So does your equipment. Don't expect it to do a job for which it was not intended. Your police vehicle, for example, is very likely a slightly modified family car with lights and a special paint job. Don't expect it to perform like a high-priced race car in a chase. It won't, and thinking that it will could get you in over your head in a hurry. The same holds true for defensive aerosols, firearms and restraint devices. Each has the ability to fail or work at less than 100 percent effectiveness. That's why you always need to have other options up your sleeve in case things don't go quite as you planned.

Make a Decision. When faced with a crisis or a real challenge, make a conscious decision to do *something*. Your decision does not have to be a flawless one. But make it rather than remaining frozen in place by indecisiveness. Problem is, if you can't or won't make a decision, you may hand the decision-making over to someone who probably does not have your best interests in mind. Make a decision. Then, act on it.

Stay in Shape. More than a few officers have died after being overpowered by a street opponent. You don't want that to happen to you. You do not have to be the biggest, strongest guy or gal in town. But you need to work at having a reasonable amount of aerobic endurance and upper body strength. That means exercising, working out, eating reasonably healthy and avoiding smoking or other unhealthy habits. Since there will always be *somebody* stronger than you are out there, you also help protect yourself by learning physical control tactics and techniques devised to help you overcome a bigger, stronger opponent.

Handcuff Properly. As one old salt put it, "if they're worth arresting they're worth cuffing." That remains true regardless of age, attitude, size or gender. *Properly* handcuffed requires that your subject must be secured with his hands *behind* him, the cuffs double-locked and snug but not circulation-ending tight.

Search Correctly. Correctly translates into thoroughly, completely and systematically, head to toe. No one is taken into custody who doesn't get searched properly. There is no "magic" number of times that an arrestee or prisoner must be searched. Rather, search him as many times as is required to make you feel comfortable that he no longer has anything on him with which he could hurt you, himself or anyone else.

Control Your Environment. Be constantly aware of what is going on around you and who is in the immediate area. Stay alert for uninvolved others to try and get involved. In addition, be light and noise conscious. Use light and sound to your advantage. If you are attempting to move stealthily and remain undetected, you do not want noise from your portable radio or jingling, banging equipment (such as keys or a baton) to announce your position. Where possible, follow the rule of "him in the light, me in the dark" when it comes to illumination. You don't want to set yourself up as a target by positioning your body in front of a light source, natural or otherwise.

Practice Tactical Withdrawl, as Required. Before you storm ahead on an ill-advised course of action, ask yourself: Is this worth dying for? Is it even worth losing some teeth over? Is it worth injury or death to an uninvolved, innocent citizen? Then, act on your answer, which hopefully always will be in the negative.

It can be hard to control the urge that says "I've *got* to get this guy *now*," but the wiser and safer route may be to wait until the odds of a safe outcome are more in your favor. That may even mean that the bad guy is allowed to escape temporarily, as in a high-speed vehicle pursuit that has started to get out of hand. There is almost always another day–assuming you're still around because you backed off when it was wise to do so.

Count on Your Good Common Sense. Trust your own, experience-based smarts. Listen to that little, internal voice that may be trying to warn you. If a given situation looks bad, sounds bad or smells bad to you, it probably *is* bad. Try something else, instead. You probably did not get this far in life by being stupid, so trust your good judgment and act accordingly.

Have a Winning Mindset. Concentrate on coming out on top. Refuse to harbor thoughts of failure when it comes to your safety and survival. Be *certain* you'll always finish as the victor. Determine now that if it ever comes down to you or the opposition going home in one piece, you always will emerge the winner.

Survive Emotionally, Too. Know now that you cannot alone solve all of the world's problems. Or even those on your own shift or beat. Just resolve to do the best you can at all times. Keep things in perspective. Do not give in to self-destructive behavior following a disturbing incident. Talk to others. Get professional aid if you need it. But know that you are a normal human being who has faced and survived abnormal circumstances. You *will* survive and grow stronger.

SOME "SPECIAL" DANGERS

There are things out there besides a bad guy's bullets that can harm you. A complete survival package involves protecting yourself from anything that could cause you injury. That includes accidents, illnesses and even vicious animals (including little Foo-Foo who bites you on a report-taking call!) It also includes the following threats:

Edged and Pointed Weapons. There is just something about a shiny steel blade that can send chills down the stiffest spine. Some peace officers have even commented that they would rather be shot than cut, although the distinction appears a dubious one.

Sharp instruments continue to be the weapons of choice for some very violent offenders, even in a land of plentiful handguns. Sometimes they are carried as a backup weapon to a gun. They're cheap, easy to hide and only loosely restricted by laws. They are quickly at hand, don't require ammunition and are easy to use, assuming you don't mind getting your hands messy. And they still result in the deaths of law enforcement officers. It is definitely worth your while to prepare well against the edged and pointed weapons threat.

Remaining conscious of your surroundings is your first line of defense against bladed weapons. Watch the hands of those around you. This includes inmates or prisoners who may be present in a so-called "secure" environment. As you know, homemade "shanks" and similar sharp instruments are a favorite of the jailhouse crowd.

Faithfully maintain a reactionary gap of at least 5-6 feet anytime you are contacting someone on the street. You do not want him to be able simply to reach out and stick you. If you have reason to suspect he has an edged weapon, back off, draw your weapon and seek cover. Order him to drop it. Actual field tests (the instructors of the excellent Calibre Press seminars do some eye-opening ones) show that a person with a knife can cross the average-sized residential room and "stab" an officer who has a holstered weapon before that officer can "fire" to save himself. Remember that the next time you are facing an adversary brandishing a knife.

Leave yourself a big safety margin (25 feet is not too much) anytime you face someone with a displayed, bladed weapon. With your handgun drawn and on target and you behind cover, if it is available, issue an oral direction: "Police! Drop the weapon! Do it now or you will be shot!" Repeat the instructions, if necessary, but stay put where you are.

Do not advance on an uncontrolled subject still wielding a blade. Keep him covered and stay alert as you wait for him to obey. Keep a line of retreat available for yourself, should you elect to back off and leave him by himself. That's assuming, of course, that he'll let you. Stay ready to fire if he attacks. If you do decide to back off, do so slowly and carefully. This is not the time to stumble and fall. Consider using natural barriers, such as furniture, etc., placed between him and you. But whatever else you do, stay ready to shoot to stop his life-threatening actions if he launches a bladed attack.

Realize that your voice and your firearm are both means of defense if you are confronted by an attacker with a blade. If the first fails, be prepared to move quickly to the next. There are a few highly-skilled officers out there who may be good enough to reliably meet a bladed attacker's rush with an impact instrument or bare hands. But the vast majority of officers do not fall into that category. Defensive aerosols such as oleoresin capsicum (OC) may also be a good option to try before you escalate to lethal force, assuming you have time and distance enough to use them safely. But do not place yourself at great risk of serious injury or death by responding inadequately or too late to an attack by a sharp or pointed weapon of any kind.

Defense Against Disease. Many of the people you contact on your job are not the healthiest specimens on the face of the earth. They can harbor skin diseases, hepatitis, tuberculosis, acquired immune deficiency syndrome (AIDS) or any combination thereof. Because of their often-unhealthy lifestyle, they also can infect you with an infinite variety of "plain vanilla" maladies, ranging from colds to heavy-duty influenza. Prevention is your first and best line of defense against all of these ailments. The foremost means of protecting yourself from illness is to maintain a healthy lifestyle. Eat right and get enough rest. (Cops often don't do well with these two!) You do not want your body's lowered natural resistance system to put out the welcome mat for any of those pesky microbes. Prevention also means taking advantage of protective vaccines offered by your employer, such as tetanus antitoxin, the Hepatitis B vaccine series and flu shots. All may provide a measure of protection.

Excellent personal hygiene is also a great defense against "sharing" diseases. Make like a doctor: Wash your hands often on the job, particularly after handling arrestees. In the field, carry a supply of the packaged, pre-moistened towelettes. Some officers favor the ones with a built-in disinfectant. Use a new one each time you clean your hands. And speaking of hands: Try to keep them away from your mouth, nose and eyes as much as possible. Hand to face is a great way to admit germs into your body. Handling the car's steering wheel or radio microphone and then touching your face is an excellent way to pick up whatever ailments are currently bothering your peers who may have used the same vehicle.

A good supply of disposable, latex gloves should be a part of your personal duty equipment. So should a good pair of gloves that are both fluid and puncture resistant. Keep them with you on the job. Clean them periodically according to the manufacturer's instructions. Try to get in the good habit of putting them on before coming to close quarters with a "client."

Give yourself some added protection against such diseases as AIDS and hepatitis by avoiding the needles drug users sometimes have on them. Wear your gloves. Before searching, *ask* the person if he has anything sharp on him that could hurt you. Some officers utilize a voice inflection that tells the arrestee that officer and prisoner alike will regret it if the searcher is injured by something said not to be present. When you search, softly pat and gently *squeeze* the clothing from the outside rather than thrusting your hands into pockets. Once you are convinced he has no weapons on him, have *him* turn all of his pockets inside out and finish emptying them.

If you do get hurt by *any* object, clean the wound with soap and water and apply an antiseptic right away. Seek medical attention promptly. A physician may decide to treat you with a tetanus shot or some other protective measure. If you act promptly, there is a very good chance you won't get sick at all. Document your injury with your employer, too.

Explosive Devices. The bombers are back. The cowards who kill and maim without having the courage to face their perceived enemies head-on never really left us, but recent years have seen a new proliferation of violent, extremist people who include law enforcement agents on their lengthy list of enemies. Incendiary, explosive or both, all of the devices fashioned by these criminals constitute a danger to you, the law enforcement officer who must face them. As always, the watchword for you is *caution*, not foolhardy heroics.

Gasoline bombs and similar devices probably remain the "poor man's" favorite bomb, even in an era of deadly vehicle-borne and letter or package devices. Often consisting of no more than a bottle of gasoline and a lighted, cloth wick, these thrown weapons can injure or kill. If you are outdoors, your best defense is to remain constantly alert for an ambush and avoid letting any burning material get on you. If you do get hit, your response is to drop and roll to smother the flames, then draw your weapon, get to cover and prepare to defend yourself from further attack. If your patrol vehicle is hit with you inside it, the danger probably looks greater than it actually is. If your windows are closed, you should be able to drive safely out of the danger zone with little chance of the flames getting into the vehicle before dying out. Then, get help on the way and prepare your counterattack. If your vehicle is disabled or your path hopelessly blocked, roll out low from your passenger-side door and get to good cover with your weapon out and ready. Stay sharp. Additional missiles or gunfire may follow.

In the past, the victims of bombing attacks have sometimes panicked and run right into a well-laid trap beyond the initial explosive device. Staying in control of yourself under a noisy and seemingly-devastating attack is a lot easier said than done, but retaining mental and emotional control under assault has saved the lives of more than a few soldiers and law enforcement officers. It works.

Even better than surviving a bombing attack is keeping yourself from being exposed at close quarters to one. With bombings on the increase these days you might do well to consider the following advice as sound protection against becoming a bomber's victim:

• Realize that expertise on how to build an explosive device is out there today. It is available from ex-military people, literature and videotapes. Equally available are the raw ingredients to build a bomb. Stolen military and commercial explosives are accessible to the bomb-maker, too.

• Take seriously all reports of planted explosive devices, including apparent crank calls, until each is proven false. The next caller just might be telling the truth.

• Also believe the subject you contact in-person who claims he has a live grenade or other explosive ordnance. Move back, take cover and be prepared to use force to defend yourself.

• Never try to play hero by attempting to move or disarm a suspected explosive device unless you are highly-trained in that skill. Evacuate the area and call in the bomb squad or military explosives experts.

• Be aware that a bomber attempting to entrap law enforcement personnel may plant a second explosive device set to go off minutes after the first one while emergency personnel are present. On-scene of a blast, keep an eye out for suspicious parcels or vehicles.

• Be especially wary of suspicious packages or vehicles left near governmental facilities, including law enforcement buildings. If you are unsure, treat it as a potential bomb, evacuate the area and summon expert assistance to investigate further.

• Look around, under and on your vehicle before you take the street and when you have been out of sight of the car on a call or contact. Know that law enforcement facilities and vehicles serve as a virtual magnet for all kinds of nuts with an ax to grind.

• Recognize that most explosive devices do not resemble a taped bunch of red sticks with "dynamite" printed in bold, black letters! A bomb can take virtually any shape or form from a stuffed toy to a radio to a mailed package wrapped in brown paper. Bombs don't have to look like bombs to do you in. If in doubt, don't touch. Get expert help.

• Realize that bombs may be found just about anywhere. You can encounter one while working the front desk, searching the interior of a just-burglarized abortion clinic or probing a marijuana grower's private field. Or you might find one while searching the residence of an illegal drug manufacturer or the "clubhouse" of a street gang or outlaw biker group. As a result, you might consider entering one of these locations from a nontraditional point while keeping a sharp eye out for trip wires and other indicators of booby traps. Touch nothing that looks suspicious.

There is no need for you to become paranoid and see an explosive device under every car and behind every bush. Just use your good common sense and recognize the potential for danger where it really does exist. Where explosive devices are concerned, some final, to the point advice should serve you well in protecting yourself and others from their dangers:

DON'T TOUCH IT.
GET EVERYONE AWAY FROM IT.
GET SPECIALIZED HELP.

LEARNING FROM EXPERIENCE

As you advance through a career in law enforcement you will pick up many additional safety tactics and techniques to add to your survival toolbox. Many of these you will develop and refine based upon your specialized training, life experience and on-the-job lessons—a few of which may have been learned the hard way. As your experience grows you also will find ways to improve on or at least personalize for your own needs some of the safety guidelines discussed in this book. That's fine, too.

A major source of officer survival knowledge you should not overlook is the combined street smarts and experience-based wisdom of your peers and supervisors. You should never pass up the opportunity to discuss safety in general or the handling of a specific call or assignment with your fellow professionals. Since life experiences and on-the-job exposures will vary widely even on the same department, these people almost certainly will have had some adventures you have not—at least not yet. Carefully evaluate what they have to say. Realize that they may have made some serious survival errors on the way to a "successful" conclusion. Then, decide which "tricks of the trade" or variances of existing practices you may want to file away mentally for possible application later, should the need arise.

Talking with as well as listening to cautious, veteran officers may bring you such common sense safety tips as:

• Take your car keys with you anytime you are going to be out of sight of your police vehicle. This is especially true if you're about to go in foot pursuit after someone. You really don't want to join the ranks of officers who have ended up chasing their own car—on foot. Save yourself some major embarrassment. Take an extra second or two and collect your keys.

• Always carry an extra, hidden handcuff key on your person. It'll help a lot if you happen to break or lose your primary key. More important, it may offer you an added chance at survival should you ever be taken hostage and secured with your own cuffs. Consider hiding places that you can get easy access to, such as taped under your gun belt or some other item of leather gear. Your wallet, waistband or a deep pocket might work, too. Do a little experimenting to see what works best for you.

• When you are on-duty, always know where you are, at least as closely as you can. If you need help in a hurry, your dispatcher will need to know instantly where to send it. "The corner of fire hydrant and big tree" won't help much, so stay constantly aware of your location and surroundings.

• Portable radios give officers a great deal of freedom and help free them from the dictates of the in-car unit. But wandering too widely without letting your dispatcher know what you are up to can spell disaster. Don't exit your car to make a contact without letting someone know where you are and what you are doing.

• Reduce the size of a target you present to a potential shooter. Don't leave something exposed that you want to keep attached. The idea is to make yourself really small, at least insofar as your opponent's sight picture is concerned. One old salt put it this way: "The thing is to get an 18-inch butt behind an 8-inch pole." That's getting to the point.

• Shout "Police!" or "Sheriff!" or whatever is appropriate for your agency anytime you confront someone and give a verbal command. It both asserts control and clearly identifies who you are to both the subject of your attentions and any nearby witnesses. If the offender chooses to resist, he will not be able to claim later that he thought he was being set upon by thugs or Martians. That remains good advice even if you are working in uniform and driving a marked car with Christmas lights on top.

• Do coordinate your moves with your partner or backup, but don't stay so close together that a single shot could take you both out. Maintain several feet of space between the two of you.

• Whether you are working on foot or in a vehicle, try to avoid developing easy-to-predict patterns in your patrol behavior. Don't eat at the same restaurant or visit the same convenience store at exactly the same time each shift. Don't do your building checks in exactly the same order or approach these structures from precisely the same direction each time. Don't sit in exactly the same spot to work traffic. or do reports every watch. The more routines you develop, the easier you make it for an ambusher to plan an attack. Vary your operations as much as you realistically can.

• Get in the practice of keeping your gun hand free and empty during a contact. You don't want to be slowed down in getting your handgun by having to stick that expensive radio or flashlight someplace when it's time to have your sidearm in your grasp. At the very least, put nothing in your gun hand that you are unwilling to drop instantly if the need arises. That would make it alright to handle things like vehicle papers and driver's licenses in your favored mitt.

• If you are fortunate enough to have a car partner, set an unbreakable rule for the two of you: *Both* of you will be out of the car and involved in either an active or a covering role on *every* contact. Nobody should be lounging in the vehicle until it's his or her "turn" to write a ticket or catch a report. The value of an always-ready backup is too great to be thrown away through laziness.

• Do not allow a subject or suspect you are "checking out" to monitor your two-way radio transmissions, either from your car radio or your portable. If he is not secured, he does not have to know your radio codes to realize he doesn't like the sound of "your subject is Code 5" from the dispatcher. That little piece of information just might goad him to flee—or attack. Keep the radio's volume turned down and keep him far enough distant that he cannot understand the spoken messages. Even when he *is* secured and in your back seat he doesn't really need to be given a crash course in your radio or computer net operations. Keep your communications secure and keep him guessing.

• While your patol car is in motion, do not allow another vehicle to linger in your "blind spot" just over your left shoulder. Alter your speed, if necessary, to change the picture. You do not want that driver's actions, accidental or otherwise, to endanger you. If you are extra suspicious about who's trailing back there, pull off the road and look him over as he passes.

• Pierce R. Brooks once remarked that one thing police recruits have to do today is *unlearn* all the misinformation they have picked up from the television cop shows and movies. One popular piece of fiction shows the bad guy being blown backwards through a plate glass window or whatever by a single blast from the hero's gun. In real life, of course, it doesn't work that way. There is virtually no round or firearm you can carry around with you that is capable of doing that to a human body. Officers involved in shootouts actually have reported being stunned when shots that they knew were hitting their adversary did not seem to be having any devastating efect. That's to be expected. Unless a round strikes the brain or spinal cord, it's entirely possible that an opponent will not react instantly to your accurately-placed gunfire. That's one of the reasons behind the officer survival maxim:

You fire to stop the deadly threat. You don't shoot to kill. You don't shoot to wound. You fire at center mass (because that's what you have the best chance of hitting) to stop the threat. You fire to stop the threat whether it takes one round or many more to have the desired effect: the cessation of the life-threatening actions on the part of your adversary. Obviously, if no threat exists, you do not have the right to fire at all.

• Remember that sound officer safety practices are not incompatible with good police-community relations. Indeed, the first rule of officer safety is to treat everyone you contact fairly and decently. It makes no sense to fight if you don't have to. It also looks a lot better for you when you can truthfully explain to your boss or Internal Affairs or the jury that you tried other options before you resorted to the use of force. There is another very practical advantage for you in using courtesy, reasoning and patience before you escalate your force options. This may very well not be the last time you encounter the ornery so-and-so you are dealing with tonight. There's a good chance he'll remember next time how he was treated this time. That may be important some day when you've got your hands full with a new problem in, say, a darkened barroom and, unknown and unobserved by you, your prior "customer" is behind you. Getting along, where possible, is always worth a try.

SUMMARY

You already know that law enforcement is a potentially dangerous undertaking. By the end of this chapter, you also should be aware of many of the practical, time-proven tactics and techniques you can employ to make your job a lot less hazardous. They have been developed over time by a lot of good officers. They *do* save law enforcement lives. Applied properly and consistently, they could save *yours.*

This chapter's safety and survival guidelines provide the backbone for everything that follows. Many of them will be repeated from time to time, in one form or another, because they apply to every single assignment you draw in law enforcement. They are worth committing to memory. Next, we will take a look at some specific threats to your continued good health as a frontline law enforcer. Even more important, we will examine some proven-effective ways to counter them.

STREET SURVIVAL CHECKLIST FOR STAYING ALIVE

1. Reread and review this chapter's guidelines for staying alive. Refresh yourself on them from time to time. They can help you save your own life.

2. Rely on specialized protective equipment and safety-smart procedures and precautions to shield yourself from infectious disease risks.

3. Realize the danger posed to you by sharp and edged weapons and employ sound tactics and techniques to defend yourself from them.

4. Recognize the special dangers posed by explosive devices and use extreme caution anytime the presence of one is even remotely suspected.

5. Learn from the street survival experiences of others in order to make yourself a more street-smart professional. Discuss your job and how to do it safely.

Chapter Four

SUSPICIOUS PERSONS AND SITUATIONS

On the East Coast, an eight-year veteran officer was fatally wounded in a 4 A.M. incident. The officer, on vehicle patrol, encountered two adult males and had placed one against the police car when the second drew a .380-caliber handgun from his coat and shot the officer in the back of the head at point-blank range.

In the West, an off-duty detective was fatally wounded in a midnight suspicious person encounter. The 18-year veteran was searching the backyard of a neighbor who had called him to report a prowler when he was shot in the neck with a 9mm semiautomatic. Subsequent investigation identified the killer as an ex-boyfriend of the woman complainant.

A city patrolman in the Northeast was killed at 3:42 P.M. after responding to a 911 call of a suspicious person. While backup officers remained outside, the officer and his partner entered a shop and were told by a man standing at the counter that everything was "alright." A hidden subject then came out from behind a wall and shot the victim officer in the head with a 9mm handgun. The partner officer returned fire and wounded one suspect.

The cold, bloody statistics tell the story. Investigating a suspicious person or situation can represent a high-risk assignment for an American law enforcement officer. During an average year, only the activity of making arrests kills more peacekeepers. In the sample year of 1994, for example, 15 of a total of 76 officers killed were murdered while investigating suspicious persons or circumstances. During the ten year period of 1985-1994, some 114 officers were feloniously killed by suspicious persons. Indeed, suspicious individuals and incidents are dangerous to you.

But *why* are suspicious persons so potentially hazardous for you? The biggest danger factor inherent in the suspicious person or incident call or contact can be found in the *information disadvantage* often experienced by the involved officer. He may, for instance, know only that Mrs. Jones called to report a "suspicious person" standing on a street corner. In another version of that scenario, he may know only that he has observed a subject standing on the corner who appears to be out of place for the time, locale or circumstances or who otherwise "just doesn't feel right." At least at the outset, that may be all the officer knows for a certainty.

On the other hand, the same "suspicious subject" knows that (choose one or more from the following) he is armed, has just committed a felony down the street, is wanted on a major warrant or is an escapee or fugitive from justice and is determined not to be taken, no matter what the cost to the officer he is about to meet. Worse still, he may assume that the officer knows or is about to learn all of these things. The stage has been set for disaster in the pending confrontation.

But the matchup between peacekeeper and criminal does not have to end in tragedy for the good guys. Over time, veteran law enforcement officers and trainers have developed and refined practical tactics and field survival procedures for neutralizing the information advantage that may be held by the offender. These techniques emphasize the importance of careful observations, information-gathering and decision-making by the alert officer, starting before the actual contact occurs.

BEFORE THE CONTACT

When you contact a suspicious person, you want to do it the right way—in all ways. That means you must do it right legally, too. Although statutes and ordinances will vary from one jurisdiction to the next (know yours!), generally you lawfully can contact and temporarily detain someone you have reasonable grounds to believe is about to commit, is committing at present or has just committed a criminal act. The manner in which you conduct this contact must be reasonable, as must the length of time you detain the individual without arresting and charging him. That would, for instance, prohibit you from holding at gunpoint a 12-year-old you only suspect of having shoplifted a cold drink. It would also keep you from forcibly detaining for an hour without arrest a person found walking in the area of a prowler call.

No matter where you work in law enforcement, you have the legal right to conduct a pat-down search of a suspicious person in an attempt to discover any threats to your safety that might be present, such as weapons. Again, your tactics must be reasonable and the extent of your search limited. You would not, for instance, be authorized to perform a strip search of an unarrested hitchhiker who has given no indication of having concealed a weapon. You also would be unable lawfully to look into a matchbox or envelope under the pretext of looking for a gun.

If your cursory search does turn up a weapon or other contraband, in order for that evidence to be admissible in court later you will have to put into words exactly *why* you felt the subject possessed a weapon or otherwise posed a serious threat to you and caused you to do a pat-down. Your law enforcement experience counts here and you can cite such factors as:

• You observe conditions indicative of a weapon, such as a bulge in the waistband or the bottom of a holster showing from under clothing;

• The subject is known by you to carry weapons;

• The contact is occurring on a call where weapons were reported present;

• The contact is occurring in a high-crime neighborhood;

• You observe furtive actions by the subject that lead you to believe he is concealing or ditching a weapon;

• The subject makes voluntary statements about the presence of a weapon, and so on.

Assuming that you have decided that it is both lawful and tactically sound to contact a suspicious person, what happens next? First of all, don't be in a big hurry to make the contact. Particularly if your presence has not yet been detected, observe your party or parties from a distance. Who is involved? What do they appear to be doing? Is there any evidence of a crime or weapon?

Find out as much as you can from your own observations as well as any other available information sources (dispatch, the complainant, license plate checks, etc.) before you make contact. Your goal here is to reduce or neutralize the information gap. What you learn may tell you that you want to get help before you make contact, or go in with gun in hand when you do. Apply all of your officer survival knowledge and tactics to what you learn.

Whether you are indoors or out, in a vehicle or afoot, try to approach quietly from your subject's rear. You want the advantage of surprise on *your* side, not the other way around. Keep your quarry in sight at all times. Keep watching his hands. Look for a weapon. Stay alert for a new threat to appear, like an additional subject you had not noticed initially. Don't hesitate to back off until help arrives if the odds appear stacked against your approaching as a lone officer.

Never, ever drive up to a suspicous person and initiate the contact while still seated in your vehicle. It's a great way to get yourself killed. Don't drive past him, stop, and walk back, either. You're again at a disadvantage if you do. Make your approach from the rear if you can. If you have a choice, pick a spot for the contact that is to your advantage. At night, that might mean a place that is well-lighted with room to get your car out of passing traffic. A spot with limited escape routes is also nice. Avoid, where possible, locations that are especially risky for you, like bar parking lots or known-hostile neighborhoods. If you must make a contact in one of these locales, be sure you have a backup quickly at hand to cover you while you are preoccupied with your subject or subjects.

MAKING CONTACT

As you start your approach to your party, remain conscious of potential cover possibilities just in case things go sour and a weapon appears. Identify yourself: "Police officer! I'd like to talk to you a minute, please!" What you say and how you say it will, of course, depend upon the situation and the degree of danger you sense. The latter might dictate, for instance, that you don't approach at all but go to cover, point your weapon and start issuing orders from there. Use your best judgment based on what you know about the pending contact so far.

Once you do make contact, carefully maintain a reactionary gap of 5-6 feet and do not allow a suspicious subject to press in too close. Order him to remain in one spot, if need be. Don't allow him to sucker you in by talking so quietly that you cannot hear him, or by holding his i.d. close to his body for you to look at. Stay sharp and refuse to play those dangerous games.

Never stand between two subjects, and do not allow anyone to maneuver into a position behind you. Remain very conscious of exactly who is where, and what they are doing at all times. Call for assistance immediately if it appears that your party is escalating or deliberately disobeying and provoking you. Don't hesitate to give clear, firm orders about what you expect your subject to do and refrain from doing. Be ready to defend yourself at all times, and make it clear via your calm, firm, in command demeanor that you will do so.

As noted, do a thorough, pat-down search if you feel your safety requires it. It is preferable to have a covering officer on hand when you do. Have the subject face away from you, legs apart and fingers laced atop his head, as you search for weapons from his rear. Be sure you keep one hand gripping his interlaced fingers as you pat him down. See that he stays off-balance, too. But don't overreach and lose your own balance.

Anytime you have a second officer to assist you on a suspicious person contact, be sure that the two of you implement good contact and cover tactics. Be a good cover officer yourself when the roles are reversed, attentive and ready to intervene with whatever force is required to protect the contact officer.

Keep a suspicious person's hands under close watch before, during and after you approach him. Any hand you cannot see should be regarded as a caution flag. But don't order your subject to remove his hands from his pockets unless you are ready to react in case he produces a deadly surprise when he does. Depending upon what you know or suspect about the contact, that may mean drawing down on the subject and issuing your orders from behind solid cover. Keep your weapon leveled on him as you order him to bring his paws *slowly* into full view. Let him know that they are to remain that way throughout the contact. You do not have to be abusive with any of these instructions; you do need to be firm and clearly in command of the encounter. Courtesy and control *can* work together.

Do not overreach your limitations. It is extremely difficult (and generally unsafe) to try to keep track of more than two persons, particularly if they are less than cooperative. Remain alert to their actions as well as your surroundings and get a cover officer on the way. Don't begin searches or attempt enforcement action with multiple subjects until that help gets there. Then, be very sure your sworn helper knows what you plan to do and what is expected of him. Any suspicious person call or contact contains within it the possibility of sudden violence, so you cannot afford to get sloppy.

If you do not take your suspicious party into custody, make your break with him a clean one. Watch him (and your back) until he is well beyond reach or attack. Do not drop your guard or get too preoccupied with filling out a contact card or other paperwork. He just may be planning to return and assault you. Stay sensitive to your environment and stay safe at the same time.

PROWLER CALLS

Because they answer so many of them over a career, for too many law enforcement officers prowler calls come very close to becoming "routine." In actuality, they are anything but. Officers have been killed on "prowler there now" assignments. "Simple" prowlers have turned out to be armed criminals about to commit or fleeing from a major felony crime. They have been young juveniles involved in mayhem ranging from burglary to sexual assault to murder. They have even been older persons or other "pillars of the community" who are desperate not to have their identity as a window peeper or pervert revealed, and are thereby willing to attack a peace officer to prevent discovery. Indeed, a "simple" prowler can turn into just about anything. Once more, the danger of the unknown looms large for the unprepared officer.

Too many officers make the dangerous assumption that the explanation for a prowler report can almost always be found in the wind, the neighbor's cat or the overactive imagination of the caller. Or they assume that if a prowler really *was* there, he'll be long gone before their arrival. As you know well, relaxing too soon as a result of any such assumption can prove fatal. Likewise, as a safety-smart officer you know better than to accept at face value any of these tried-and-failed excuses from an intercepted prowler:

"I was just looking for a dark spot to relieve myself."
"I was looking for my cat, dog, mongoose, etc."
"I'm at the wrong address; I got lost."
"I'm just drunk and confused."
"I was taking a shortcut."

"I was hiding from muggers, gang members, Martians, etc."

"I live here."

Just a bit more investigation on your part should serve to confirm or debunk any such proclamations of innocence. Make careful inquiry.

Prowler calls require the same attention to good officer safety practices that you apply to your other interactions with unknown risks. Because it is impossible to assess completely the potential for danger at the beginning of the assignment, prowler calls should always require the presence of a backup or second officer. Do not cancel that assistance until and unless you are positive you will not need it. In addition, do not hesitate to search for weapons or a suspected prowler you have detained, even though you may not have yet developed sufficient probable cause for an arrest. It's your safety that is at stake here. You can always explain truthfully and even offer an apology, where appropriate, if you later determine that your subject is clearly innocent of any wrongdoing. Your survival, however, must remain your first consideration.

There are several precautions you can take to increase your chances of capturing a criminal while you protect yourself from injury, accidental or otherwise, on a prowler assignment. They include the following:

Your goal is to surprise the prowler, if he is still present, not have things happen the other way around. Arrive quietly and inconspicuously. Avoid sirens, racing engines, squealing tires and slamming patrol car doors. Turn your radio volume down. Remember that little sounds can travel a great distance at night.

Park several addresses away from your target address and move in on foot, first quieting any noisy personal equipment, such as jingling keys, a banging nightstick or a squawking portable radio. Be sure that your dispatcher lets the caller know when you are on-scene so that you don't get shot by a nervous complainant. Once you start to move in, prevent an ambush by avoiding the most obvious (and probably the most visible) pathway to where you're going. Instead of marching straight up the sidewalk, for instance, move through the front yards closer to the cover offered by the structures.

Search in tandem with a backup officer. If you don't have a partner already with you, await the arrival of the second unit before you begin a detailed search. Be sure everybody among the good guys knows where everyone else is, where they're going and what they are doing. Cops have been shot by other cops on prowler calls.

Limit the use of your spotlight and flashlight once you are on-scene. They announce your presence and they just might give an adversary a bright target to aim for in the dark. Hold your hand-light away from your body and don't keep it illuminated the whole time. Just use it when you really need it.

If you can, find out from your dispatcher or the caller if there are special hazards on-scene that you need to be aware of: dogs, holes in the backyard, clotheslines and (especially) other persons who may be outside looking for the prowler. Your dispatcher already should have discouraged any vigilante searches and asked the reporting party to stay inside and on an open telephone line to your communications center. The caller also should be queried about any weapons he may have armed himself with. He should be encouraged to put them down now.

Your search for hints of a prowler's presence must be a complete and careful one. Be alert for tracks in snow or wet grass and listen for neighborhood dogs that may betray a prowler's location or direction of travel. Look for other clues of something amiss, like a suspicious vehicle parked nearby or someone loitering in the area. Don't put a possible threat behind you until you have checked it out and discounted it as a danger. When you move, use cover to your advantage. Stick close to the wall of the structure when rounding a corner, but don't pass the corner at all without first peeking around it, quick and low, while the rest of your body remains behind cover. Don't proceed mindlessly into an area where you cannot see the "lay of the land" and any hazards (including prowlers) that might be lurking there.

Your prowler search should be slow, careful and thorough. Conduct it systematically with your search partner. Prowlers have been known to conceal themselves in some pretty amazing places (in a doghouse, high in a tree, on the roof), so don't overlook *any* likely or unlikely hiding spots, such as:
  • under stairs and inside window wells,
  • in or under parked vehicles of all kinds,
  • under stacked lawn furniture, boxes and other objects,
  • inside sheds, garages and outbuildings,
  • under shrubs and bushes, and
  • just about anywhere a human body could be concealed.
Again, do not bypass any potential hiding spot without first clearing it carefully for offenders. Get sloppy and the "best" that will happen is

that you'll fail to find the offender. The worst case scenario could be bloody indeed.

Your decision about whether or not to have your sidearm in hand during your probe for a prowler should depend on what you believe you are facing from the information you have. If you have reason to believe your subject is armed, you obviously should be working with a backup officer and sticking extremely close to cover with your gun drawn and at the ready. But as in any other search operation where a lethal threat is not in evidence, keep your finger away from the trigger and outside of the trigger guard. Otherwise, an accidental discharge could occur if you stumble or are startled. If no deadly threat is believed to be present, leave your sidearm snapped into its holster as you search. Be prepared to draw quickly should a lethal threat suddenly present itself.

In sum, *expect* to find danger when you go searching for a prowler. Plan your every action towards effectively countering it if it's present. If it is, you will protect yourself even as you hold the offender accountable for his actions.

FOOT PURSUITS

Whether he turns out to be a prowler or some other variety of suspicious individual, your subject may respond to your intervention by fleeing on foot. If he does, you are again facing a challenge with considerable potential for a dangerous confrontation. By the very nature of a foot chase, the risk of accidental injury of one degree or another is also present, as virtually hundreds of officers discover to their discomfort every year. Others escape an accidental injury only to be attacked and hurt (or worse) by a subject they caught up with but lost the struggle to. Obviously, just catching up to a fleeing offender is only part of the challenge. What happens when you get there will have a lot to say about whether you make it through the encounter alive or not.

The veteran street cop utilizes time-proven techniques for bringing his quarry safely into custody at the end of a foot chase. You can use some of the same "tricks of the trade" to take some of the danger out of your own pursuits that just happen to be on foot. Try on the following advice from the veterans:

Whether you are alone or not, never begin a foot pursuit without first radioing your dispatcher where you are, what you are doing, why you are chasing and your direction of travel. If possible, add a quick description of your subject. It takes a bit of time, but it's *vital* that your listening peers as well as your dispatcher know what's up. Your brief radio message will get help on the way fast and just may be the determining factor in keeping you safe even as your suspect is brought into custody.

If you happen to have a partner or assist unit on-scene when the chase begins, do not split up to chase multiple suspects or try to cut off a single, fleeing individual. More than a couple of officers have been killed by a subject they were chasing after voluntarily surrendering their advantage of having superior manpower at hand. Don't give up your strength of numbers advantage. Stick together and guarantee that you get at least one bad guy, and safely at that. If you are alone when the chase begins and must start the pursuit alone, be sure you get help on the way before you commit yourself to a solo chase operation. Be cautious and realize that you are alone without another set of senses and muscles yet there to help you. Respond carefully.

If you are about to commence a foot chase after a subject who has just fled from a vehicle, never run past the stopped car without first slowing way down and clearing it carefully for other suspects. You don't need to get attacked from behind once you go by. If the vehicle still contains suspects, deal with them first and let the runner go for the time being. Do stay alert for him to return, however, just in case he decides to come back to assist his partners in crime. Be sure you've got backup help coming, too. The foot chase should resume only after anyone left behind has been checked out and secured.

Take your car keys with you when you begin a foot chase. You don't want to discover you're now afoot when you return for your wheels. Fleeing offenders have been known to double back and drive off in police vehicles left running. Officers also have lost cars to additional subjects left behind in the suspect's vehicle as well as to larcenous passersby. Don't put yourself in the embarrassing position of having to explain that one to the chain of command or your colleagues. Grab your keys. Lock your car.

If you believe your foot pursuit quarry to be armed with a deadly weapon, consider holding off on the chase until you get plenty of help on-scene to set up a broad perimeter around the area in which he was last seen. (Caution: don't set your perimeter of helpers too small. A properly motivated crook can cover a long distance in an extremely short time.) Any searching you do should be done with a partner and extreme caution. If you are pretty certain your suspect has a gun, a better option would be to set up a strong perimeter with plenty of helpers and summon a SWAT or tactical unit to do the searching. If one is available, consider using a law enforcement aircraft to help with the spotting duties. A trained police tracking dog and handler can be an invaluable help, too. Be resourceful.

During a foot pursuit, try to follow the same general path as your fleeing subject. Let *him* find the hidden obstacles, such as clotheslines, wires and cables, holes and sprinkler heads. Hit a fence at about the same place he did, but take a quick peek before you go over just in case he's waiting on the other side. Pursue him in control of yourself and let *him* push it until he screws up. It's a lot safer for you that way.

Keep in contact with your assisting officers as the chase continues by using your radio, whistle or shouted directions. Your communications may help another officer get ahead of the party to cut him off. Shout at the subject that you **ARE** the police and that he must freeze in place. He just may start obeying you if he becomes convinced he is not going to get away. But he might also decide to turn things around by attacking you. Keep your guard up at all times. Be prepared for a sudden change in tactics by your opponent, such as a frontal attack or an ambush. Expect the unexpected.

If you completely lose sight of the subject you are chasing, slow down and be extra cautious. He may be waiting for you. If you think he is armed, do not cross a big open area without cover if you know he has already succeeded in reaching his own cover on the other side. Wait for help before proceeding with a partner. Then, rely on the building search technique of one officer covers while the other moves. It's okay to slow things down. It's more important that you stay in one piece than capture the offender at any cost. If need be, there generally will be another day to collar him—when he doesn't have the advantage and a healthy head start.

When you are searching for a vanished runner, look carefully in tandem with a partner officer. Check every place a human form might be concealed, and then search again. Do not put any unsearched hiding places behind you. Clear them before you move on.

During a foot pursuit be sure that your sidearm stays snugly strapped into its holster. If you have it in your hand you run too great a risk of an accidental discharge, or having it taken away from you if a struggle develops unexpectedly. There's really no good reason to have a gun in your hand in the first place during a chase. Warning shots are dangerous, ineffective and have little use in modern law enforcement. If your subject is the one displaying a gun, you should be behind cover with your own firearm out and ready to respond.

If you have kept yourself in as good physical shape as you should have, you have nothing to fear from a lengthy foot chase. In actuality, a long chase can prove to your advantage as your subject wears himself out and makes careless mistakes as you remain fresh to make the eventual collar. At the very least, a protracted foot pursuit gives you time to radio for assist officers who can set up a perimeter ahead of your fleeing subject. At this point, you may need to lose the notion that you must personally seize the fleeing individual. Teamwork is what it's all about. After all, your initiative and directions made it possible for the whole thing to come together. It's perfectly alright if one of your peers is the one who puts the *habeas grabus* on your offender.

Don't overlook the importance of maintaining your self-control and sense for caution throughout a foot pursuit. You cannot afford to throw all caution to the wind as you throw yourself blindly after your subject. If you do, you could miss some danger signs that should tell you to slow down and alter tactics because the nature of the chase has just changed: the suspect has vanished, a weapon has appeared, additional threats are present, the subject has stopped running and turned on you, and so on.

By thinking while you run, you are pursuing smart. You are keeping your senses on full alert for additional threats and other changes in the situation. By remaining thus in control, you increase your chances of catching the offender at the same time you guard your own safety. As the old salts say: Pursuing fast is good. Pursuing fast *and* smart is better.

When you catch up to your fleeing subject, another period of potentially high danger is at hand for you. It is at this point—the actual "laying on of hands"—that more than a few officers have been injured or killed by a previously-fleeing offender who attacked rather than surrendering. You absolutely must utilize top notch street survival techniques as the chase ends and the distance closes between you and your target. If he is going to try and assault or disarm you, this is probably his best opportunity to do it. Be extremely careful.

Many officers who end up being killed, hurt or disarmed by a fleeing person become victims after grabbing and going to the ground with the subject. Experience has shown that you probably will be better off safety-wise staying on your feet, if at all possible. As you overtake a fleeing party, consider body blocking him or shoving him hard to the ground rather than grabbing onto his clothing or person and trying to wrestle him into custody. If you grab him while you are both upright, you may open yourself to a roundhouse swing or a blade attack. If you go to the ground with him and wrestle for control there, you run the risk of him getting on top of you and taking your weapon away in the struggle. Instead, block or shove him to the ground and step back with whatever weapon ready as is appropriate for the circumstances. Instruct him in clear and certain terms as to what he is to do next: "Don't move! Now, turn onto your stomach! Place your hands behind your back! Don't move again!" If possible, you should then wait until a covering officer is in position before you move in closer to cuff and search him. Remember that even though he's on the ground and apparently compliant, he nevertheless continues to represent a real threat to your safety. Stay alert.

Naturally, bringing your runner into custody won't always be that simple. If, for instance, your subject widens the distance between you and is able to get behind cover or into a structure such as a house before you catch him, think about keeping your distance and remaining behind cover yourself until backup help can arrive. Then proceed with extreme caution as you would in any area or structure search for a hidden and possibly dangerous offender.

In the final analysis, being safety-wise during a foot chase means executing the pursuit on your terms, not his, to the extent possible. Pursue only when you feel it is safe to do so. Pursue in control. Get plenty of help. And back off for the moment anytime your survival sense tells you that things may not be quite as they appear, that the danger quotient for you may have just gone up. It may be time to rethink, revise and redeploy. That's the best way to reduce your risks at the same time you increase your chances of safely apprehending a fleeing offender.

SUMMARY

Because of the lack of solid information you may experience at the outset, suspicious persons and suspicious situations are potentially risky affairs. Your best bet for your continued safety is to utilize sound tactics and procedures designed to offset the initial information advantage that may be held by the subject(s) you are contacting. Gather as much information as you can *prior* to the contact. Stay alert and continue collecting observations as the contact proceeds. Position yourself carefully. Don't let your subject get too close. Get assistance en route quickly if anything at all looks, sounds or smells "funny."

Watch their hands and stay sharp for surprises. Realize, too, that foot pursuits and prowler calls represent varieties of the suspicious person or suspicious situation assignment that require the application of specialized survival tactics to help keep you safe. Finally, disengage carefully if you decide not to take your suspicious subject(s) into custody. Watch for danger from any quarter until the focus of your attention is totally out of your presence. Stay suspicious yourself—and help keep yourself healthy!

STREET SURVIVAL CHECKLIST FOR SUSPICIOUS PERSONS AND SITUATIONS

1. If at all possible, observe the person or situation from a place of safety for a time before you initiate contact.
2. Use all of your skills of observation and information-gathering to alert you to who and what you are dealing with.
3. Check out the "lay of the land" and attempt to contact a suspicious person at a location that is to your advantage, not his.
4. Watch your subject's hands and remain alert *throughout* the contact.
5. Where appropriate, pat your subject(s) down thoroughly for weapons.
6. Watch your positioning (and that of your weapons) in relation to the subject you are contacting. Keep a generous distance buffer between the two of you.
7. Recognize that a foot pursuit is a high-risk undertaking that calls

for caution, restraint and the application of good tactics and techniques.

8. Know that "simple" prowler calls can turn into something much more dangerous that requires all of your field survival skills and instincts.

9. Never stop looking for one more threat or danger on any suspicious person call or contact.

10. Disengage carefully following any interaction with suspicious persons. Watch your back.

Chapter Five

VEHICLE CONTACTS

The Deputy Chief of a town police department in the Southwest was killed after making a traffic stop on a vehicle with expired plates at about 7:30 P.M. He obtained the adult male driver's paperwork and ran radio checks from his patrol car. Upon learning the subject's license was suspended, the officer was reapproaching the stopped vehicle when the driver shot him in the face with a 9mm semiautomatic pistol. Captured later, the killer was charged with drug offenses in addition to murder.

Shortly after 6 A.M. in the Rocky Mountain West, a county sheriff made a traffic stop on a vehicle containing two burglary suspects, a man and a woman. The sheriff and his backup subsequently learned via radio that the plates on the vehicle were reported stolen. The sheriff then approached the driver's door for the second time, this time with his hand on his holstered weapon. The backup, with his weapon drawn, went to the passenger's side. The sheriff was at the driver's door when the male suspect fired one round into his heart with a .44-caliber weapon. The sheriff died at the scene. The two suspects escaped but were later found dead.

In the Northwest, a patrolman contacted a suspicious vehicle in a high school parking lot at about 2:30 A.M. The officer then learned from his dispatcher that the vehicle had been reported stolen. As the patrolman approached the juvenile male driver, he was shot in the face and chest with a .25-caliber pistol and died of his wounds.

There is no such thing as a routine traffic stop or vehicle contact. One officer after another has died because he mentally applied the word "routine" to a vehicle-involved situation that turned out to be something much more. There are really only two kinds of vehicle stops or contacts: *unknown-risk*, because you have no way of knowing what awaits you at the vehicle you have just contacted, or *high-risk*, because you already are in possession of information or observations

65

that tell you that you are dealing with danger. The traffic stop you make on an as yet unremarkable vehicle and driver for going 55 in a 40 mph zone is an unknown-risk stop, simply because you don't yet know for sure what awaits you: an apologetic minister, a fire-breathing jailhouse lawyer or an escaped killer. A high-risk contact, frequently referred to as a felony stop, would not surprisingly include your coming to grips with a known or suspected robber, burglar, rapist or other armed and dangerous individual, or a carload of them. You will, of necessity, make most of your unknown-risk vehicle contacts alone. On the other hand, a high-risk contact mandates that you have one or more backup officers with you from start to finish.

There are several reasons why vehicle contacts can represent hazardous undertakings for the officer carrying them out. First, officers are frequently confronted with the "familiarity breeds contempt" danger. Uniformed officers make a great many vehicle contacts, day in and day out, probably over a period of time that can run into years. Because they do them a lot, and because most vehicle occupants don't physically attack the uniformed symbol of the law who has intercepted them, there is a natural tendency for officers to begin to shift into "automatic" mode when interacting with a vehicle and the people it contains. These same officers frequently develop shortcuts for writing a ticket or a field contact card, and over time shortcuts that may neglect safety needs become ingrained into behavior as bad habits.

The subconscious mindset of these officers becomes something like "the last 999 traffic violators haven't come after me, the next one won't either." These officers have, of course, now set themselves up for a successful attack by a drunk driver, certified crazy or criminal opportunist who is coincidentally traffic violator number 1,000. In the time it takes to pull a trigger, a traffic stop has brought about a law enforcement funeral. Officer complacency has been the killer.

Second, traffic and vehicle contacts are inherently risky because of the data disadvantage experienced by the officer initiating the contact. (Here the vehicle contact is closely akin to the suspicious person or suspicious incident assignment.) The officer may have little information about who he is about to come to close quarters with. The vehicle occupant, on the other hand, knows that he has just committed a violent felony (or is wanted, is holding drugs, is armed, is an escapee, or whatever) and fears that he is about to be found out and arrested. Barring the intervention of some safety-smart strategies that this chapter will teach, the stage may have been set for tragedy for an officer who believes he is simply stopping a speeder.

Third, a motor vehicle by its very nature adds an element of risk to the encounter. The vehicle itself can be a powerful and deadly weapon in the hands of an offender. Peace officers are intentionally killed and seriously injured by vehicles on a regular basis. The vehicle's collection of compartments, dark corners and out-of-sight areas creates any number of hiding places for weapons as well as offenders. While officers have been slain by handguns pulled out from under seats, they also have been killed by offenders concealed in the backseat, the trunk or the truck bed. Indeed, vehicles can prove to be dangerous things.

On the brighter side, like every other sort of activity engaged in by law enforcement personnel, vehicle stops and contacts can be made imminently survivable by the consistent application of proven tactics and techniques crafted to return the advantage to the man or woman with a badge who is handling the assignment. The safety steps will vary a bit depending on the anticipated degree of danger contained in the contact. The most frequently-occurring type of vehicle interaction--the unknown-risk contact or traffic stop—will be examined first.

UNKNOWN-RISK CONTACTS

The same, basic officer survival practices that help keep you safe as you go about your other law enforcement duties should serve you well on an unknown-risk vehicle stop or contact, too. Take nothing for granted beyond the reality that a vehicle, whether occupied or apparently empty, embodies some element of risk for you. Watch the hands of anyone you contact. Never relax too soon. Practice excellent weapon retention techniques. Steer clear of tombstone tactics and false, cowboy courage. Keep watching for the red flag indicators of danger. Beyond the basics, also apply the tactics discussed below to assure your continued well-being through a whole host of unknown-risk vehicle stops and contacts.

Learn as much as possible before you make contact. For your own safety, you need to know as much as you can about the vehicle and person(s) you are about to contact *before* you actually commit yourself. Use all of your senses to pull in as much information as possible. Are there indications of trouble present, like missing license plates, wired-on plates, fresh damage to the vehicle or furtive actions by the occupant(s)? If you have the capability to do so, run the vehicle's plates through the computer. The return message may tell you that you are dealing with a "hot" car or a vehicle associated with a crime or wanted party. Keep watching and gathering additional data as long as you can before you commit yourself to action. If the vehicle is stationary, you may be able to observe from a distance, hopefully unnoticed, for several minutes. What you see or otherwise learn in the meantime may cause you to change your whole plan of approach. It may tell you, for instance, that you'll want a backup on hand before you approach.

Keep observing and collecting additional information once you make contact with the vehicle and its occupant(s). Run them through the computer system for records and wants. Observe what's in and around the vehicle. Is there evidence of criminal activity? How about weapons? What you detect may change the incident from an unknown-risk to a high-risk contact requiring a quick revision in your tactics.

Communicate effectively. Before you make the stop, notify your communications center as to where you are and what you are doing. Radio or log the license plate and/or vehicle description. Get the location right, and tell your dispatcher if it changes. That scrap of information alone could make all the difference in the world if you have to summon help suddenly. Stay in touch with your dispatcher throughout the contact to let her know that you are alright and what you are doing. Let her know if you have a prisoner aboard or are leaving one location for another. She is, after all, your lifeline to safety. Let her know when you are finished with the contact, too.

You also must communicate your directions to the vehicle occupant. When you have all the information you expect to get for the moment, pull your vehicle into position several car-lengths behind your subject's vehicle, activate your emergency lights and tap the horn to draw his attention. If you get no response after a couple of attempts with the horn, hit the siren instead. Watch out for a sudden or "panic" stop when he sees and hears you. Realize that he may be confused and will require you to make eye contact and direct him with hand motions where you want him to go. During all of this, remain alert for any indication that the vehicle occupants are behaving strangely. Now is not too early to call for a backup car if you don't like what you are seeing. Watch for odd behavior from other vehicles in the vicinity, too. Other drivers may be either seeking to avoid you or rubbernecking to see what you're up to.

At night, direct your spotlight and takedown lights into the interior of your subject's vehicle once it becomes stationary at the right side of the roadway. You want him in the light while you remain hidden in darkness for as long as possible. Unless you are far out of passing traffic, keep all of your emergency lights operating throughout the contact. They can not only help protect you from a rear-end collision, they also can help backup officers find you in a hurry, if need be. Meanwhile, keep watching the vehicle occupants for unusual behavior. Take your time here; you don't want to miss something that could alter your handling of the situation.

Approach and position yourself and your vehicle carefully. Direct the vehicle you are stopping out of traffic and, preferably, clear off of the roadway. (A parking lot is nice if one is conveniently available.) Stop with your front bumper at least a car-length behind the subject's rear bumper. Offset your vehicle about half a car-width to the left of the violator's left vehicle side. This allows your vehicle to block off at least a minimal "safe lane" for you to walk and stand in on the left side of the subject's car. This protection from oncoming traffic is minimal, however, so be sure you keep glancing to the rear for traffic hazards from time to time while you are out of your own car and in the "safety zone."

If heavy traffic or other conditions do not permit a safe approach to the driver's side of the vehicle you have stopped, approach from the right side, instead. Some officers like to use this approach with a driver they are a bit suspicious of, as it permits them to arrive by surprise in many cases. It also permits them to see if the driver is holding a weapon to his right side, awaiting an approach to his left window. It additionally may offer an improved view of a right-side passenger's actions.

Stay alert for wayward traffic and other dangers as you slowly approach the violator's car. Avoid the area between the two vehicles. Standing there is a great way to earn a couple of crushed legs if your patrol vehicle is rear-ended and shoved forward. As you move, visually check to see if the trunk lid is secure on the subject's vehicle. (Yes, officers really have been killed by offenders secreted in the trunk.)

Glance into the rear window and into the truck bed or rear cargo area if you are dealing with a pickup truck or van. Don't pass by the backseat without visually checking out what's there. Don't continue to walk and put a backseat passenger behind you if you are concerned about what he's up to. If at any point in your approach you see something that could be a threat, immediately retreat to cover and get help on the way. Depending on what you detect, it also may be time to draw a weapon.

Keep your gun hand empty of anything you would be hesitant to drop in a crisis—like a flashlight or radio. Licenses and registration papers are okay there. If you have sighted no threats so far, stop just short of the leading edge of his door so that he has to turn slightly over his left shoulder to see and talk to you—or point a weapon. In that position, he also cannot disable you by striking you with his car door. Consider conducting all of the business of the contact from this position. Keep your peripheral vision on alert for hazards such as bizarre traffic behavior or a pedestrian wanting to get involved in your business.

If you are going to be writing a ticket or other paperwork, consider getting the driver's documents from him and returning to your own vehicle to do the writing and check him out for wants and driver's license status. He stays in his own vehicle and thereby has less opportunity to argue or attack. Never put an unsecured traffic violator or other offender into your own front seat while you write him up. That's a great way to get disarmed and shot with your own gun.

Whether you do it twice or half a dozen times, treat every approach back to the violator's vehicle as your *first* approach. Check things out all over again. The situation just may have changed since you were there last. Your subject may now be displaying an attitude—or a weapon. Proceed cautiously each and every time.

Watch for danger signs. Look for hazard flags that tell you all is not well. Detecting one or more hazard warnings may mean it is time to call help, go to cover, produce your sidearm, or all of the above. Every officer's list of vehicle-related danger signs will vary from the next's, but most will include at least the following indicators that something may be dangerously amiss:

• Weapons are seen
• The vehicle occupant(s) are obviously drunk, high, mentally unstable, etc.

• Evidence of a crime present (like a punched ignition)
• Furtive movements; hiding or switching places among driver and passengers
• Hands not visible
• Oral threats or menacing body language from the vehicle occupants
• Escalating emotions; vehicle occupant tensing up visibly
• Known history of violence by the involved party.

None of these signs and symptoms of possible trouble mean that you are about to be attacked, of course. But they may well tell you to alter your approach, such as by calling for a cover car or staying behind cover yourself. Trust your good judgment. Don't ignore them.

Keep the violator contained to the extent possible. Unless you believe he has a weapon in his vehicle, you are often better off to leave your subject sitting in his car while you retreat to your own vehicle to run checks and complete your paperwork. Ask him to stay put. That way he's out of your face and unable to argue or do something worse, like go for your gun. By keeping him contained you also keep him out of passing traffic, one more complication of a vehicle stop or contact.

Again: whatever else you do with him, keep an unsecured, not-in-custody subject out of your car while you take enforcement action. You don't need a bullet in the side or back of your head. Generally speaking, he shouldn't be in your vehicle unless he's in-custody, secured and searched. Don't cut corners on this piece of advice. Officers have perished doing just that.

Get sufficient help. Get help on the way anytime things cease to look, sound or feel right. Call a backup if you encounter verbal resistance that threatens to go physical. Back off, if necessary, until your help gets there. Vehicle contacts are not the place for cowboy courage and tactics. Call as much help as you believe you will need. Make the best use of the help you have. In other words, implement careful contact and cover tactics throughout the interaction. Be sure your cover knows the plan and his role in it. Then, proceed with your business.

Remain alert and continue to assess. There is no guaranteed safe moment during any vehicle contact. Officers handling unknown-risk vehicle stops have been shot to death before they even had a chance to get out of their car. They have been murdered while walking up to the driver's door or killed after they got there. Officers have been slain while sitting in their vehicle writing a ticket or talking on the radio. A contact that began unremarkably enough can change quickly as a cooperative driver turns arrogant, passengers get involved, dispatch advises you of a warrant for the driver, a hostile crowd starts to gather, and so on.

Whatever the situational change, you must be alert and sensitive enough to react to it instantly with an appropriate alteration in your tactics and techniques. That may mean backing off, drawing your weapon, calling for assistance, going to cover or all of the preceding. Whatever your safety sense tells you to do, act promptly and decisively. But you won't know to act at all unless you have remained constantly tuned in to everything relevant that is going on around you during every stage of an unknown-risk vehicle contact. That alertness remains your secret to staying safe.

Use cover intelligently. You must "think cover" during the whole time you are on-duty. That includes the many minutes you spend on vehicle-related business. Think about where you could go for cover quickly should a weapon appear or things otherwise start to go downhill violently. Your car door and metal wheels offer at least some protection from incoming rounds, and getting behind either is better than shooting it out while standing in the open. Your car's engine block represents good cover, too. But don't be limited in your thinking to just your vehicle as a means of protection from bullets. What else is good, solid, and very close by? Keep thinking cover during every vehicle contact. Those thoughts just may save your bacon one day.

Break it off, if necessary. Tactical withdrawal is almost always an option. The need for it can arise quickly in a traffic-related incident. You may, for example, be a lone deputy confronting a whole carload of rowdy, threatening drunks on a lonely country road. Your best bet may be to let them go for the time being if your backups are, say, half an hour away. There may be a chance to grab the driver at a later date, or even pick the whole bunch up with plenty of help down the road. Yes, they could hurt someone in the intervening time period. Or they might not. That's the decision you have to make. But your good common sense should tell you that your chances of coming to grief are pretty good if you elect to take on a whole carload of belligerent inebriates by yourself. Let your common sense be your guide.

A common sense application of your tactical withdrawal option may require you to ask yourself: "Is this arrest worth dying for? Is it even worth losing some teeth over?" Hopefully, your answer always will be in the negative. It's up to you to then act on the answer you come up with. There is more than one way to make a collar. Waiting until the odds are on your side indicates good sense, not cowardice. It shows a good survival mindset and a devotion to saving lives—including your own.

Remain focused. It can happen all too easily. You get so caught up in writing a summons, running a subject on your in-car computer terminal or carrying out one of the other half-dozen tasks of a vehicle contact that you lose track of your violator, even if only momentarily. That amounts to a harmless lapse if your subject isn't looking for a chance to take you. If he is, the break in concentration could lead to a police funeral. Yours.

Use at least your peripheral vision to keep your subject vehicle and its occupants under surveillance at all times. Keep your head up, not down towards the radio or the console. Do your writing with your materials up against the steering wheel, not down on the seat. Stay focused to the maximum extent possible on the primary threat to you: the target vehicle and its occupants.

Make a clean break. Officers have been attacked while returning to their car at the close of a traffic contact. They have even been followed from the stop site by angry subjects intent on getting in the last word—or blow. In other words, you cannot afford to relax even a little until you and the subject of your actions are thoroughly separated. You don't have to walk backwards to your patrol car after writing a summons. But you should be glancing over your shoulder as you return. You should be visually checking for your subject until one of you has left the area. Even then, you should remain alert for a return engagement from a worked-up violator.

Particularly if your last contact involved a belligerent or uncooperative subject, you should consider driving well out of the immediate vicinity before you park to complete your paperwork or resume traffic surveillance. Getting yourself out of the neighborhood may literally remove the temptation for an offender to push his luck just a little farther. Even so, stay alert for surprises, just in case you have been followed. It has happened before, occasionally with tragic results.

Get better and better. You get more skilled at handling unknown-risk stops and contacts by doing a lot of them the right way and learning from your successes and shortcomings. Mentally review each one when it's over. Examine with a critical eye your safety tactics as well as your people skills. What worked well and what didn't? What changes might you make on the next one to make it go even smoother? Experiment a little to discover what feels right and works best for you. Compare notes with your peers, too. You may be able to take advantage of their victories and losses without experiencing any attached pain!

HIGH-RISK CONTACTS

High-risk vehicle stops and contacts used to be called felony stops. Many officers still refer to them that way, and that's just fine. Remember, however, that a vehicle contact or stop may qualify as a high-risk event even though a felony-level crime is not (yet!) known to be involved. An example could be cited in a carload of known gang members who may or may not be armed, or in a mental subject who is driving a vehicle and has promised to commit suicide by cop if contacted by the law.

Many of the safety tactics and practices appropriate for a careful unknown-risk vehicle stop or contact can be applied to a high-risk affair, too. Information-gathering, positioning and communication, as examples, are still extremely important. But the known, high-risk contact requires some additional tricks.

There are, no doubt, as many variations on making high-risk vehicle stops and contacts as there are law enforcement agencies in the nation. Certainly there is more than one effective and safe way to do them. But the key is that every member of each agency know exactly what is expected of him or her when a high-risk stop goes down. There is safety in consistency, and this book will teach one effective and consistent way to handle a high-risk vehicle contact. Make whatever changes your agency may require, if any. Just be sure you and your cohorts all do it the same way and understand each other's responsibilities. Confusion and danger will result if you don't. You need to retain flexibility for the varying conditions you can encounter from one high-risk stop to the next, but the basic, core tactics should remain the same.

Before starting any high-risk vehicle contact you should endeavor to learn as much as possible about what you are getting into. To the extent that you have the time and resources available, attempt to answer such questions as:

• What kind of crime is believed involved? Has violence occurred?

• Who are the offenders and how many are there?

• Are weapons involved and, if so, what kind?

• How much assistance will I need? How about the need for specialized help, like a K-9 or SWAT?

• Where can I make the stop with the least degree of added danger from traffic, unfriendly neighborhoods and the like?

• What kinds of added hazards may exist, like vicious dogs or innocent parties in the vehicle?

• Have I gotten the odds as heavily stacked in my favor as I can expect? Is the help I have with me sufficient for the job?

When you have as many queries answered as possible in the time you have available, move on to setting up the contact itself. Do not attempt a high-risk vehicle contact alone, even if that means delaying or even missing the apprehension of the bad guys. No stop, no suspect is worth your dying for, and that's what you're risking if you act alone. Backups on-scene are absolutely mandatory.

Use the police radio to make sure that all of your team members know what they are expected to do on the contact. The officer setting up the stop—in this case you—normally should be the one issuing directions to the others. The same officer will normally issue instructions to the suspects, as well. Once your help is with you, get a couple of car lengths behind the suspects' vehicle and activate your emergency equipment. Tell your dispatcher what is transpiring and where. Keep assessing the contact as it progresses. Sudden changes (such as the appearance of additional suspects) may require you to summon additional cover officers or even back off until the odds are back on your side.

Keep your patrol vehicle to the rear of the suspects' car. Never pull alongside or in front of the bad guys' vehicle. Peace officers have been shot to death doing exactly that. Leave the ramming maneuvers to the TV cops, too—just stay behind and stay alert. Never stroll up to the suspects' vehicle once it has stopped. That action has resulted in unnecessary law enforcement deaths, also. Operate from behind good cover and eventually bring the offenders into *your* area of control. Whatever else you do, remain flexible throughout the contact and be prepared to adjust your tactics as required for the threats you are facing. Once more, for this to work every officer involved must be kept abreast of what's going on and what he or she is to do next. This is not a good time for independent enforcement action.

As the cars come to a halt, positioning of the law enforcement vehicles is very important. The front of your car should be at least a car-length off of the rear of the target vehicle. You should be directly behind the subject's car with the front of your vehicle canted slightly to the left. This positioning is intended to give you a bit of additional protection from your vehicle's left front tire and wheel as well as some of the engine block.

Your first backup should park to your car's left with about six feet between the two police cars. Another backup, if there is one, should park to your immediate right, again with about six feet between your cars. Any additional police units should be parked to your rear, with their headlights extinguished at night so as not to put light behind you and make you a target. The officers belonging to these vehicles can flank out to the sides behind cover so as to assist in a foot pursuit or provide additional firepower if shooting develops. If that much help is available, it's also a good idea to have one car and officer about half a block behind the action with emergency equipment activated to stop traffic from coming into your area of operations.

You and your peers should seek immediate cover behind the left front fenders of your cars approximately even with the left tire and wheel. Or, if the positioning provides better cover in a given situation, locate yourselves behind the driver's door of the police car. A passenger officer in a two-person car should seek cover behind his car door. But again, do not hesitate to abandon a car for better cover if it clearly exists close by. At night, be sure the spotlights and takedown lights from all the up-front police vehicles are directed into the offenders' car. Then, with the vehicles at rest and all law enforcement personnel behind cover with weapons drawn and leveled in the direction of the suspects, the lead officer (you, in this case) issues oral instructions to the bad guys in a loud, clear manner:

"Police! Put your hands on your head!"

Fear or confusion may have prevented your subjects from complying immediately, or they simply may not have understood you over the traffic noise. Repeat the instructions, if necessary. When you do gain initial compliance, continue:

"Driver, remove your keys and drop them out the window! Now put your hands back on your head!"

If things have gone smoothly so far, it's time to begin emptying the suspects' vehicle. Be sure your covering partners know what's going to happen next, then bring your subjects out, one at a time:

"Driver, reach outside and open the door with your left hand! Step out facing the front of your car! Step to the side, away from the car! Freeze right there! Don't turn towards us!"

With you and your backups continuing to cover any remaining occupants in the vehicle, the driver is brought into your area of control to be secured:

"Driver, walk backwards slowly towards us! Move! Everybody else keep staring straight ahead!"

The driver is guided rearwards by your instructions to a point about 10 feet in front of and between your vehicle and your backup's car on your left. Now you issue another order:

"Go down on your knees! Now! Keep looking straight ahead! Don't look back at us! Leave your hands on your head! Cross your ankles! Don't move again!"

You now become cover as you motion your first cover officer forward to handcuff the kneeling subject, do a pat-down search for weapons and bring him back to a waiting police car, where a more detailed search is completed. It's up to you and any other backups to keep watching to the front for any activity from the stopped vehicle as well as any resistance from the seized subject. If you spot danger from any quarter, shout a warning to the exposed officer and be prepared to react with force to defend him. Even if the vehicle now appears empty, keep watching carefully for offenders who may have so far remained hidden.

As noted, any officer who spots a weapon or other threat during the contact is responsible for shouting a warning to his peers. An oral warning should also be given to the possessor of the item:

"We see the weapon! If you touch it you will be shot!"

The necessarily harsh warning just might save the life of a poor, misguided criminal. The whole set of exit instructions and control actions are then repeated with each additional occupant of the suspects' vehicle. Generally speaking, the same officer retrieves and secures each subject, one by one. If sufficient vehicles are on-scene, he puts each one in a separate car. An officer is also detailed to watch the whole crew once the arrests are made. The key is to have only one suspect moving or on the ground at a time so that you can focus your attentions appropriately. Nevertheless, be alert for diversions created by the offenders. If one runs, let him go until the others can be dealt with. You do not want to pursue him past a car that may still contain deadly threats.

Once all known suspects are in custody, issue a bluff challenge, still from behind cover:

"You! Hiding in the car! We know you're there! Sit up with your hands on your head or else!"

If you get no response, your first backup officer moves quietly up on the left side of the suspects' car under the cover of the other officers present. When he has cleared the car at gunpoint, he so advises his peers. It's now time to clear the trunk, if there is one. While the same officer who just cleared the interior of the vehicle waits with weapon drawn at the left side of the vehicle, facing the trunk, you advance quietly, retrieve the keys, and position yourself beneath the car's rear bumper. You then reach up and insert the key into the trunk lock and turn it, allowing the trunk lid to come up. (You should check to see if there's a trunk release control in the vehicle before you try this.) As you stay low and out of the line of fire, your partner is able to see into the trunk for bad guys from his forward, left-side position. No vehicle belonging to high-risk subjects should be towed or impounded until the trunk and any other hidden compartments have been cleared for offenders at the site of the stop.

"Special" vehicles can pose special problems during a high-risk contact. If you are contacting a van with rear doors, for instance, you will have to cover these added locations from which a suspect could fire or emerge. If you are effecting a high-risk stop on a van with right side cargo doors, a second backup should be assigned to watch those points for danger from the right rear of the subject vehicle.

Stopping a tractor-trailer rig also will require that a second backup officer be available to watch the right side of the vehicle in case an attack is launched from that side or the underside of the trailer. Any vehicle with heavily-tinted windows can also pose a problem for you. If you can't see who's inside, you may want to order the driver out and to the left side of his vehicle while you remain behind cover at your car. You can then direct him to open the vehicle's left-side doors as he slowly backs up towards you. *Ask* him who else is in there, just remember to take what he tells you with a grain of salt. Try your bluff order to the other occupants if he says there's no one there. If there are people inside, put them through the high-risk contact exit and control drill one at a time. If you still don't know the full story inside, an officer will have to cautiously approach along the left side using available cover to clear the vehicle. You might consider moving a patrol car forward on the vehicle's left side to be used as cover for you if there is absolutely no other protection available.

Motorcycles, especially groups of them ridden by people who don't think much of the law, can present another high-risk stop difficulty. The bikes themselves can present a threat, since some of their owners like to hide their weapons there. But it remains the outlaw bikers themselves who merit your greatest attention. Watch them and their hands throughout the contact. Watch any female passengers, too, as they may be the ones holding the weapons and drugs. Consider having the group remain astraddle their bikes, kick-stands up, for the duration of the contact. It will put them at a real disadvantage if they want to get froggy yet want to protect their favorite possession, too.

Subjects who refuse to exit a vehicle during a high-risk contact can cause extra trouble for you. Remain patient, stay behind cover and continue to order them out. Keep watching for hostile actions. This is in reality a barricade situation, so handle it that way. Keep up communications with the vehicle occupants and tell them that unless they exit they will be assumed to be armed and will be treated accordingly. That means you are willing to use special tactics, including the application of gas, to bring them out, so tell them so. Call in SWAT and continue to hold your perimeter with the help of your backups if your subjects decline your invitation to come peacefully into custody. Take your time in your role as a negotiator. Allow your subjects some time to realize the predicament they are in. They may decide to come out before you have to do anything more drastic.

SUMMARY

There is no such thing as a "routine" vehicle contact. Whether it is an unknown-risk or a high-risk interaction, each one will require that you bring into play everything you have learned about staying safe on the street. In order to survive a lot of vehicle contacts over a lot of years you will have to call upon all your powers of observation to help you identify the danger signs and react promptly and effectively to them. You will have to remain alert, get your facts together, stay in close communication with your dispatcher and fellow officers, watch your approach and positioning, get plenty of help when you need it and constantly assess for situational changes. Additionally, making a vehicle contact in safety will require that you utilize cover wisely, follow contact and cover procedures with your backup, remain alert throughout the contact and handle arrestees carefully. Finally, surviving a career full of vehicle contacts will necessitate that you never treat a vehicle containing suspected felons or violent offenders as "just a traffic stop."

You owe it to yourself and your loved ones to come home intact at the end of a shift or a career. Respecting the potential for danger contained within every vehicle contact and acting appropriately to neutralize the threat will help you get it done.

STREET SURVIVAL CHECKLIST FOR SURVIVING VEHICLE CONTACTS

1. Realize that there is no such thing as a *routine* traffic stop or vehicle contact.
2. Stay in close touch with your dispatcher before and during a vehicle contact. Be sure that someone knows where you are and what you are doing.
3. Learn as much as you reasonably can about who and what you are contacting before you initiate the stop.
4. Watch for situational changes that could indicate you are dealing with something other than what you initially thought.
5. Summon sufficient backup help to carry out your vehicle contact plans in safety.
6. Whenever you have a backup present for a vehicle stop, implement contact and cover procedures.
7. Mind your approach and positioning during any vehicle contact. Treat every approach to the vehicle as your first, as new threats may have appeared.
8. Never execute a high-risk vehicle contact alone. Allow suspects to escape for the moment rather than go after them with insufficient people resources.

9. During a high-risk vehicle contact, be sure that everyone involved—officers and suspects alike—knows exactly what is expected of them. Instructions must be clear and direct.

10. Do not expose yourself unnecessarily by approaching high-risk suspects who are still inside their vehicle. Remain behind cover and order them out and into a position of disadvantage within *your* area of control.

11. Do not lower your guard at any point during a vehicle contact. That includes the time during which you are returning to your own vehicle at the stop's conclusion.

Chapter Six

PRISONER HANDLING FOR SURVIVAL

In a big city in the Southwest, a 26-year-old officer with a year on the job was shot twice in the back of the head while transporting two robbery arrestees in the rear seat of his patrol car. The officer had missed a .380-caliber handgun concealed on one of the suspects. The officer died from the wounds he received in the 3:30 A.M. incident.

At about 2 P.M., a deputy sheriff arrested a fugitive at a bar in the northern U.S. The deputy placed the subject in the patrol car's back seat and got into the driver's side in front. The male pulled a .22-caliber, single-shot handgun and shot the officer in the right temple, then reloaded and shot himself fatally. The deputy died the next day.

Two West coast patrol officers were shot to death at about 11 P.M. after making a vehicle stop. The officers had not contacted their dispatcher prior to the incident. A struggle ensued when the officers attempted to restrain the driver outside of his vehicle. The driver, later determined to be a gang member, was able to get to a 9mm handgun and shot one officer in the head and chest and the other officer in the neck, face and back.

Making arrests and handling prisoners are among the most dangerous activities engaged in by this country's law enforcement officers. During recent years, peace officers were slain at virtually every stage of the custody and handling process, ranging from the initial approach to the offender, during an attempt at handcuffing, during transport and even while booking was in progress. In addition to the arrest site itself, officers have been killed by prisoners inside their own police vehicles. They have been murdered in hospital emergency rooms after escorting an "ill" prisoner there for treatment. They have been slain within the law enforcement building or lockup facility itself.

At times, officers were killed by their prisoners after failing to find a deadly weapon stashed on the person of an arrestee. Other officers had their own weapons taken away by prisoners and used on them with deadly effect. Still others fell victim to makeshift weapons (one corrections deputy was beaten to death with an oxygen tank in a jail infirmary) or were fatally assaulted with prisoners' personal weapons, like hands and feet.

Officers killed by their prisoners committed one or more of almost all the identified fatal mistakes that can be committed by a peace-keeper. They put unsecured prisoners in their police vehicles, performed poor (or no) prisoner searches, failed to handcuff or hand-cuffed sloppily and neglected to employ good weapon retention practices. For all of these reasons and more, otherwise good lawmen and women died.

Prisoner handling is made all the more hazardous for you, the offi-cer who must do it, because it is often impossible to say which prison-er will hurt or kill you if he or she gets a chance. It's easy to spot as potentially dangerous the fire-breathing resister who tells you to your face that he's going to kill you and every member of your family. You are naturally going to be extra careful around him. Problem is, the quiet, polite, unassuming and small-statured prisoner on the other side of the booking room may be even more intent on hurting you if he gets the chance. And while it may help a bit by raising some red flags for you, the nature of the offense charged against your prisoner is not a foolproof guarantee of his danger level, either. While the prisons are full of murderers who have attacked a law enforcement officer, among their other crimes, the lockups are also home for people who killed a cop over a traffic ticket or an animal-at-large citation. Consequently, you must assume that *every* prisoner you come in contact with repre-sents a potentially lethal threat to you. That includes the "happy" drunk, the out-of-touch with reality mental subject and the strung-out druggie whose lowered inhibitions and reduced self-control could enable them to slice and dice you without even fully realizing what they have done. It also includes the otherwise "good citizen" you have arrested for a really embarrassing or heinous crime. He may seek to kill you to preserve his disguise of respectability.

You keep yourself from being murdered by your prisoner by refus-ing to become careless or complacent. You protect yourself by calling for assistance whenever a prisoner handling assignment displays indi-cators of impending violence, resistance or anything else out of the ordinary (like allegations of misconduct against you made by a prisoner of the opposite gender, for instance). But you can do much, much more.

APPROACH AND POSITIONING

It's no secret that you are at your most vulnerable when you have to move in close to a subject you have contacted to make a physical custody arrest. That's a given. It's at this moment that you can be assaulted, disarmed and shot to death with your own weapon. It is equally true, however, that the regular application of some sound safety tactics and techniques will greatly reduce the dangers you face when coming into close proximity to an arrestee. Those sound tactics and techniques include the following guidelines for survival-smart approach and positioning:

• Remain aware of cover possibilities as you move in to take physical custody of your soon-to-be prisoner. Know where you can go if a weapon comes into the picture.

• Whenever possible, work with a cover officer when you have to make a full-custody arrest. That obviously will not be possible or practical for every "minor" offense arrest you make. But when the arrest is for a crime of violence or a felony, a backup officer should always be present. The same holds true for any subject who is belligerent, threatening to resist or is known to have resisted custody in the past. Ditto for someone who is believed to be mentally unstable or is under the influence of alcohol or drugs.

• If the subject to be taken into custody does not already know who you are, your approach should commence with your identifying yourself and giving initial, controlling instructions: "Police officer! Don't move!"

• Your verbal instructions will vary depending on the specifics of your situation, like the involvement of a major crime or a weapon. If a weapon *is* believed present, the initial confrontation should take place with you behind solid cover, pointing your sidearm at the offender's center mass. Keep your directions clear and simple. Direct your subject to turn his back to you, spread his legs and lock his fingers together atop his head. If you have not already had an opportunity to view him 360 degrees for a possible weapon tucked into a belt or waistband, you may now want to instruct him to turn slowly around, ending up facing away from you again. Visually inspect him for weapons while staying well beyond his reach and behind cover. (You should be no closer to him than five to six feet at this time.) If you do see a weapon, let him and any other officers present know what you've spotted: "We see the weapon! Don't touch it or you will be shot!" It's not necessary to scream, bluff or bluster. Just let him know what will happen if you are menaced. The calm but firm tone of your voice should transmit that you mean what you say.

• Assuming for the moment that so far your arrestee is apparently compliant and no additional dangers have as yet materialized, you are ready for the next step in the custody process. Advise your subject that he is under arrest. Tell him to stand still and continue facing away from you as you move in from his rear, preferably under the covering eyes of a backup officer. Stay ready to back off and draw a threat-appropriate weapon if you detect resistance or an attack developing from either your subject or anyone else. Depending on what you spot, that temporary retreat may call for you to go to cover and order up additional assistance. If none of that develops, you're almost ready to snap on the handcuffs.

HANDCUFFING

Law enforcement personnel are still dying while attempting to apply handcuffs to subjects they are trying to take into custody. They are sometimes slain even *after* the cuffs are in place. That should serve as ample reminder to you that even the highest quality prisoner restraint devices (the only kind you should carry) are *temporary* controls that can fail you. They can be broken, shimmed, unlocked or slipped out of by a particularly limber or clever arrestee. None of the preceding is intended to cause you to lose faith in a vital piece of law enforcement equipment, because the vast majority of the time quality handcuffs do work as intended to partially immobilize a prisoner, *if* they have been properly applied in the first place. Just be aware of their limitations and do not get lulled into a false sense of security just because you have succeeded in getting the proverbial bracelets on an offender.

There are a number of effective handcuffing techniques out there, but none of them can be learned fully by reading something or watching a videotape. Each requires in-depth, hands-on instruction under the supervision of a skilled instructor. That instruction must be followed up with regular refresher training to assure that your skills stay sharp. All the same, there are a number of "handcuffing for survival" principles you can learn right here. They will complement what you learn in your hands-on training and should serve to keep you safe while you are dealing with a variety of arrest and prisoner control situations.

• If you work the street, carry a couple of sets of quality cuffs on your duty belt. Bad guys frequently don't come solo. Also carry some plastic ties or a strong nylon cord for securing an arrestee's ankles if he's trying to kick you or your car windows.

• In addition to your duty key, carry an extra handcuff key hidden on your person. It can save you a lot of trouble if your primary key is lost or broken. More important, if you locate it where you can get to it while cuffed yourself it could save your life should you be taken hostage and secured with your own handcuffs.

• Check your cuffs from time to time to see that they are undamaged and operate smoothly. Replace them if they are damaged or hard to operate smoothly.

• Follow the general guideline of "handcuff first, search second." Although a handcuffed prisoner can still harm you, his abilities to do so will be limited once he is properly in cuffs and kept under close visual surveillance.

• Once your subject has been placed in a position where he is clearly off-balance, approach from his rear and cuff one hand at a time behind him. Try to first slip the cuffs through his belt or otherwise secure them behind him so that he cannot later step through them if he's especially limber. Be sure he remains off-balance while you maintain yours during the cuffing and the followup searching process. If at any time resistance or an attack develops, back out of his reach quickly and draw the weapon appropriate for the circumstances: baton, defensive aerosol or firearm. Be prepared to defend yourself as you order him back into cuffing position.

• Keep a tight grip on the cuffs throughout the handcuffing procedure. A loose and swinging cuff can be a vicious weapon.

• Do not try to "slap" the cuffs against a subject's wrists. It works better if you press the cuff arm firmly against the wrist, one at a time. Assuming you've kept obstructions such as coat sleeves out of the way, the cuff arm should swing smoothly around and engage the metal teeth on the other side. You can then tighten the cuffs up as necessary.

• Check the snugness of the cuffs to see that a prisoner cannot pull his hand through them. Also check that they are not so tight that they impede the blood circulation in the subject's hands. Check them from time to time during a long transport, and advise the prisoner not to sit on them or otherwise apply pressure to them. Investigate *carefully* if he claims they're too tight. He may be luring you into position for attack.

• Double-lock the handcuffs right away according to the manufacturer's instructions. Check them to see that they really are double-locked. If they are, they should not tighten up any further when you put pressure on the outside of the cuff arm.

• Never handcuff yourself to a prisoner. That's a great way to get hurt or killed. You are better off to hold onto your prisoner's arm as opposed to the handcuffs when you are walking at his side (with your gun side turned away from him). Otherwise you could get your hand badly pinched and bloodied should your subject decide to trap your fingers by maneuvering the cuffs.

• While you would rarely be justified in handcuffing a prisoner with his hands in front of his body, an injury or similar circumstance might occasionally require it. If you do, be sure his hands are cuffed back to back and the cuffs are slipped beneath his belt to anchor them. Move the belt buckle around to his rear. Better still, use a cord or plastic ties to place a makeshift belt around his middle to hold the cuffs at waist-level in his front.

• Practice your handcuffing techniques from time to time under the supervision of a qualified instructor. Motor skills are perishable and must be refreshed periodically.

SEARCHING FOR SURVIVAL

Normally, a prisoner search will commence once the subject has been secured with handcuffs. The searching process is accomplished to assure that you, your prisoner and others in the vicinity remain safe by removing from the prisoner's custody a weapon or anything else with which he might inflict injury on anyone. Incomplete or totally skipped searches remain major contributors to peace officer deaths—

deaths that could have been prevented by the application of basic, common sense safety practices.

Generally speaking, each subsequent search completed on a prisoner should be done with an increasing degree of thoroughness. He is searched once, primarily for weapons, immediately after being arrested and handcuffed. He is searched again, in even more detail, before he is placed in a police vehicle for transport. He is searched again and in great detail for weapons, contraband and evidence once he reaches the place where he is to be booked and/or incarcerated. There is no "magic" number of times a prisoner should be searched. Rather, he must be searched however many times it takes for you to be convinced that he is free of anything with which he could hurt himself or someone else. That means removing from his control things like belts, ties, keys, pens, pocketknives, lighters, matches, medications, necklaces, pagers, etc.

Prisoner searches may be one of the few areas in law enforcement in which routine can be a good thing. Your prisoner search should be systematic and done essentially the same way every time. Wear gloves that are both fluid and puncture resistant. Precede your search by *asking* the subject if he has any blades or needles on him. Tell him that you will be "extremely unhappy" if you hurt yourself on something he said wasn't there. Consider starting with the hair and headgear and working down from there. You are looking for anything out of the ordinary that just doesn't look or feel right. Search from his rear while he is off-balance, but don't reach around him too far and lose your own balance. If possible, have a second officer cover you during the search. If your subject has shown any indication of being violent or resistive, you'll *always* need to have a cover officer present.

Work downwards from outer garments to clothing next to the skin. Bag and inventory whatever you take off of your subject and place it out of his immediate reach. Check around his waist area and in the small of his back and crotch for hidden weapons or contraband (the latter two locations are favored hiding spots.) Don't forget to check inside footwear, another good hiding area.

Follow the dictates of good judgment and common sense as well as your jurisdiction's laws and your agency's policies governing skin searches and the search of members of the opposite sex. Obviously, any search of a bodily orifice must be conducted by medical professionals. On an arrest scene, you certainly have the right and the obligation to go after a weapon if you have good reason to believe one has been concealed on the person of a member of the opposite sex. If you do so, try to have a witness to your actions and state clearly in your report of the incident exactly what you did and why you had to do it.. Otherwise, restrict your search for weapons to a pat-down of the subject done from the outside of the clothing. The prisoner should then be kept under close observation and searched as soon as possible in even greater detail by an officer of the same gender.

Good searches can make your job a lot safer. Doing them right will aid you in protecting others you are responsible for even as you shield yourself from surprise dangers.

TRANSPORTING IN SAFETY

From the moment you take custody of a prisoner until you deliver him into the custody of someone else, you are responsible for his safety and security, your own and that of anyone else in the immediate vicinity. Those major obligations require that you remain alert and extremely sensitive to your prisoner and what is going on around you at all times.

Prisoner transport duty can be especially hazardous for two kinds of officers. One group hauls dangerous prisoners so often that the assignment becomes routine and those handling it can get careless. The second group is seldom involved with prisoner transport and its inexperienced members can be unintentionally careless when it comes to moving bodies from one place to another. You do not want to belong to either group because the members of either can quickly become casualties of the prisoners they were transporting.

A "routine" prisoner transport can quickly turn into a tragedy for you if you are not totally attentive to your duties. That means practicing excellent weapon retention as well as getting help when you need it. It also means keeping a firm grip, literally and figuratively, on the individual you are moving from Point A to Point B. If a prisoner is resistive or simply refuses to go with you, you may need to apply a compliance hold or "comealong" to one of his wrists. (This is a technique you should practice with your arrest and control instructor.) The idea here is not to punish the individual for giving you a bad time.

The purpose is get him to comply with your lawful and reasonable orders without a big screaming, thrashing fight in the middle of the floor. You should tell him simply: "Your discomfort will cease when you come along peacefully. I don't want to hurt you and you're not going to hurt me, either. Don't resist."

Your prisoner must be carefully searched for weapons before he is put into a police vehicle for transport. Your vehicle should have been searched by you prior to that time to ascertain that no "surprises," like deadly weapons, were stashed there by the last passenger. The cuffs are then checked for snugness and your prisoner is properly belted in for the ride. When the subject is removed from the vehicle at the conclusion of the transport, the area where he was seated is checked again to see if he stashed something on you, like drugs or a weapon. The cuffs are examined again, too.

If the person you are transporting is actively resisting and violent, you may need one or more officers to ride in the caged backseat area with him to be sure he does not hurt himself or someone else during the trip. If he's trying to kick the windows out of the police vehicle, you may need (with help) to secure his ankles together with plastic ties or cord. Do not tie his handcuffs to his ankle restraints, however.

You need to be aware of the dangers of something called positional asphyxiation that may have played a role in several in-custody deaths. It may occur after a violently resistive prisoner has been placed on his stomach, possibly with his feet pulled back behind him and secured to his wrists, with an officer putting pressure on his back with a knee or otherwise. A prisoner could have difficulty breathing in such a position and may, in fact, cease to breathe at all. An officer putting continuous weight on a subject's chest also could have fatal results. A subject who is in actuality struggling to get oxygen could be mistaken as being resistive by officers who then apply even more pressure.

The presence of drugs and alcohol in the prisoner's system may figure in some of these in-custody deaths. The message for you here is to see that any prisoner who is displaying symptoms of respiratory distress or complaining of illness or shortness of breath be rushed to emergency medical care immediately. He should not be hog-tied nor should he be left lying restrained on his stomach either before, during or after transport. If at all possible, he should be kept in a sitting position during transport with at least one officer next to him to monitor him and provide restraint, if necessary. Transportation by paramedics should be considered here, with an officer going along for security purposes during the trip. In addition, there are some new restraint systems on the market that permit you to either strap or wrap a violently resistive prisoner without hog-tying. Consider checking them out for your own application.

There is no good reason why you, your prisoner or anyone else should come to harm during the transport process. By applying what you have learned here and carefully monitoring your prisoner and your environment you can prevent bad things from happening while you safely and successfully carry out a very necessary but potentially risky assignment.

WEAPON RETENTION

Excellent weapon control is never more important than when you are handling prisoners. You must remain constantly aware of your sidearm in relation to everyone else in the vicinity, particularly prisoners. Be alert to the presence and location of weapons carried by your colleagues. Officers who had properly controlled their own weapons have been killed when an arrestee snatched a firearm from a less-careful officer nearby. Of course, once you are in a "secure" facility and your prisoner has been searched for weapons multiple times, your own weapon should be locked away beyond the reach of *any* unauthorized person.

While you are armed, always keep your gun side away from a prisoner or prisoners you are escorting. Do not walk between two prisoners, even though they appear securely handcuffed. Don't walk in front of them either, if you don't want a nasty surprise from the rear.

You also can improve your weapon retention capabilities by wearing a top-quality safety holster that features one or more safety thumb snaps to keep the gun secure. The weapon should be kept snapped down unless it is being drawn. Beware of the so-called "super fast draw" holster. If you can draw a weapon from it really fast, it's just possible an offender can get it out quickly and easily, too. You want excellent security over great speed.

With a partner and under the supervision of a competent instructor, practice your weapon retention moves with dud weapons. Practice how you would react if a prisoner got his hands on your gun. Remember that if it ever happens for real, there are "no holds barred" in the struggle to regain control of your own weapon and possibly save your own life. Your goal should be to make your attacker uncomfortable enough that he forgets all about wanting to take your firearm. There is plenty of time to be nice once you regain control of your gun.

SUMMARY

The close quarters contact required in prisoner handling makes this law enforcement activity one of the most dangerous for you. But it is not inevitable that you should come to harm at the hands of someone lawfully in your custody. By remaining alert, handcuffing properly and searching thoroughly you can help assure that you do not fall victim to the hostile actions of your prisoner. Meanwhile, you also can keep yourself safe by making use of the services of a backup officer whenever you feel it prudent for seizing, transporting or otherwise handling a prisoner.

As you know, complacency kills. Do not get careless or apathetic around *any* prisoner, at *any* time. If you do, it could become your very last mistake. Never relax fully when there is a prisoner nearby. Never stop seeking the next hidden weapon, the next concealed threat. It's the only way to avoid becoming a victim of someone who is *supposed* to be under *your* control.

STREET SURVIVAL CHECKLIST FOR PRISONER HANDLING

1. Handcuff first; search second. Hands should be cuffed behind the back and the handcuffs should be double-locked and checked for appropriate snugness.
2. Search a prisoner as many times as necessary until you are certain he possesses nothing with which to harm himself or someone else. Remove any and all items he could do damage with.
3. Keep your prisoner off-balance and at a disadvantage while you search in detail from his rear. Do not overreach while searching and lose your own balance.

4. Do not allow friends or relatives of an arrestee to come in contact with him at the arrest site or in your vehicle once he is in your custody.

5. Do not try to control alone more prisoners than you can safely handle. Depending upon the circumstances, that limit may be one prisoner.

6. Watch your weapon retention practices around prisoners. Never allow an unsecured prisoner to get in close to you.

7. Search every prisoner who comes into your custody. Never accept someone else's word that "he's clean." Double-check for yourself.

8. Remain constantly alert for threats during the prisoner transport process. More than a few prisoners have chosen this time period to attack.

9. Maintain a high level of alertness the entire time you are in the presence of *any* prisoner. Take nothing for granted based on the crime a prisoner is charged with. Realize that peace officers have been murdered by every kind of prisoner.

10. You are responsible for your prisoner's welfare while he is in your custody. Question him to see if he has medical problems requiring immediate treatment. Observe him carefully for signs of injury or illness and seek medical help if in doubt.

11. Remember that prisoners who are intoxicated, on drugs or violently resistive may be in danger of respiratory arrest, particularly if required to lie restrained on their stomachs. Avoid hog-tying prisoners. Transport them in an upright position with an officer next to them for monitoring and control purposes.

Chapter Seven

"UNDER THE INFLUENCE" PEOPLE

In the Midwest, a 16-year trooper stopped his patrol car beside an interstate highway to investigate two apparently intoxicated men standing outside a parked vehicle. After learning by radio of an arrest warrant for one of the men, the officer was handcuffing him when shot in the chest by the second subject. The officer died from injuries inflicted by the .25-caliber bullet. The killer, arrested later the same day, was found to be a 45-year-old parolee.

In the Midwest, a 38-year-old police sergeant was intentionally run down by an intoxicated driver while working crowd control. At approximately 2:30 A.M. the officer was standing at a street barricade when a male adult drove by, made a U-turn and then accelerated his vehicle through the barricade, striking and killing the sergeant and a civilian bystander.

In the West, a patrol officer stopped a suspected drunk driver at approximately 11 P.M. While the 29-year-old officer was conversing with the drunk outside of his vehicle, the subject produced a .380-caliber semiautomatic pistol and shot him in the shoulder and head, fatally wounding the policeman.

For the law enforcement officer faced with confronting a person who is intoxicated or "under the influence" of alcoholic beverages or drugs, licit or illicit, one thing remains certain. Anytime a diminished capacity human being is involved, the potential for real danger is inevitably present. As any veteran officer can tell you, the person who has had his judgment scrambled and his inhibitions weakened by alcohol or drug ingestion is capable of doing things—including attacking a police officer—that he might never even consider while straight or sober. With her judgment impaired by the effects of drugs or booze, a 90-pound woman may take on three burly officers; a normally shy and retiring man may elect to shoot it out with deputies.

Alcohol and drugs kill on a regular basis via accidents, suicides and homicides. Too often, law officers are among the victims. One study

95

undertaken by the Behavioral Science Unit of the Federal Bureau of Investigation found that about 76 percent of the convicted cop-killers interviewed said they were in some way involved with drugs or alcohol at the time they murdered a law enforcement officer. You should require no additional evidence that these people can prove extremely dangerous to you, the officer sent to "fix" the problems they have caused.

Every year the statistics and anecdotes reported in the FBI's *Law Enforcement Officers Killed and Assaulted* publication include case histories of peace officers murdered by drunk or drugged people. Nevertheless, officers continue to die at the hands of these individuals because they underestimated the potential for harm they posed. Too many of these officers made assumptions–dangerous assumptions–that proved to be tragically false. They may have assumed, for instance, that a drunk will never put up serious physical resistance to arrest. They may have died finding out that just isn't so.

RECOGNIZING INTOXICATION

Your observation that someone is intoxicated or "under the influence" of alcohol constitutes a danger sign indicating the need for increased caution and protective measures on your part. But if intoxicated or "under the influence" behavior is a warning indicator of increased danger for you, what are the clues that someone is drunk or "under the influence" in the first place?

The drunk depicted by the mass media is often stumbling in both speech and gait. He is frequently shown as either naughtily hilarious or nastily evil. He may in reality be all of the preceding–or none of the above. As life experience as well as your training and on the job encounters have taught you, the presence of an "under the influence" or drunken condition also may be signaled by a wide variety of other symptoms. If you are to spot potential danger in time to protect yourself from it, you must be able to detect the inebriated or drugged individual with the help of other possible indicators, too. Learning to protect yourself long enough to help this person depends at least partially on your ability to spot him or her early-on as someone in trouble–and potentially troublesome. Although they can vary widely from one

person to the next and may appear very differently displayed on the *same* person on different occasions, the signs of being "under the influence" of alcohol or drugs include the following:
- Loud, boisterous, perhaps profane language
- Clothing disarranged and soiled
- Watery, bloodshot eyes
- Either dilated or pinpoint pupils of the eyes
- Strong smell of alcohol on the breath and person
- Needlessly belligerent attitude, mannerisms or speech
- Poor motor skills and balance
- Slurred, hard to understand speech
- Visible needle tracks on the body
- Alcohol, drugs or drug paraphernalia in the subject's possession
- Presence of empty containers of drugs or alcoholic beverages
- Display of emotional extremes, such as laughing or crying without apparent reason
- Abnormally passive or aggressive behavior
- Staggering, stumbling, lurching walk
- Hallucinations or delusions; bizarre actions
- Swaying or nodding when trying to stand still
- Difficulty performing "fine" tasks with the fingers, such as extracting a driver's license from a wallet
- Difficulty in understanding or following instructions or explanations.

No single indicator or group of them *guarantees* that a given individual is "under the influence" or intoxicated. But the presence of one or any number of them indicates a need for you to inquire and observe further. While there may be another reasonable explanation for your observations, you certainly have adequate grounds to believe you are confronting a diminished capacity person who may be drinking, drunk or stoned.

Naturally, you generally can confirm the degree of intoxication of an "under the influence" person by a chemical test of his breath, blood or urine. On-scene, your options will be more limited. If you are schooled in the technique, the results of a horizontal-gaze nystagmus test will tell you a lot. Or you may have to collect information from results of the old-fashioned but very revealing heel-to-toe walk, stand on one foot and recite the alphabet exercise, or the stand still with your head tilted back and your eyes closed routine, all designed to tell you if your test subject is exhibiting deteriorated balance and motor skills. Whatever tests you employ, demonstrate and then apply them only under the watchful eyes of a cover officer. Resist the urge to get too exotic or difficult in your testing methodology. It would be embarrassing, at best, to fall down while demonstrating your "special test" on the street—or in the courtroom!

But even as you gather in the probable cause indicators that spell out "drunk or drugged," there's something else you should be thinking about every time you deal with someone who may be either.

DANGER OF UNPREDICTABILITY

If you remember nothing else about drunk or drugged people, remember this: *they are absolutely unpredictable.* And because you can never know for sure exactly how they will react in a given situation now that their judgment and inhibitions are shot, each and every one of these people must be viewed as a potential threat to you. Experience has proven that all too many of them are *that dangerous.* Never forget that a drunk who is 100 percent cooperative one moment can be a spitting, clawing, punching monster trying to kill you the next. It can and does happen all the time.

Also realize that a drunk or drugged person's promise to do or refrain from doing anything is meaningless and must be viewed by you as such. The drunk driver you just stopped may truly mean it when he says he won't drive further if you'll just let him "sleep it off" in his car. Ten minutes after you've driven away, he may have completely forgotten his promise as he steers his death machine back onto the highway. Taking at face value the statements of a diminished capacity person can get you into a great deal of trouble. It additionally can result in a great deal of bloodshed for you or some other innocent party.

Unpredictability also may surround an apparently intoxicated person's condition—and how he got that way. It is urgent that you know that a number of illnesses, medical conditions, and injuries can produce symptoms that closely resemble "under the influence" or intoxicated behavior in a human being. Insulin reactions, diabetic conditions, stroke, mental illnesses and closed head wounds, among other things, all can result in behavior that mimics intoxication. Diagnosing the problem can become even more difficult for you if the person you are observing has been drinking or taking drugs *and* is suffering from one of these maladies. You handle the situation best by making all the careful observations you can and gathering as much information as possible. Interview friends, family or witnesses about the affected party, if any are available. Look for medical bracelets or cards on the subject's person that may describe a medical problem or condition. Is the smell of alcohol strangely missing? If you have any thought at all that something besides booze or drugs may be causing the problematical behavior, keep the subject under close observation and get him or her to medical attention. Never, never simply lock up an unconscious or violently ill subject. Seek medical attention before you do anything else.

An alcoholic individual also may exhibit another medical problem that can pose a danger to the both of you. An alcoholic who has been deprived of alcohol for some time may display bouts of uncontrollable shaking, trembling and wild hallucinations. The individual likely is suffering delirium tremens, popularly known as the "DTs." He may display signs of terrible fright at the dangers he "sees," and may cry, shake or cower in fear. He's dangerous to himself because he may engage in self-destructive behavior to escape his torment. (One man suffering from the "DTs" burned down his own house, with fatal results for himself, to drive out the demons he believed were residing there.) He's dangerous to you because in his tortured mind you may be among the threats he feels he must destroy in order to survive.

Any person you contact who appears to be exhibiting the symptoms of delirium tremens is experiencing a medical emergency. He must be secured, kept under surveillance and transported to medical aid without delay. The "DTs" may constitute a lethal threat for the sufferer and those around him, including you. Observe carefully and act promptly.

You can always resume processing your party for the appropriate charges and handling *after* he has been cleared by a medical professional, if that turns out to be the case. Take no chances with your prisoner's life and your own peace of mind and future.

ALTERING YOUR TACTICS

Reason and logic may not work on someone whose judgment has been destroyed by drugs or alcohol. You may be justly proud of your ability to reason with the "clients" you encounter on your rounds and thereby achieve compliance with your requests and orders. Realize, however, that reason and logic may have very little influence on the drunk or stoned individual you meet. When that happens you must remain patient and repeat your instructions as many times as you feel necessary, but you also must have alternative strategies ready to go if words fail you. That may mean resorting to minimal force to bring an uncooperative inebriate into protective custody. No one can tell you exactly how many times you must repeat instructions or explanations and how much time you must spend before resorting to control tactics with an "under the influence" person. Each situation will be at least somewhat different than the last or the next. You will have to decide based on your training, observations and experience when it is time to abandon one approach for another. But it's almost always worth *trying* the least coercive route first. It not only makes for fewer injured cops and inebriates, it also looks better in court when you can honestly testify to everything you tried *before* you resorted to more forceful methods.

An individual whose senses have been dulled by chemicals may fail to react as expected to a pain compliance hold or "comealong." Defensive aerosol sprays may fail to have much effect on someone who is deeply "under the influence," too. Not dissimilar to the case of the very mentally disturbed person, the inebriate's nerve cells are *trying* to tell his brain that he's hurting; the message just isn't getting through. As a result he may keep fighting you until overcome by superior numbers and/or tactics. The important thing is that you do not panic when normally successful subject control tools or techniques fail for you. You instead go on to the next option, which in many cases means that you and one or more backups must wrestle the subject into custody by "muffling" his resistance with minimal force. Occasionally, that may mean that you have to back off temporarily until you have adequate assistance on hand to overcome unlawful resistance. But remember to stay sharp throughout the contact. An initially-cooperative subject may become wildly resistive and violent without warning as the alcohol or drugs he ingested before you got there start kicking in and affecting his behavior. Watch him, too, for evidence that the load of chemicals he has on board may be interfering with his respiration and heartbeat. If he evidences difficulty in breathing or goes unconscious, emergency medical assistance is indicated. Don't delay getting him to professional help. That often will mean calling paramedics to your location.

A final—and important—note about drunk or drugged people who refuse to go along with the program for you: "Under the influence" people can be especially adept at discovering how to "get your goat" and exploit your vulnerabilities through obscene, threatening, or simply belittling and demeaning comments directed at you. Some of these individuals also can take the art of "passive resistance" to a whole new level. You can never win by arguing with these people or engaging in a trade of insults that doesn't faze them but demeans you. Don't waste your energy in pointless verbal sparring. Just deal with them as quickly and professionally as possible and get them out of your hair.

A person does not give up any of his rights simply because he is obnoxious and "under the influence." Standards of probable cause for bringing one of these people into legal custody are no less strict than those required to lawfully seize a sober person. Protect your case in criminal court at the same time you shield yourself civilly by playing it "by the rules" any time you are handling a drunk or drugged subject. You survive legally by following the guidelines provided by statute as well as by your agency's rules, policies and procedures for handling these "diminished capacity" individuals.

Naturally, you must *never* respond with physical violence except to defend yourself or someone else. If you slip and react to a verbal attack with a physical assault, you risk an end to your career and criminal charges, to boot. Career survival is a part of your total survival package. Keeping your cool around "under the influence" people helps you protect yourself in more ways than one.

SAFETY IS PARAMOUNT

As every veteran law enforcement officer knows, drunk and drugged people are very frequently involved in murder, rape, assault and other crimes of violence, ranging from bar brawls to parking lot fights. Add to that violence the diminished capacity individual's willingness to take on a peace officer and you begin to get the full picture of the danger involved anytime you must deal with one or more of these persons. As a peace officer, your contacts with the drunk and drugged will be frequent. You must realize now that real hazards accompany each and every one of those interactions. In addition, you must apply sound officer safety tactics devised to reduce the dangers posed by these "under the influence" subjects. There is much you can do in the interest of safety:

Follow the basics. Remembering the fatal errors that result in the deaths of law enforcement officers and following every pertinent officer survival technique you ever learned can help keep you safe when you are dealing with "under the influence" persons. Watch your approach and positioning around an inebriate. Don't get too close, too soon. Maintain a reactionary gap in case he decides to attack. Keep watching his hands and look out for furtive movements as well as weapons. Keep your gun side turned away from the subject and the weapon well out of his reach. Practice excellent weapon retention. Think about the location of cover, just in case you suddenly have need of it. When you take an inebriate into custody, be sure you handcuff him and then search from his rear while he remains off-balance. Once he is in custody, watch him carefully. No less care and caution will suffice when you are working with a drunk, stoned or "under the influence" person.

Try to calm your subject. A calm, quiet, yet firm voice may help you in controlling an "under the influence" person. By also applying a good deal of patience you may be able to avoid a struggle with the party who is the focus of your attentions. Try to appear nonthreatening, but tell the truth. Remain firm but fair. You may have to deal with this subject again and he or she just might remember you–for good or ill.

Take your time. Be patient. Go slow. Do not invade the inebriated subject's personal space or lay hands on him until adequate help is on hand, just in case violent resistance develops. Give clear, simple explanations for what you are doing and why, but realize that you may not be understood or obeyed.

Get help. Realize that a diminished capacity person may seem insensitive to pain. And because his pain tolerance is greatly increased, he may seem to have superhuman strength. If possible, get assistance before attempting to take him into custody, protective or otherwise. Meanwhile, be ready to defend yourself if resistance develops. It just might.

Keep him in sight. Do not allow a diminished capacity person to leave your sight during the contact. If you let him wander into the next room "to get my coat," he just might return with an unpleasant surprise in his hand. Go with him if you elect to let him move. But do not allow him to reach into any areas beyond your control.

Secure and search. Handcuff properly and search carefully and repeatedly any drunk or drugged person you take into custody. Remove from his person and his control anything with which he might hurt you, himself or anyone else. Try to have a cover officer present anytime you carry out any of these tasks. Never stop looking for one more threat or hazard when an "under the influence" person is the object of your attentions.

Follow careful prisoner handling guidelines. Whether he is in protective custody or charged with a crime, the diminished capacity individual must be handled carefully and monitored virtually all the time he is around you lest he attack or become critically ill himself. Either scenario is possible. Also, watch for any indication (breathing difficulties, passing out, etc.) that might indicate your prisoner may require emergency medical care. Naturally, you must continue to observe him carefully to prevent a surprise attack on you either on the street, in the car or after you arrive at a "secure" booking facility. Remain constantly alert to defend yourself against a surprise attack. Virtually any given drunk is capable of mounting one.

Take him seriously. Until and unless you disprove them, take at face value the threats an "under the influence" person makes against you. If he is promising to kick your butt "once these cuffs are off," have backup on hand whenever the handcuffs are removed. It's always possible that it really wasn't "the booze talking." He really meant it. Don't accept verbal challenges to fight a drunk. Instead, beware of the diminshed capacity person who is making threats against anyone. He is probably a danger to himself and everyone who comes near. Look to your officer survival tactics for responding in safety to him.

Drunk drivers are dangerous, too. One particular variety of "under the influence" person represents a special threat to you. Consider the following evidence of his danger towards everyone using the public roadways, you included:

• A drunk male adult, driving at high speed while headed the wrong way on an expressway, collides head-on with a compact car containing two young girls. Both girls die; the drunk is hospitalized.

• A family of three, headed home from a visit with relatives on a holiday, pauses at a city traffic light. Their stationary vehicle is crushed from behind by the car of a speeding, intoxicated driver. The husband and father is killed; the drunk escapes with minor injuries.

• A state trooper assisting a stranded motorist is struck by a swerving, speeding van while standing at the roadside. The officer dies instantly. The van's driver is later found to have been legally intoxicated at the time of the collision.

As the slogan goes, *drunk drivers kill.* Sometimes law enforcement officers are among their victims, intentionally or otherwise. As a first-line responder, you are at risk from these dangerous people because your duties require you to share the streets with them, often at times of peak danger, such as the bar closing hour. You also are at increased risk because your duties take you out of your vehicle on or near the same roadways that these dangerous people travel while piloting their vehicles through a drunken haze. Finally, you also are at risk because drinking and drunk drivers are in at least one respect no different from the other inebriates you encounter on the job: Their conduct is unpredictable and they may direct violence at you when you make contact with them.

You protect yourself from the drinking, drunk or drugged motorist by watching for the red flag indicators that one is nearby, possibly on a collision course with your push bumpers—or your rear pants pockets. These telltale warning signs of a possible "under the influence" driver include:

• Vehicles out of pace with other traffic, moving too fast or too slowly for the norm

• Vehicles moving without lights at night

• Vehicles with fresh crash damage, perhaps indicated by dragging, scraping parts or leaking fluids

• Vehicles swerving or weaving across traffic lanes or repeatedly wandering within a single lane

• Vehicles running stop signs or signals

• Vehicles being operated on the wrong side of the road

• Vehicles striking the curb or center median, perhaps repeatedly

• Vehicle windows open in inclement weather (the driver may be trying to sober up in the onrushing air)

• Vehicles moving with windows mostly covered by ice or snow

• Brake lights on constantly on a moving vehicle, or being applied intermittently without apparent reason

• Driver overreacting, as by going into a panic stop when no real threat exists

• Driver clutching the steering wheel in a "death grip" while staring straight ahead

• Driver following too closely behind another vehicle

• Vehicle stopped well inside an intersection, or at an unusual distance back from it

• Obvious arguments or blows being struck inside a moving or stopped vehicle

• Driver vomiting out the window of a moving vehicle, or beside a stopped vehicle

• Driver actively attempting to avoid a police vehicle, as by dropping back in traffic or turning off on a side street

• Driver drinking from an alcoholic beverage container

• Vehicle failing to move ahead with other traffic when the signal changes or the way is clear (the driver may be passed out or dozing).

There are other indicators of "under the influence" driving, of course. And none of the preceding symptoms constitutes proof positive of a drinking or drunk driver. But, once more, all give you the right and obligation to investigate further to ascertain the reason for the out of the ordinary behavior. There's a good chance that a drunk or impaired vehicle operator is at the heart of the problem.

You must utilize excellent officer safety tactics around all known or suspected "under the influence" motorists. They may attack you because their judgment is impaired or because they're just plain mean when they're drunk and don't like cops anyway. Or they could hurt you accidentally because they have such poor control of the potentially deadly machinery they are operating. Use extra caution from the moment you pull in behind a suspected drunk driver and activate your emergency equipment. Don't get too close. He may engage in all sorts of bizarre driving behavior, ranging from a sudden swerve across the centerline to a panic stop to slamming it into reverse to fleeing at high speed. Be ready for just about anything. Do not ride his rear bumper or get too close too soon. When both vehicles have stopped, watch for backup lights or vehicle movement that indicate he's coming in your direction. Also be ready to exit quickly should he jump out and start back for you. This isn't the time to get caught sitting down.

Never, ever place yourself between your car and the possible drunk's vehicle. Approach to the side and out of traffic. Watch for threats from drunken passengers who may want to get into the act. You can back off temporarily and wait for help if things don't look or feel right. Always get help on the way before you extract the driver for questioning or roadside sobriety tests. When you do make contact with the driver, tell him to turn off his engine to at least reduce somewhat his immediate potential for further harm. Ask him to hand you his keys if he appears particularly smashed, but do not reach into the vehicle to retrieve them yourself. That's a great way to get dragged to your death.

Follow the same safety precautions with a suspected drunk driver that you would apply to any other traffic-related contact. Keep an eye on passing traffic. Keep yourself and the subject off of the roadway. Look out for weapons and other surprise threats. Maintain a healthy reactionary gap between the two of you just in case he suddenly feels froggy. Be conscious of your sidearm's location and keep it turned away from him and safely snapped into its holster. Keep a wary eye on passengers. Move the driver away from them and instruct them to remain in the vehicle. Get emergency help on the way if they disobey you or otherwise appear about to get involved. Back off, if need be, and be prepared to defend yourself.

Don't place yourself at a tactical disadvantage by demonstrating field sobriety tests until you have a backup officer there to cover you. Be sure there's a backup on-scene before you make an arrest. When you do arrest, *always* handcuff and carefully search your alcohol or drug-involved offender. Even after he or she is secured, remain alert for new threats to your safety. One drunk driver managed to shoot and kill two state troopers inside their own testing facility *after* they had searched him for weapons, locked up their own handguns and removed his cuffs. Don't let a drunk or drugged driver add you to a growing roster of law enforcement victims of "under the influence" persons.

SUMMARY

The safe and humane handling of "under the influence" persons can prove a serious challenge for the most experienced, skilled, compassionate and safety-conscious law enforcement officer. In a society that presents a steady flow of these sometimes sad, always unpredictable and not infrequently dangerous people, as a first responder you are destined to face that challenge on a regular basis whether your work environment is urban, rural or somewhere in between. Become sloppy in your tactics or apathetic in your demeanor and any one of these encounters could end badly for you.

Whether they have alcohol, drugs or a combination of the two on board, intoxicated or "under the influence" people represent a real threat to themselves and others they come into contact with while they are in their diminished inhibitions and befuddled judgment state. Those endangered "others" include you and your peers who must deal with their irresponsible and sometimes violent behavior. Via constant vigilance and the regular application of basic officer survival practices, you can drastically reduce the threat. That's how best to go about surviving a career full of "under the influence" people.

STREET SURVIVAL CHECKLIST FOR HANDLING "UNDER THE INFLUENCE" PEOPLE

1. Remember above all that intoxicated or "under the influence" people are unpredictable. Any one of them can prove dangerous to you.

2. Learn to recognize the symptoms of intoxication or "under the influence" behavior brought about by either drugs or alcohol. These signs can serve as red flags of danger.

3. Always get a backup for dealing with an intoxicated or diminished capacity person. Doing so could save both of you from injury.

4. Realize that the demeanor and actions of an "under the influence" person can change quickly and radically without apparent cause or warning.

5. Handcuff and search any intoxicated or impaired individual you take into custody.

6. Closely and continuously monitor the physical condition and actions of an apparently "under the influence" person you have taken into custody. Realize that some injuries and illnesses can mimic intoxication and that any hint of such a condition requires that the subject receive immediate medical attention.

7. Never ridicule or needlessly antagonize an intoxicated person. You could provoke an unnecessary fight.

8. Take nothing for granted and carefully watch an "under the influence" person for assaultive as well as self-destructive behavior. Be prepared to intervene promptly.

Chapter Eight

CRIME IN PROGRESS CALLS

In the West, a 47-year-old officer with 16 years of service responded to a 1:40 P.M. silent alarm at a business. As he was approaching the scene, three men ran in front of his vehicle towards an apparent getaway car. The officer exited his car and ordered the males to halt just as a fourth man ran by, pulled a 9mm handgun and shot the officer fatally in the head and chest.

In a southern town, a juvenile male sniper began firing a rifle in a residential neighborhood. Three residents had been wounded when officers arrived at the 4:30 P.M. call. As the 48-year-old victim officer rounded a corner in his police vehicle, he was struck in the head with a rifle bullet and killed. The sniper was subsequently shot to death by other officers.

At approximately noon, officers on the West Coast responded to a "man with a gun" call at an unemployment office where a 33-year-old man had entered and then shot seven persons, killing three. He fled the arriving officers and a vehicle pursuit ensued. When his route was barred by heavy traffic, the subject stopped and fired two rounds from a rifle with a telescopic sight at the pursuing police. A 35-year-old officer was 200 feet away but was struck fatally in the head. The chase resumed and the subject was eventually killed by other officers.

Thanks to improved technology, including instant silent alarm systems, portable law enforcement radios and computer-assisted dispatching, peace officers are doing a better job than ever of arriving at major crime scenes while the perpetrators are still present. In some jurisdictions, improved patrol deployment practices also have speeded up officers' response to serious crimes in progress. As a consequence, more confrontations between cops and armed and dangerous crooks are taking place in the U.S. today. The good news is that more serious offenders are going to prison. The down side is that these increased confrontations are sometimes resulting in casualties among law enforcement's first responders.

Perhaps more so today than at any other time in the nation's history, it is by no means a given that criminals will surrender when confronted by authority, even though that authority is armed and wearing a badge. A physical assault on the officer or even gunfire in a crowded store parking lot may be the response from an offender who has decided he has nothing to lose by taking on the law. This particularly violent and uncaring sort of modern day offender requires careful handling by the peace officer determined to stay safe and survive the rigors of the street. But first that officer needs to have some understanding of what makes the crime in progress call a potentially dangerous one.

WHY THEY'RE DANGEROUS

A crime in progress assignment contains built-in hazards for the officer sent to deal with it. The danger is real for a number of reasons, and it begins for the peace officer even before he or she arrives on-scene. While the regulatory specifics will necessarily vary from one jurisdiction to the next, a crime in progress call not infrequently requires an emergency response from the officer sent to resolve it. That often translates into a Code 3, lights and siren run over perhaps several miles of busy streets. Sound emergency driving techniques will make the trip safer for the survival-smart peace officer, but the unpredictable reactions of other drivers sharing the road will not permit the danger to be removed completely. Thus, the need to get there quickly but safely represents the first safety challenge for the officer answering a crime in progress call.

The lack of information so often found in critical law enforcement calls for service presents another threat to the first responder. A lack of data about exactly what is happening on-scene can set an officer up for disaster unless that officer applies everything he or she knows about defusing the danger of a high-risk assignment. The officer also must confront changes—perhaps drastic ones—that may have occurred on-scene between the time he last received information and the time at which he arrives to face a confrontation. Lack of information can kill.

The officer arriving on the scene of a crime in progress may encounter a number of unknowns—all of them amounting to potential safety risks. How many offenders are there? Exactly where are they? Are they armed? If so, *how* are they armed? Are there additional, unknown offenders, like lookouts or backup crooks, somewhere on-scene? A failure to ferret them out in time could have fatal consequences.

An officer answering a crime in progress call has no way of knowing how an interrupted or startled offender will react to being challenged by the law. Will he fight? Might he flee on foot? Will he resort to gunfire? Will a high-speed pursuit ensue if he is able to get to a vehicle? Will he turn an innocent person into a hostage to facilitate his escape? Or could a barricade incident result from an interrupted crime? Escalation is always possible when a criminal realizes that his predatory actions have been interrupted by law enforcement.

Any number of on-scene complications can make the first-responder's job harder—and more risky. It may be difficult to make a safe approach to the scene, out of sight and behind cover. Victims or bystanders may react in unpredictable ways, placing both themselves and the responding officers at increased risk. Misidentification problems may occur on both sides. (In one tragic case, a store proprietor grabbed a robber's gun away and ran outside brandishing it, whereupon he was shot fatally by the officers waiting outside.)

Indeed, there are plenty of reasons why a crime in progress call means danger for *you* if you are the law enforcement officer sent to handle it. But handle it you can, and without exposing yourself to unnecessary risk of injury or worse. As you might suspect, that requires the application of some risk-reduction tactics designed to markedly defuse the danger.

TACTICS FOR HANDLING

Your personal tactics and techniques for handling any kind of crime in progress must acknowledge the very real elements of danger present in the assignment. That principle holds true whether you are in uniform or out, on-duty or off, working a radio car or holding down an extra-duty security job at a local business. As a matter of fact, there is evidence that you may be especially at-risk if you intercede in a crime in progress incident while you are off the clock and without some of the benefits that being on-duty brings you (like radio communications and quickly available backup, for instance).

You safely and effectively handle a crime in progress call with tactics and procedures similar or identical to those you employ in successfully resolving a number of other law enforcement "field problems." You ask questions, make observations and gather information. You plan, approach and deploy carefully. You communicate, coordinate and confront from cover. In the end, you gain safe control over the offender(s) and start getting ready for the next encounter. In more detail, it looks like this:

Answer some key questions. Even as you and other police units are being dispatched to the scene of a reported crime in progress, your Communications Center call-taker should be asking a number of questions in order to provide you and your peers with as much data as possible before you get there and must confront potential danger. The questions will, of necessity, vary somewhat depending upon the type of crime involved. But with virtually any crime you will need to know as many answers as feasible to such vital queries as:

• What is the exact location or address of the incident?

• What is happening now, and what has happened since the start of the incident?

• Who are the offenders, if known, and how are they described? Clothing?

• Where, exactly, are the offenders? How many are there?

• What kinds of weapons, if any, have been seen?

• Have shots been fired? Are there casualties? If so, where are they now?

• Has a lookout or a getaway vehicle been seen? Where? Description?

• What was the direction of travel, if the offenders are leaving or have left?

• Who is the source of the information, and where is the reporting party located?

If your dispatcher is not relaying to you the available answers to these queries, don't be bashful about asking. In addition, you as the frontline responder must be aware of at least one other key query: What *don't* I know about this situation that could prove hazardous to me and my backups? Realizing in advance that you will probably *never* have all the answers should help to keep you cautious—and alive. There is plenty more to do, too.

Arrive in your "stealth" mode. You should use some of the information you receive while en-route to plan your approach so as to avoid detection by the offenders. What you are seeking is sometimes referred to as "invisible deployment," and it requires that you approach quietly, park around the corner or down the street so as to avoid drawing attention to yourself and move closer on foot by using available cover and concealment to keep the element of surprise on your side. As you move, you must avoid having the "surprise" turned around on you. Move quietly and cautiously and watch for anything that looks out of place. Especially at a robbery or burglary in progress, there could well be a lookout posted nearby. Do not move past a suspicious person or parked vehicle until you have satisfied yourself that neither poses a threat to you. If you determine that either may be a part of the problem, you must deal effectively with the danger before you proceed to get closer to the reported crime in progress. You cannot afford to leave a threat behind you.

With even the best alarm systems and smoothest dispatch functions, there is a built-in delay for you in getting the information on any crime in progress. Accept that as a given and realize that you realistically could encounter a fleeing suspect or suspect vehicle blocks or even miles from a crime scene where you believed an offense was still in progress. Be prepared to use high-risk contact tactics in challenging anyone or any vehicle fitting a possible description of the offender(s). Take no chances here. Be sure you have help with you before you initiate a confrontation, and then do so using high-risk contact tactics that emphasize the importance of superior manpower and good cover.

Your knowledge of your beat and your jurisdiction should help you make an "invisible" close approach to the trouble site. That familiarity should tell you where plate glass windows, doors and other vision points would give a bad guy a chance to see you coming. These are obviously the sides of the structure you will want to avoid as you approach the scene. Remember that it's certainly worth walking a ways to increase your safety margin.

Unless people are clearly being harmed right in front of you, your approach should *not* include entering an involved structure before you have help on-scene. Even then, it remains preferable to take good cover and allow the subject to come out to you as opposed to going in after him. You can often reduce the complications—like the likelihood of hostages—by waiting for the offender to move onto ground that is to your advantage.

Plan for safety and success. Have a plan for what you'll do once you get on-scene. Hopefully you have done some contingency planning and thought about a similar scenario before, as well as how you would respond to defuse it. Communicate your plans to your responding peers. If you are the officer responsible for setting up the call's response and deployment, get on the radio to let your helpers know where you want them to set up and what you want them to do once they get there. It should be made known to everyone that no independent actions or heroics are wanted. Teamwork will be required to bring the situation to a safe conclusion. In your deployment instructions, be sure that all escape routes from the site of the incident will be covered. Two officers on diagonally opposite sides of a building can maintain containment if you are dealing with a small structure; more help will be required if you are working with something like a big, open field or a large, irregularly shaped building. The idea behind setting up a good perimeter is, of course, to assure that no one gets in or out without being challenged by an officer from behind solid cover.

While it is highly desirable that your presence remain a secret until you are ready to confront the bad guys on *your* terms, realize that many crooks are pretty good at their "business," too, and there's a very real chance that you'll be discovered before you want to be. Plan for that eventuality. Recognize that gunfire or hostage-taking may be the result of an interrupted crime. Respond with force to protect yourself, but don't be rushed into an assault that doesn't *have* to take place. The point at which the offenders become aware of law enforcement's presence remains one of the most dangerous times during any crime in progress incident. If you are carefully behind cover and gunfire does not result at that point, there's a good chance the offenders will calm down again as the police-controlled standoff continues. That's precisely what negotiating from a position of strength seeks to accomplish. Very often it works well for the good guys in that the offenders eventually call it quits after realizing that (1) they're not going to be killed unless they harm or threaten to harm someone and (2) law enforcement is in control and their chances of escaping are virtually nil. Even an offender who has fired shots and perhaps hurt someone *may* calm and eventually be talked into surrendering. It will be up to the officers on-scene to assess the continuing violence potential of the criminal(s) involved and respond accordingly.

Plan and execute a safe arrest process. It's important enough to state one more time: Whenever feasible, you do not go inside a building to confront an offender. You instead wait for him to exit (assuming he doesn't know you're there) or order him outside onto your turf (assuming he *has* discovered your presence) where it's safer for you because you're behind good cover and he's not. Once he's outside, even if he has a hostage it's generally best that he not be allowed to leave the scene. That holds true in spite of his promises of safety for his prisoner. Once he leaves with someone, there is virtually no way you can guarantee that individual's continued survival. A SWAT sniper may be one solution to the problem, but every situation you encounter will be at least a little different from another. It's up to you to act in good faith on the totality of the circumstances you have laid out before you. And that may require you to exercise the lethal force option against an offender who is clearly threatening the lives of innocent others.

In most cases your arrest and control decisions will not be such drastic ones. The main concern for you here is that you and your peers remain safe while bringing a criminal, possibly an armed one, into secure custody. To do that you start with a plan. If the bad guys do A, you'll do B; if the offender does X, you'll do Y, and so on. Mentally preparing for the various possible scenarios will help you handle what does develop for real. Whatever your plans may be, it is vital that each member of the law enforcement team knows what he or she is to do, and how.

The basic safety measures you employ in any other potentially high-risk arrest are appropriate for the crime in progress response. You avoid a confrontation, if possible, until sufficient backup is in place and behind cover. Only one officer directs the operation and issues instructions to peers and suspects alike. Oral instructions to bad guys are direct, to the point and given from a place of cover. Soon-to-be prisoners are ordered into a position of disadvantage, kept off balance and approached from the rear for handcuffing and searching purposes. The securing officer is closely guarded by peers who remain behind cover, utilizing sound contact and cover principles. Finally, all officers remain alert for the next, undetected threat even as prisoners are secured and carefully searched for weapons. Even then, you should question victims and witnesses to be sure you've really located all of the crime's participants and there are no further hidden dangers present.

"MAN WITH A GUN"

A call of a "man with a gun" represents one more example of a crime in progress assignment, but it's one that contains real danger for you if you're the officer sent to handle it. While every crime in progress call *may* be dangerous, you know going in that this one most certainly is because a tool for murder and mayhem already has been reported involved. Obviously, all of your plans and actions will have to take this information into account and be devised accordingly.

Here's a sobering thought for you to consider, too. In one California study of peace officer killings done several years back, a number of murdered officers who *knew in advance* that they were responding to dangerous calls in which weapons were likely involved proceeded to those calls *and died anyway* in spite of the radio warnings of mortal danger. The message for you here would seem to be that it's not nearly enough to know ahead of time that danger lies in wait. To stay alive, you also need to do something positive with the information, like significantly altering your approach and deployment tactics, or waiting for the arrival of plenty of backup before committing yourself to action, whenever possible. There's more you can do, too.

Virtually all of the tactics you would employ in responding to other sorts of crime in progress calls should serve you well on a "man with a gun" assignment, also. Invisible deployment is vital. So is exceptional coordination and communication among you and adequate numbers of assist officers, whether they are two or ten in number. Good use of physical cover and the application of wise contact and cover tactics are critical, too, as are careful arrest and prisoner control practices. All of these techniques make up an effective officer survival package for safely handling a "man with a gun" incident.

But there's more. You can do much to get ready for a "man with a gun" call before you ever receive one. It all goes back to mental preparation for the challenges of your job and the contingency plans that you make for responding to those challenges when they appear. When you have some "down" time on the job, *think* and then make some tentative plans for how you might respond to:

• a "man with a gun" reported seated in a local restaurant having a meal;

• the same "man with a gun," only this time he's reported arguing loudly with the teacher in a classroom full of youngsters;

• a subject brandishing a pistol and quoting the Bible on a crowded bus or commuter train;

• an apparently intoxicated police officer, visibly armed but very cooperative as the driver of the speeding vehicle you've just stopped;

• an individual reported to have a holster protruding from under his jacket, seated quietly in the midst of a crowd at the local city council meeting;

• the man reported to be taking target practice with a .22-caliber rifle—on his neighbor's cats.

The scenarios you could develop tailored to your own job and locality could be endless. Thinking about them now and formulating plans for how you would respond to them could well make all the difference should you one day face a similar event for real.

As in any other variety of crime in progress call, information gathering will have to be a big part of your effective handling of a "man with a gun" challenge. You will need all the data you would glean for those other crime in progress assignments, but with extra special emphasis on such questions as:

• Who is the armed subject? What is his description? Where is he right now?

• Who else is involved? Does the bad guy have help? If so, exactly where are the other subjects?

• How is he armed? Have shots already been fired? How about known casualties? Where are they?

• Are there hostages involved? Where are any bystanders and uninvolved others located? How will their presence affect my plans for solving this crisis?

• What appears to be the cause of the problem? Interrupted crime? Suicidal person? In-progress raid or arrest involving another law enforcement agency?

• Could there be an "innocent" explanation for what is happening? (Examples: an off-duty officer who doesn't realize that his holstered firearm has been spotted while he was standing in a supermarket checkout line; a hunter sitting on his back porch cleaning his rifle, etc.)

• What is my safest approach to the armed subject's location? What are the cover options?

• How much help will I need? Exactly how should I deploy it?

• What provisions do I need to make for evacuating or protecting in place others in the vicinity who may be at risk?

• What kind of weapons can I bring into play here? (A buckshot-loaded shotgun in a crowded shopping mall probably would not be the best choice, for instance.)

• What kind of crime is known to have been committed so far? Would forcing a confrontation right now make matters worse? Should I wait until he goes outside, gets out of the car, moves down the block, etc.?

• Does the bad guy realize that I'm on-scene? Do I still have the element of surprise on my side? Does he seem to be *wanting* a confrontation with law enforcement?

As in every other sort of assignment you face, you will never have all the answers you want before tangling with a "man with a gun." Just answer the questions you can from the sources you can tap and the personal observations you can make in the time you have available.

On a "man with a gun" assignment, isolating the offender from everyone else at risk is important. Be sure you have sufficient manpower on-scene to accomplish containment of the suspect. How much help you will need could depend on the nature of the location where the problem is occurring and the type of weapons believed involved. An armed subject inside a convenience store will not call for as many assist units as an armed man loose with a gun "somewhere" in a shopping center. Call in as much help as you need to throw a secure cordon around the involved area. The idea is to make it impossible for an armed subject to get outside your perimeter without being confronted by officers who have good cover and an excellent sight picture of the bad guy. The message you are sending is a simple, direct, yet effective one: *We are prepared to deal with you. Give up now to preserve your safety.*

Naturally, the weapons involved also will affect the size of your armed perimeter. A subject brandishing a handgun generally won't require a perimeter that is city blocks across. A subject firing or threatening to fire a rifle certainly may.

The actual, oral message you deliver to an armed offender can vary depending on the circumstances, but it should remain direct. In as few words as possible, identify yourself and tell the subject precisely what he is to do: "Police! Don't move until told! Turn away from us! Lay the gun on the ground! Do anything else and you will be shot! Put your hands on your head! Interlace your fingers! Back up towards us! Get down on your knees! Don't move again!" Or whatever else works well for you to get the suspect safely separated from his weapon and into handcuffs. Naturally, all of your instructions should be shouted at gun-point and from behind cover.

In a situation where a subject is reported to be armed but you do not currently see a weapon in hand, frame your oral instructions to avoid giving him reason to touch any weapon he does have. In other words, don't tell him to produce the gun and lay it aside. Just secure him under the covering watch of a backup officer and then search him carefully to recover whatever it is he might have.

Finally, unless your "man with a gun" already has harmed someone or is in the process of doing so when you arrive, do not be in too big a rush to force a confrontation. If you can observe and assess from good cover without tipping him off to your presence, do so. Give your assisting officers time to arrive on-scene and deploy, if you can. If your subject is agitated, he may calm somewhat. If he is now in a crowded area, he may move to a spot that better enables you to isolate him. Given time, he may get careless and provide you with a better (and safer) opportunity for confrontation and control.

Rely on your common sense and good judgment in deciding when, where and how you elect to assert control over a "man with a gun." Remember that in the majority of armed confrontations, time is on the side of law enforcement. Act when you're ready and in a position of tactical superiority. That's how you turn a "man with a gun" into one more arrestee, safely disarmed and in custody.

SUMMARY

Responding to a crime in progress call may well mean that you are heading for danger, simply because the criminals who caused the trouble in the first place are still there to confront you. You control the danger factor by the application of intelligent preparations and planning for what you'll do when you get there. You further protect yourself from harm by arriving and deploying silently and invisibly for the offender or offenders. Once you're on-scene, you stay safe by using cover properly and utilizing excellent contact and cover tactics along with adequate law enforcement reinforcements. You remain alert as well as patient and take on the bad guy on ground and terms that are advantageous to you and your backups. By the tactics and techniques

you choose you seek to gain every advantage for yourself while deny-
ing them to your adversary.

Of all the crime in progress calls that you may face, the report of a
"man with a gun" may be the most potentially hazardous of all. You
defuse the danger by following your established crime in progress procedures while you isolate and eventually confront from cover the
source of the danger. Meanwhile, you rely on your own proficiency
with firearms, proper use of cover and ability to work as part of a team
to keep you safe as you neutralize the armed threat that a criminal
"man with a gun" brings to the community.

STREET SURVIVAL CHECKLIST FOR CRIME IN PROGRESS CALLS

1. Begin your contingency planning for safely handling a crime in
progress call long before you receive it. That includes physical,
mental, emotional and equipment preparations.

2. Plan your approach and deployment to keep your presence and
whereabouts a secret from the criminals.

3. Communicate and coordinate your response and on-scene
actions with other police units.

4. Be on the alert for additional threats–lookouts, getaway vehicles,
possible accomplices–as you arrive in the area of a crime in
progress.

5. When you respond to a serious or violent crime in progress, do
not go in after the offender alone. Get as much help as you think
you'll need. Then, let him come out to you, if at all possible.

6. Expect the participation of more criminals than you were
advised of when you were dispatched to a crime in progress. Keep
looking for new threats.

7. On a "man with a gun" call, get plenty of help and try to isolate
the subject from the surrounding area. Realize that you may have to
do some quick evacuations, especially if the subject has been firing.

8. Whenever possible, try to maneuver to confront a "man with a
gun" outdoors and away from numbers of innocent persons. Unless
he is in the process of hurting people, avoid going inside after him.

Chapter Nine

SAFELY DEFUSING DISTURBANCES

On the East Coast, a 39-year-old city patrolman was shot and killed on a disturbance call. The manager of a restaurant had requested that police remove a man who was harassing his former girlfriend, a waitress at the establishment. At about 7:50 P.M. the officer approached the subject at the bar and asked him what he was carrying in a waist pouch. The man suddenly drew a .45-caliber pistol and shot the officer in the chest. Shortly afterwards he also shot to death his former girlfriend and himself.

In the northern U.S., two officers arrived at the scene of a disturbance purportedly involving two brothers at a private residence. Outside the home, the officers focused their attention on a man carrying a rifle. A second subject began firing at the officers from behind cover and the subject with the rifle began shooting also. Both officers were killed.

A 34-year-old state trooper was shot to death at approximately 10 P.M. after responding with a second trooper to a neighborhood disturbance concerning a vehicle blocking a driveway. The officers arrived, exited their vehicles and were rounding the corner of a storage building when the victim trooper was hit in the abdomen with a .308-caliber rifle round fired by a 68-year-old male positioned nearly 100 yards away in some woods. The officer died the next day.

Handling disturbance calls can be as hazardous as experienced law enforcement officers have long assumed it to be. According to statistics compiled by the Federal Bureau of Investigation, during the example year 1994 alone, eight of the 76 American law enforcement officers murdered that year were killed while handling disturbance assignments. Over the longer period of 1985-1994, 119 peace officers were slain while working disturbance calls that ran the gamut from bar brawls to domestic disputes to "civil situations" to large scale disturbances that became virtual riots. During the same, ten-year time span,

121

over 36 percent of the 587,474 officers assaulted but not killed were attacked while on disturbance-handling assignments—the largest number assaulted on any kind of police business.

Not surprisingly, many of these disturbance call assignments telegraph their potential for danger. They look and sound as dangerous as they are. On occasion, however, fatal danger can hide in situations that at first glance appear more bizarre than risky. In a recent case, a 29-year old patrolman with a northern U.S. police department responded to a 4:30 A.M. report of a man creating a noise disturbance *while feeding birds*. The officer, who was wearing soft body armor, arrived and confronted a 48-year-old subject in an alley behind the man's home. Shortly thereafter, the officer radioed that he had been shot. When backup officers arrived, they found the two-year patrolman dead from nine 9mm bullet wounds, two in the head. The killer was eventually wounded and arrested after barricading himself. Indeed, even a disturbance assignment that sounds "harmless" enough can prove fatal.

As veteran officers know, so-called "civil disputes" also can turn instantly deadly. Hardened criminals and crazies get into disputes with tow truck drivers, restaurant managers and landlords, too. When they do, the result can be violence. The smart officer will realize that what started as an argument over an unpaid bill or vehicle repossession could have turned into a violent confrontation with shots fired before the law arrives. That same smart officer will tailor his response, arrival and tactics accordingly to deflect the dangers of the unexpected.

"Civil disputes" can indeed be hazardous for you. Consider this real-life example of a "noncriminal" disagreement gone awry. A 17-year veteran officer and his partner responded to a rent dispute call. As he was getting out of the patrol car, the 48-year-old officer was struck fatally in the head with a .30-06 rifle round. The 57-year-old male killer then barricaded himself with a hostage before surrendering three days later. It was subsequently learned that the man had killed his landlord just before the police arrived.

But if it is agreed by most veteran officers that disturbance calls *are* potentially risky affairs, exactly what makes them so? In actuality, several factors may come together to increase your exposure to harm while you are striving to restore some degree of peace to the situation. Perhaps first among the factors pushing up the danger quotient for you is the presence of powerful emotions on the parts of the disturbance participants. Whether they are family fight combatants or barroom brawlers, the "players" probably have already had their "fight or flight" mechanisms activated, with a resultant adrenaline dump firing them up for action. In other words, while you are present with the intent of calming things down and restoring order as painlessly as possible, your potential opponents are mentally and physically ready to do battle. It is quite possible that they have already engaged in all-out combat before you arrived. Now, to them you represent only one more busybody to fight. If you're not really careful, you have been set up to be a victim before you've even gotten involved.

A second element of danger for you on the scene of a disturbance call may be found in the frequent presence of deadly weapons. The Hell-raiser who knows that he's likely to get into an altercation not infrequently has equipped himself in advance for a confrontation. That may have lead him to stash a pistol in his glovebox, or stick one in his coat pocket. It may have caused him to hide a knife in his boot, or tuck a club under his car seat. Whatever the weapons of choice for the combatants, all remain dangers for you, the peacekeeper sent to "fix" things.

There is at least one more key factor frequently found at the site of a disturbance that makes handling the incident in safety an especially critical challenge for you. It's intoxicated or under the influence behavior by at least one and possibly all of the dispute's participants. It is not unusual for a veteran nightwatch officer to have a hard time recalling the last disturbance call he attended where drunk, drinking or drugged disputants were *not* involved. As you know, the presence of alcohol or drugs in any assignment you undertake underscores the potential danger for you. When lowered inhibitions and shot-to-Hell judgment come into play, the normally compliant individual may elect to take you on physically. Add to that lack of self-control the escalating feelings often present at any disturbance call and you have a situation practically guaranteed to result in a blowup—assuming, that is, that you do not respond promptly and effectively to prevent a dangerous explosion of violence. You can and must do that. Here, in detail, is how it's done.

REDUCING THE DANGER

The survival practices that help keep you safe on a number of other high-risk assignments can protect you on a disturbance call, too. While specialized safety measures can be appropriate for certain kinds of disturbances, like bar fights and large scale disputes, a set of general disturbance survival guidelines should serve you well at virtually every scene of controversy and mayhem. These steps for surviving a disturbing scene include the following:

Plan Ahead. Your planning should begin before you arrive and continue through your departure from the disturbance scene. Think about your safest route of approach and arrival to preserve the element of invisible deployment for surprising your subjects. If you have been to the place before, where are the known hazards and complications, such as good ambush sites? Who are you likely to find present? Outlaw bikers? Gang members? Or who? Plan your actions and arrange for the help you will require. It's not too early to begin planning on the tactics you will need to solve the problem in safety, based on what you know so far. Remain flexible, however. Your handling of the situation could change drastically depending upon what you discover on-scene.

Only Fools Rush In. Don't be in too big a hurry to charge into the midst of potential danger. Seldom will you have to act immediately upon arrival to save a life. If you can arrive quietly and observe unnoticed for a few minutes (don't park right out front) you may be able to learn things that will help you solve the problem in safety. Your auditory observations might tell you, for instance, how many people are involved, who the aggressor is, whether or not there are weapons involved and the emotions and demeanor of the parties entangled in the situation. Thus armed, you and your backup(s) should be able to handle the call with greater effectiveness and safety once you do announce yourselves. One pair of officers, listening undetected outside the front door of a residence where a domestic beef was in progress, made a quick change in plans after hearing the male party state "I'm going to get my gun." They forced a quick entry and controlled the subject before anything nastier could transpire. There are plenty more true stories out there of peace officers who bided their time, observed carefully and then acted effectively and in safety on what they had learned.

Watch Your Approach and Positioning. Keep an eye out for good, solid cover in case gunfire should threaten as you approach a disturbance call. Park away from the address and move in afoot along the fronts of the neighboring structures. Try to avoid the most obvious routes of approach, such as the front walk, just in case a disturbance participant, alerted to your arrival, might be waiting in ambush. Do not stand directly in front of a door you are knocking at. Rather, stand off to the side and against a wall. Once you have announced your presence, maintain a generous reactionary gap of several feet between yourself and the disturbance participants. Keep your gun side turned facing away from them as you keep your weapon covered with your elbow or arm. Beware of anyone who wants to get close to you, as he may be planning an attack or weapon takeaway attempt. Tell him where you want him to be and direct him (as courteously as the situation permits) to stay put.

Control Your Environment. Control the scene rather than allow it and the disturbance participants to control you. Do not allow them to duck out of your sight or keep their hands out of your view. Don't let them get behind you. Remain aware of each person's location, what is in his hands and what is going on around you at all times. The cover officer on-scene will be responsible for watching the primary officer carefully as he or she goes about gathering information and taking concrete action to resolve the dispute. Meanwhile, you must attempt to clear the area of uninvolved people who might at some point want to take sides and intervene. (It is very doubtful that they will be on *your* side if they do get involved!) In a crowded establishment such as a bar, it may be easier to guide the main actors outside so you can investigate further there. Your safety demands that you stay out of crowds to the extent possible whenever you are handling a disturbance of *any* kind.

Get Sufficient Assistance. It's been said repeatedly throughout this book and will be stated yet again. It's that vital to your survival. Do not attempt to handle any kind of disturbance call without adequate law enforcement resources on-scene to help you. A disturbance call ranks near the top of the list of law enforcement assignments that must never be worked by a lone officer. Call as much help as you believe you will need if your dispatcher has not already provided you with adequate cover. Then, wait for it to get there before you enter the fray, if at all feasible. Do not, on the other hand, join the list of officers who have called for a backup but failed to wait for its arrival before committing to action. Some of these courageous but unwise peers of yours have been found dead or dying when their help did get there.

Control the Discussion, But Let Them Talk. It is up to you and your backup(s) to stay safe while you learn enough to determine what you are going to do, how you are going to do it and who you are going to do it to. One good means for doing that is to control the flow of information. These are the facts that you eventually will be required to act on. Be prepared for all participants in the dispute to want to bend your ear with their version of events and advice on what you should be doing next. You and your cover officer should separate the speakers so that the primary or contact officer can interview each without interruption. Although you should seek to position each participant beyond the hearing of the others, you nonetheless should take care to remain close enough to your backup to allow each of you to watch one another at all times.

During your information gathering session be sure that you listen more than you talk. Take your time. Get it handled the first time so that you or another officer do not have to return to do it all over again an hour later. Let your subjects vent, but also steer wandering speakers back to the present when they want to tell you about everything the opposition has done wrong over the past ten years. Remain patient. Now is the time to gather the information you shortly will need to decide on a course of action. Find out everything relevant that you can in the time available.

Stay Alert for Big Changes. Disturbances can get worse instead of better, sometimes even after you arrive. Watch for the individual who looks to be getting more agitated as the investigation proceeds and it becomes apparent even to him that he may be headed for jail. Keep watching for new threats, like weapons or additional players, to appear without warning. Call more help if it looks like it might be needed. Adjust your tactics as required, even if it means temporarily backing off until more help can arrive.

Take Appropriate Action. Based on your assessment of the observations you have made and the facts you have gathered, act decisively to solve the disturbance problem at hand. If a full-custody arrest is the option you have selected, all officers present should know in advance what is to happen next. Be fair, but act firmly. If a subject convinces himself that you are unsure of yourself or don't know what you are doing, he may try to take control of the call away from you. To put it another way, realize that if you cannot or will not make a decision in a confrontation, you turn the decison-making over to someone who likely is not your friend. Say what you mean and mean what you say. Take whatever lawful action is called for by the facts to quell the disturbance and return some degree of normalcy to the scene. Act with authority, but act in safety.

Follow Careful Prisoner Handling Tactics. Think about the officers killed and assaulted statistics the next time that you respond on a disturbance call. They tell you that the people you'll meet on disturbance assignments can be very dangerous indeed. Some of them end up injuring police personnel even *after* they are in custody. Resolve now not to be hurt by *your* disturbance call prisoner. While working with an alert cover officer, properly handcuff your subject from behind while he remains off-balance and at a disadvantage. Search him carefully, as many times as you feel you must, to assure yourself that he has nothing with which he could injure you, himself or someone else. Stay alert for a surprise assault from even a previously cooperative prisoner. His attitude and intentions easily could change without warning. Keep your weapons secure and well out of his reach. Officers have lost their guns—with fatal results—to *handcuffed* offenders in the past. Remember that your disturbance call prisoner represents a real threat to you until he is finally and safely behind bars or is otherwise totally removed from your presence. Relaxing too soon could have disastrous repercussions for you, so don't do it.

Is It Really Over? Make your break from the disturbance site quickly and cleanly. Do not remain in the vicinity unnecessarily to complete paperwork or discuss the call with another beat car. Go somewhere else to write or talk, just in case a disturbance participant or one of an arrestee's pals decides to track you down to resume the altercation. Even after you leave the area, keep an eye on your rearview mirror for any "tails" you may have picked up at the scene. It doesn't hurt to stay cautious.

Get Better For the Next One. Experience is of no value if you fail to learn from it. Think about your handling of a disturbance assignment when it's all over. What worked well for you? What didn't? While every disturbance will be unique from all the others you will handle, be your own harshest critic in reviewing and revising your tactics and techniques to do it even better the next time. Add some tools to your growing bag of tricks based on what you learn and experience. One of them may turn out to be just what you need to save your own life the next time a disturbance call beckons.

BAR BRAWLS

The bar.

You know which one it is. There's probably one (or more) in your jurisdiction where the patrons remind you of nothing so much as the inhabitants of the cantina scene in *Star Wars*. When a disturbance takes place in this environment, you *know* it has the potential for real danger for you, the officer assigned to bring order out of drunken chaos.

Bar calls are hazardous for several reasons. First of all, you may be dealing with disputants whose judgment and inhibitions have been largely destroyed by alcohol. These people may be capable of just about anything. They are highly unpredictable. And they just might decide to take you on.

Second, bars can be dangerous places due to the weapons often found there. The regular patron of a sleazy establishment knows there are others of a character similar to his own there. He knows well that they may be violent. He's not about to be caught dead without his "equalizer" readily at hand. If he's drunk, mean or desperate enough when you confront him, he very well might be willing to use it on you.

Third, the environment of the bar itself may help set you up for attack if you're not careful. Attacks can develop without warning from a number of dark, hard to see places. Attackers can escape in the roiling crowd and ensuing confusion of humanity. There are also plenty of obstacles for you to fall over in the semi-darkness if you get into a struggle while attempting to take someone into custody.

In addition, bars can be risky places because you and authority in general may be seen as outsiders here. The anti-law enforcement attitude that prevails in some of these joints can make it psychologically easier for a customer to attack or resist you, perhaps with help from his fellow bar dwellers.

It is up to you to offset these hazards with survival-sound tactics of your own that will help protect you when your duties take you into these establishments. Whether you are responding to a call of a bar fight in progress or simply doing a liquor law compliance inspection, a few bar survival guidelines should aid you in staying healthy. Consider the following:

Know What You Are Facing. It's important that you know what's on your beat, bars included. Learn the safest routes in and out of "your" bars, paying special attention to back doors and out of the way places. Practice approaching them without being detected. Then, when trouble does arise for real, do not use the most obvious entry point where an ambush may be waiting. Also, try to learn in advance where any special hazards might be located, such as the bartender's hidden club or handgun. Learn about "secret" rooms and other areas where an offender might hide–or launch an attack.

Don't Pass Up a Problem. Realize that with the built-in delay involved in the call to 911 and the dispatching that follows it you may encounter the suspect in a bar problem some distance away from the establishment itself. Do not overrun danger. Realize that a bar fighter who knows you are coming just might hide in the parking lot or elsewhere nearby to elude or attack you. It has happened before. Stay sharp and keep looking for danger.

Stop, Look and Listen. Wait outside a bar where a problem is supposed to be occurring until your backup(s) can catch up to you. As you wait, allow your senses to gather in as much of what is happening as you possibly can. How many voices can you hear? What can you see from outside, if anything? What appears to be going on right now? Use what you learn to plan your intervention in safety. What you find out may cause you to alter drastically your planned response. It may, for example, result in your calling in a lot more help.

Wait for Help, and Use It Wisely. A bar disturbance calls for no fewer than two officers to handle it. It could require a good many more. Stand by for your help to catch up to you before you get involved. It's safer for everyone that way. Once your help is with you, apply careful contact and cover tactics. The concept holds regardless of how many officers and subjects are involved. Covering officers should maintain surveillance from a position (Ex: back against a wall) where no one can get behind them. The cover officer does not participate in the handling of the call other than to provide a very visible deterrent, shout a warning and intervene with threat-appropriate force if a contact officer is endangered. Get as much help as you need to the scene promptly. Keep it there until you are through.

Stay Alert for Danger. Do not relax your guard for even an instant in a bar setting. Danger can emerge quickly. Watch the hands of those you are dealing with. Keep watching for new "players" and new threats to appear. Look out for weapons, makeshift or otherwise. Be aware that previously uninvolved drunks may jump on your back, go for your weapon, try and whip up the crowd or otherwise deal themselves in on the action. Practice excellent weapon retention here.

Get Out Quickly and Safely. It is to your advantage to move the subject(s) of your attentions out of the bar as quickly as feasible. You are still at risk outside, of course, but you probably have reduced the danger from friends, allies and enemies of the person you may now be taking into custody. Getting a recalcitrant offender out of the place can naturally be a task in itself. If possible, consider waiting until you get outside to handcuff him. It may be safer and less emotional there. Do perform a pat-down search for weapons immediately upon contacting your subject, however. Do so under the watchful eyes of your cover officer and keep your cover advised via word or hand signals as to what you plan to do next. Following your weapons search, advise your problem subject that you need to talk with him further outside. Guide him ahead of you to help clear a path as you point him towards the door. Your cover should walk behind you to protect your blind side. Ideally, one officer should be present for each individual needing removed from the bar. One or more cover officers should bring up the rear of the procession and continue their surveillance outside in case problems develop there.

Make Your Break. Don't hang around the bar environs once you have finished your business there. The bar parking lot is not a great place to loiter and do your paperwork, especially if you have a prisoner aboard. You or your "guest" might draw the attention of someone with considerable ill intent. A prisoner rescue attempt also remains a possibility if you are unwise enough to remain in the immediate neighborhood. Be smart—make a clean break and then keep an eye out for trouble that could have trailed you from the cantina scene.

LARGE SCALE DISTURBANCES

Some peace officers tend to see large scale disturbances as nothing short of full-blown riots and mass civil disorder, requiring huge numbers of officers and perhaps the National Guard to restore the rule of law. These kinds of big problems can indeed happen, however infrequently they may occur. When they do, everything you have learned about surviving on the street will be required to keep you safe. At the same time, much more common and likely to occur in most jurisdictions is the big, out-of-control drinking party turned nasty, the sporting event crowd turned destructive or the planned or unplanned clash between two or more groups of protestors or zealots convinced that their way is the only way. "Regular" domestic disputes can escalate into a battle involving the whole building or the entire neighborhood before you get there.

Even worse, the number of disturbance participants can grow vastly *after* you get on-scene and attempt to take action not to the liking of the principals and their backers. What started as a domestic involving two people can get out of hand in a hurry as various friends, relatives and other "supporters" of the warring parties get involved. Change the setting for this dispute to a rowdy bar or a drinking, after-wedding reception or similar event and you have all the makings of a full-scale donnybrook in which law enforcement officers are all-too-often injured. It's happened many times before.

The dangers for you on a large scale disturbance scene are multiplied because of the increased numbers of participants present. Simply put, there are that many more human threats to deal with, and that many more directions that danger can come from. Unless you are cautious, a roiling mass of humanity will make it easier for someone to get next to you to take your gun, or slip a blade into your back. A large crowd can separate you from your backups and virtually carry you along, thereby setting you up for a disarming, a beating, or worse. There is even the risk of being knocked down and trampled by the throng. Finally, there is the added element of anonymity which, combined with mob psychology and the perceived safety of numbers, may cause someone or several someones to attack you who would never even think about it while facing you one-on-one.

The same, basic officer safety tactics and techniques that will shield you from the other disturbance call dangers of the job will serve you well when the numbers of potential attackers are much greater. In addition, some "special" large scale disturbance handling techniques can help you remain even safer. For instance:

Know What You Are Facing. Collect information, where possible, *before* the trouble breaks loose. Intelligence-gathering is key. Keep the lines of communication open to your informants in the community. The information you learn may help you prevent a problem from occurring, or respond to it more effectively if it does. By keeping your intelligence "feelers" out you may be able to learn of planned major events, who's mad at who about what, who the players are and otherwise sense the pulse of the street. But you'll learn none of this unless you ask questions and listen carefully to the answers. Stay tuned in to help yourself stay safe.

Make Some Plans. This advice applies to entire law enforcement agencies as well as you as an individual officer. Plan ahead for handling all the various big disturbance scenarios your active imagination can dream up. Determine in advance how quickly you could get additional personnel resources, and where you would secure them from. When should your plans include tactical withdrawal until more help arrives? Are formalized, mutual aid agreements needed? Who is to be in charge of a multi-agency operation? Are there plans and facilities for handling large numbers of arrests and prisoners? Exactly how is it to be done? Excellent contingency planning is a must for responding effectively to a large scale disturbance.

Get Help. It's been said many times before, but it remains a key principle of officer safety and survival, particularly at the scene of a big disturbance involving a violent or potentially violent crowd. Get your help on the way early before the situation you are dealing with gets out of hand. When assistance does arrive, try to commit your added people resources as an organized unit as opposed to piecemeal where the impact will be diluted. When you commit your forces, do so with a plan in mind as to what you intend to accomplish (arrest the ringleaders, disperse the crowd, etc.) Be sure each of your people knows the plan and his or her role in it.

There is some evidence that a show of force in the early stages of a mass disturbance or civil disorder can contribute towards a quick resolution of the problem. Many of the participants may decide that they really don't want to continue their involvement as badly as they thought, since it has now become apparent that the law means business. Stage your forces near the trouble site and let your potential opponents see that you really *are* serious.

Don't Intervene Alone. Controlling a large scale disturbance is not accomplished via cowboy tactics. Teamwork backed by adequate resources is the only way to get the job done in relative safety. Wait for your help to get there, even if a rowdy crowd is committing law violations in your presence. You help no one, particularly yourself, if you charge into a hostile crowd alone and get attacked and disarmed in the process. Pause until sufficient help is on-scene to do it right. Use the intervening time span to gather information via your observations and then formulate your own plan of attack.

Assess a Crowd for Danger. Monitor a crowd at a disturbance scene for indications that it is collectively getting drunker, noisier, larger or more threatening. Are threats of violence towards officers being shouted? Have bottles, rocks or other missiles been hurled? Has the group begun to engage in vandalism or other property damage? Can you determine by watching and listening who the obvious leaders or agitators are? You may want to identify them now for removal later when you have adequate assistance with you. Report what you observe to the officer in charge of managing the disturbance-busting operation.

Avoid Crowds. It's worth saying one more time: Neither you nor any other lone officer should charge into a potentially hostile crowd in pursuit of a rock-thrower, epithet-shouter or other offender. Doing so is an almost certain shortcut to the local emergency room–at best. Instead, note who you want and go after him with a plan and a solid wedge of officers once you have plenty of help on hand, assuming you still consider getting him to be worth the effort required.

Weapon Retention Is Vital. Remember that any time any officer must enter a crowd at a disturbance scene, all weapons and other personal equipment must be securely strapped or snapped and covered with an appropriate body part (arm, hand, elbow.) Keep your gun-side arm tucked securely over your sidearm. Be alert for a quick grab for your weapon, and instantly meet any such assault by locking your weapon in its holster with at least one hand as you launch a no-holds-barred counterattack on the would-be gun thief. Practice your weapon retention skills, too. They may save your life one day on the scene of large scale disorder.

Apply Contact and Cover. Naturally, there is nothing that says contact and cover involves only two officers. Contact and cover principles are absolutely appropriate for large scale disturbances. Adjust the relative numbers as the situation dictates. A large scale problem may call for the use of six contact officers and two covers, for instance.

But the principle remains the same. The contact officers may make the arrests, remove prisoners and disperse crowds. The cover officers watch out for the safety of the contacts and get involved only to protect these primary officers from attack. Remember that you must think past the numbers. A really large scale disturbance could call for the use of 200 contact officers with 20 covers, and so on up the scale.

Avoid Entrapment Attacks. Beware of ambush attacks at or near the site of a large scale disturbance. Don't get suckered into a location where you will be badly outnumbered and subject to being overwhelmed. Work only with your partners and covering officers. Realize, too, that following the dispersal of a disturbance some of the disgruntled participants may try to set a trap for you elsewhere, perhaps to "get even." Be wary of "odd" calls to out-of-the-way places at such times. Decline to meet a would-be informant at such a location. Consider varying your patrol routes and operations to frustrate someone who may be laying a trap for you.

Maintain Your Self-Control. The survival-smart officer (that's you!) will smile, talk little, and maintain his professional's calm demeanor at the scene of a large scale disturbance. When you must use force, you will make sure it's the minimum amount required to do the job of overcoming unlawful resistance in safety, and no more. You realize that engaging in debates or shouting matches with your tormentors is a waste of energy and brain cells, so you will do neither. By keeping control of yourself and your emotions you thereby deprive some unfriendly elements in the news media of having the graphic videotape images of "brutal, out of control cops" they so desperately desire. By making sure that you do not overreact, you also avoid inflaming an already overheated crowd that may be looking for an excuse to escalate the violence against law enforcement. Most important of all, you will know that by maintaining personal discipline and solid self-control you have done the *right* thing.

Have the Right Equipment. Every officer responding to a large scale disturbance should be properly equipped for the threats he may confront there. For you, that equipment includes gloves, baton, aerosol defense spray, soft body armor, a helmet, an adequate number of prisoner restraint devices and a quality safety holster that keeps your sidearm in your own possession. Remember to secure all of your personal equipment against a sudden grab by someone in an unruly or violent crowd, too.

At a violent large scale disturbance, the decision may be made to deploy chemical munitions (CS, pepper gas, etc.) to disperse the crowd. If chemicals are to be used, personnel who understand how to properly employ them must be involved in the operation. If chemicals *are* deployed, it will first be necessary for law enforcement personnel to be equipped with adequate gas masks and the knowledge of how to work while wearing them. The decision to use gas is a big one, however, and it is normally reached no lower than the mid-manager level in the law enforcement agency.

Tell Them to Leave and Let Them Go. There may be a select few you want to grab, but a generally effective principle for safely defusing a large scale disturbance is this one: Allow the members of the crowd ample opportunity to depart. Tell them to leave and advise them they are subject to arrest if they do not go. Repeat the order several times. Give them time to obey your instructions. Most want to be in on the action, but have no desire to go to jail. By giving them repeated orders to disperse and allowing them the means to do so (an escape route), you also legitimize any reasonable force you may eventually have to use to remove the hard core troublemakers who remain behind.

Never block a crowd's exit from a disturbance scene. A cornered group of rowdies may very well fight you. This may be an excellent occasion to ignore minor violations (Ex: open container of alcohol) for the time being to get these people away from ground zero. Save your law enforcement resources to deal with the real problem people.

Target the Agitators. It's another valid principle of crowd control. Assuming you have adequate resources to do so and your agitator targets have committed solid violations of the law for which they can be lawfully charged, a wedge of several officers can move into the remaining crowd under the watchful eyes of the cover officers and arrest the problem people. These arrestees must be immediately secured and transported out of the area before a rescue effort can be mounted by their compatriots. Fingerprint and photograph them for future identification. If existing conditions make it impossible or unwise from a tactical standpoint to arrest the primary troublemakers, seek to at least identify them for followup charges at a later time.

Protect Your Equipment and Facilities. To avoid having your transportation vandalized and immobilized, leave a force of officers to guard your police vehicles parked near a large scale disturbance. Try to group your vehicles in one spot to make the task of maintaining security easier. Also realize that a disorderly crowd may follow you to the police station or jail to advocate for or bail out their arrested pals from the initial disturbance. Security should be heightened at your physical plant with uniformed officers visible in strength to deter vandalism or violence. Stay alert for a new, large scale disturbance to erupt inside or outside your building. Be prepared to deal effectively with it, too. Just as in the original disorder, properly applied chemical munitions such as pepper gas may be a viable alternative. Again, you cannot afford to relax too soon.

SUMMARY

Unless handled with all the care and caution you can bring to bear from your training, experience and officer safety awareness, a disturbance call could result in your violent death. While that's not a particularly nice way to say it, it nevertheless happens to be the deadly truth. All of the emotions, willingness to do violence and (oftentimes) drug- or alcohol-induced complications that can accompany a disturbance assignment have stacked the deck against you unless you are *ready* for the challenge in every sense of the word.

To be ready as well as safety-smart, you must plan your response and arrival to surprise your potential adversaries as opposed to getting surprised yourself. You must secure sufficient help to aid you in safely defusing the crisis, and you must wait for that help to get there before you go into action. You must continuously assess who and what you are dealing with and remain highly sensitive to situational changes, like a subject escalating in his belligerence towards you. You have got to control the scene and keep track of *all* of the participants involved in the situation, as well as any "players" on the periphery who are not yet involved–but may want to be. You absolutely must stay sharp and expect the unexpected at every moment. To stay safe, you are mandated to determine the action appropriate for the handling of the incident, act decisively and then disentangle yourself from a less-than-happy environment as quickly as possible. Any prisoners who come into your custody must be correctly secured, thoroughly searched and closely watched every second they are in your presence.

Disturbance calls and the violence that attends them can spell serious injury or death for the unwary, uncautious or just plain lazy law enforcement officer sent to handle these critical assignments. You can never afford to fall into one or more of these categories of misguided and endangered officers. No matter what kind of disturbance you are confronting, by adding the officer safety tactics and practices you have learned in these pages to your own, good common sense and decision-making abilities you *can* bring order from chaos and restore peace in the face of violence, all without sacrificing your own safety in the process. In pulling it off, you will be more than a safety-wise law enforcement professional. You also will be a winner in the biggest contest of all: The daily struggle to survive the rigors of the street.

STREET SURVIVAL CHECKLIST FOR DISTURBANCE CALLS

1. Do some careful planning and information gathering before you arrive.
2. Approach the disturbance site inconspicuously and try to remain unnoticed while you collect additional information and observations.
3. Get enough help on-scene *before* you commit yourself to intervening in any kind of disturbance. Don't leap in over your head.
4. Control the scene and the discussion once you commit to action. Stay alert for situational changes and surprise dangers.
5. Watch your positioning and that of your weapons around others. Follow excellent weapon retention practices at all times.
6. Act decisively, take whatever enforcement action you elect to take and make a clean break from the scene. Don't remain nearby afterwards.
7. Realize that a "civil situation" dispute can prove just as dangerous for you as any other kind of disturbance call.
8. While handling a bar brawl, keep a sharp eye out for weapons and other dangers to appear from dark corners and surprise directions.
9. Know that you are at increased risk while inside a bar. Disengage as quickly as possible and watch your back as you do so.
10. At a large scale disturbance, never enter a volatile crowd alone. Make your plans and get adequate help on-scene before you attempt enforcement action or crowd dispersal.

11. Leave the crowd an escape route on the scene of a large scale disturbance.

12. Practice excellent contact and cover tactics while handling any kind of disturbance call or assignment.

13. Be prepared to implement a temporary tactical withdrawal at any disturbance if your common sense tells you that the odds are weighed heavily against you and you do not have sufficient resources to regain immediate control in safety.

14. Maintain your professionalism and self-control on a disturbance-solving assignment. Don't respond to taunting or baiting behavior by your antagonists.

Chapter Ten

DOMESTIC VIOLENCE INTERVENTION

At about 11:30 P.M., a patrol officer responded to a domestic disturbance call at an eastern U.S. residence. She was the first officer on-scene. She had knocked twice at the door when the home's inner door was opened and she was shot fatally in the throat with a .380-caliber semiautomatic pistol. The 50-year-old killer went back into the house and shot his girlfriend to death. He then exchanged fire with an arriving backup officer without effect, fled in a vehicle and was captured the next day.

In the South, a 45-year-old sheriff's deputy was slain in a 10:30 A.M. incident involving a domestic dispute. The deputy had accompanied a woman to her home so that she could get some clothing after her common law spouse had threatened her. The officer was standing in the carport in front of the residence when he was hit by a 12-gauge shotgun blast fired from a pump house about 30 yards away. The 61-year old assailant then shot his wife and returned twice more to the fallen officer to fire at him again. The last round was a .38-caliber bullet fired into the officer's head. The killer was later wounded and arrested.

At approximately 6:15 A.M., two patrol officers were murdered while handling a domestic disturbance. The officers arrived at a home where a 53-year-old male was reportedly violating a restraining order. The officers were directed upstairs by the suspect's daughter. When they opened the door to a bedroom, both were struck with rounds from a .30-caliber rifle. The subject then shot his wife, son and each of the officers again before turning the gun on himself.

By some estimates, an act of domestic violence occurs every 18 seconds in this country. The advocates for victims of domestic violence assert that this crime is the leading cause of injuries to women in the U.S. They estimate that 4,000 women die from domestic violence injuries each year in America alone. They further guess that perhaps as many as six million women are in some manner assaulted or harmed by their "intimate partner" on an annual basis.

139

Although women are most often the victims of domestic violence, men can be victimized, too. Same-sex violence from a domestic or "intimate" relationship also is a reality. Juvenile violence in which a teenaged boy brutalizes his girlfriend or the other way around also falls under the broad definition of sexual or "intimate" partners who cause harm to a significant other and thereby become perpetrators of domestic violence.

With all of that threatening, shoving, hitting, kicking, biting and, sometimes, shooting and stabbing going on, there is little wonder that you as a law enforcement practitioner are endangered when you intervene to stop it. But what, exactly, makes these assignments so potentially risky for you? The contributing factors are several.

WHY ARE THEY DANGEROUS?

When you intervene in a domestic violence incident, you are stepping into a virtual minefield that may have been days, months or even years abuilding. The dynamics of a domestic violence incident (or, more likely, a series of incidents) often involve a long period of separate attacks against intimate partners and, perhaps, offspring of the offender or victim. The pattern of violence may be a continuing one that in the past has involved threats, bruises, abrasions and, perhaps, broken bones and even life-threatening injuries. The more serious injuries may have come to the attention of law enforcement and resulted in prior intervention by officers, possibly helping set you up by creating an offender who already hates cops, expects to be arrested and is willing to respond violently to prevent your interfering with "his" property. (Although domestic violence offenders obviously can be of either gender, the generally larger, stronger male is most often the aggressor and so the term "he" will be used to represent the criminal in these pages.)

Most law enforcement jurisdictions have responded to victim advocate-driven legislative mandates by implementing something similar to a "required arrest" policy in substantiated cases of domestic violence. While this reaction appears to be an effective one for answering this especially cruel kind of criminal violence, it well may have the unintended side effect of increasing the likelihood that a domestic violence offender will attack you. Whereas a few years ago the violator may have counted on you to back off or give him a warning if his line was smooth enough and his victim was intimidated into silence, his recent experiences with law enforcement may have convinced him that he's automatically going to jail anytime the law shows up in response to a domestic pounding. That may have told an offender whose judgment has already been affected by booze and/or drugs that his only real chance for escape is to attack the law enforcers at his door. In other words, you've been targeted before you even made contact.

You can add the dangers of that sort of offender thinking to another threat almost always present on any kind of disturbance or assault call. Emotions and adrenaline are likely already running high as a result of the altercation or violence that occurred before you got there. An offender who has already attacked one or more other people may see you as simply an additional, interfering target to be assaulted, with or without deadly weapons. As one experienced patrol sergeant put it: "His blood's up. He's already licked somebody, even if it's his 90 pound girlfriend. What makes you think he's not ready to pound on you, too? Badges don't mean too much to these guys except to make 'em madder." It is often true enough.

But you do not have to become a punching bag or an animated paper target for the fists or bullets of this dangerous, unpredictable criminal. By applying a set of proven, sound officer survival tactics and techniques you can protect yourself as you bring a violent offender into much-deserved custody. It works like this.

TACTICS FOR HANDLING

Arrive inconspicuously. It is vital that you keep the element of surprise on your side when you are responding to a domestic violence call. You want to have time to gather some initial information, assess what you are dealing with and have help with you before you commit to action. As a consequence, you do not announce yourself with red lights, sirens, racing engines and slamming car doors once you get close to the scene. Instead you arrive quietly, parking several addresses away. You move in on foot, staying alert for anything amiss in the area, like an alerted offender waiting to ambush you. Keep your radio turned down and silence any other noisy equipment on your person.

Maintain good communication. Stay in constant touch with your dispatcher and backup officer(s) once you are on the scene of a domestic violence incident. Be certain that it's known where you are and what you are doing the whole time. Your life is at stake here. Let your radio dispatcher and peers know when you arrive, how much more help you need, when the situation is under control and where you are going next. Let your assist officers know about any special problems they may face, like additional parties involved or an armed suspect loose in the area. As in so many of the other kinds of calls you handle, a lack of information could get you killed. Keep your information lifeline working for you and stay safe.

Carefully execute your approach and positioning. Keep thinking about quick cover possibilities as you approach the location where the problem is supposed to be occurring. Once you get inside, continue to watch for weapons and remain mindful of where you could go for cover in case gunfire suddenly erupted. Cover awareness could well save your life if things go downhill in a hurry.

Consider approaching in a not-so-obvious manner, as by walking along the fronts of nearby houses rather than strolling along the sidewalk or street. If the violence is believed to be happening at a bar or other business, you might try the rear door rather than the obvious entry point, just in case your arrival is anticipated. Meanwhile, stay alert for surprise dangers outside as well as inside the target address.

Don't stand in front of a door when you announce your presence. Stand to one side and remain close to the wall just in case someone has some shooting on his mind. Once you have let people know you are there, don't be in a hurry to get too close. Maintain a healthy reactionary gap of several feet between yourself and everyone else on-scene. Move in close for arrest and control measures only when you have help on-scene and your subject is off-balance and at a disadvantage, if at all possible.

Be cautious about your positioning in relation to everyone else there. That includes the apparent victim, who may have a change of heart once you start enforcement action and turn on you. Keep your weapons covered and away from a sudden grab. Do not position yourself between victim and offender or let people get behind you. Remember that "uninvolved" others can get involved without warning, so stay sharp for new threats to appear.

Stop, look and listen. It certainly can happen that you must intervene to save a life the very second you arrive on-scene of a domestic violence call. But it is unlikely to happen very often. Generally you will have at least time to gather in everything your senses can tell you as you size up the situation from a place of safety, *before* you announce your presence and commit yourself. By peeping through a window, listening at a door and otherwise learning everything you can, you may be able to answer such key questions as:

Who is doing what? Who is the aggressor? How many people are present?

Are there obviously weapons involved?

Is there a struggle currently in progress?

Has someone been hurt already?

How much help will I need to deal with this?

By pausing to gather information you give your backup time to catch up to you. Once he or she is there, the two of you can formulate a plan of action to keep you safe as you intervene effectively.

Postponing a giveaway of your arrival until you are really ready to act will boost your safety and effectiveness on-scene. Whenever the situation allows it, slow down to avoid leaping in over your head at the outset. It just makes good survival sense.

Get enough help. Never attempt to handle a domestic violence intervention alone. There already have been way too many law enforcement deaths among well-intentioned but misguided officers who tried to do just that. There are too many directions for danger to come from to permit you to go it solo on a domestic violence assignment. Don't do it, not even if the information you have from your dispatcher or victim tells you that the perpetrator already has departed the scene. Nothing says he cannot return—with a vengeance towards the nosy outsider who is meddling with his "property" and his business. Peace officers have been killed by domestic violence offenders who left temporarily, only to return with a weapon to "even things up" with all concerned.

Be sure to get *enough* help. There's nothing special about the figure *two* when it comes to the number of officers required to handle in safety a domestic violence situation. If past experience tells you that a minimum of three officers will be required to handle the involved offender, that's the smallest number of people you should have on-scene when you confront the guy this time. If you learn that there are a number of people present, unfriendly to the law or otherwise, you again will need more help than can be provided by a single backup officer, even one who provides superior contact and cover support. Call more help than you think you'll need rather than the other way around. You can always send it away if it really proves unnecessary.

Separate the players. You and your backup officer must separate the parties involved in the incident and keep them a room or more apart as you interview each one about what transpired prior to your arrival. If at all possible, each officer should be able to see the other's back as the information-gathering from the respective participants continues. Continue to keep the parties well-separated by distance and under your watchful eyes until you are through taking enforcement action and are departing the scene. All the while, remain on the lookout for an attack from the original offender or a counterstrike from the aggrieved party, directed at either you or the tormentor—or perhaps both of you.

Get rid of the extra people. Attempt to convince uninvolved friends, relatives, supporters and opponents of the involved parties to leave the area of the call. At least make an effort to get them to go next door, take a walk down the street or go wherever to give you time to handle the problem without their interference. You don't need any extra bodies getting involved in a replay of the original crime, or jumping on you when you take enforcement action. If you cannot get them to leave, be sure to isolate the primary players from the others present as much as you can. Have a watchful backup officer—or more than one officer—keep a close eye on these people the whole time you are on-scene. Keep these people informed, to the extent possible. Learn what they have to say for whatever value it might have in helping you determine what happened before you got there. But do not allow these individuals to dictate your actions. Let them know—courteously, if possible—that they are subject to arrest, too, if they physically interfere with your duties. Then, have plenty of help to keep them under surveillance until you depart the area.

Remain alert. Stay sharp the whole time you are on the scene of a domestic violence intervention assignment. Keep watching the hands of those present. Look for where a new threat might come from at any moment. With your partner covering you, do a pat-down of the participants for weapons if you have any reason to believe they might be involved. Watch out for situational changes, such as an aggressor working himself up for a fresh attack—possibly with *you* as the new victim. Let him know that you see potential trouble coming and are prepared to deal with it. Call more help, if you feel it's necessary. Be prepared to go to a chemical spray or impact weapon to defend yourself from an attack. Or back out temporarily, if you are clearly overmatched or outnumbered and the quantity of help you need isn't there yet. You can always reassert control when the odds are back on *your* side, assuming you don't get killed or injured by acting rashly before adequate resources are at hand. Remain alert and remain alive.

Act decisively–and safely. If you act like you're not quite sure what you are doing on the scene of a domestic violence assignment you just might set yourself up for an attack by a newly emboldened offender who thinks he can take you. To prevent such a personal disaster from ever occurring you must not only know what you're doing, you must look and sound like it, too. Self-confidence that does not stray into arrogance is what's called for here. You'll need to put on your best take-charge face, make your enforcement decisions and go from there. Once you've determined that you have legal grounds for an arrest and have determined that it's your most reasonable course of action, it's time to make it happen. Be sure your backup knows what you are about to do. (Some officers use verbal codes or hand signals to tell peers that a full-custody arrest is about to take place–cover me.) By this time you have hopefully maneuvered your offender away from others present, including the victim, and are in a position to give him the bad news. Don't bluff or make idle threats or promises. Just get him off balance, tell him he's under arrest and then make it so. This is not the time to engage in debates or arguments, so don't get dragged into those pointless games. Act and be prepared to deflect and control an opposing reaction.

Follow excellent arrest and control practices. By the nature of the offense you are there to investigate, you already know your soon-to-be prisoner has the capacity to be violent and potentially dangerous to you. You don't want to give him the opportunity to add you to his victims list. Get him cuffed and searched from behind while you are covered by an alert backup officer. Remove from his person anything with which he might harm *anyone*, himself included. Keep him under close observation and get him away from the arrest site quickly, even if that means another officer must transport him while you complete your on-scene investigation. Speed is essential here to reduce the opportunities for him or someone else to resume the violence that started the whole mess in the first place. Watch your back as you depart. Don't linger in the neighborhood to do paperwork in your car. Get yourself and your prisoner to the station or the lockup and complete your work there. You must remove the temptation for another player to come up to your car with the intent of continuing the argument, assaulting you or your prisoner or mounting a rescue attempt for the individual you have in custody. Get out of there fast and remove the source of focus for any unhappy folks who still happen to be nearby.

Watch your mental health survival, also. Responding repeatedly to the same addresses and people on reported instances of domestic violence can prove depressing as well as frustrating to a law enforcement officer who truly wants to protect the innocent and lock up bad guys. In a scenario in which the victim may offer little in the way of thanks for the protection rendered and may even turn physically on the rescuer, your reward probably will have to be internal. You know you did the right thing. You know you intervened to save an innocent person from injury or death. You may have to self-generate the only real praise you are to receive on this type of assignment. Little wonder, then, that you don't look forward more to handling these sorts of calls.

But in most all situations, you really *did* help, even if it was only to give the victim a few more hours reprieve to make up her mind to leave an abusive partner. That may be the best anyone could have done under the circumstances, so do not sell yourself or your abilities short. You did what you could. You did your best under very trying conditions. You helped give a victim a little more time to think and respond to a predicament, even if it was only for a day. That realistically may have to be enough.

In order to keep yourself mentally and emotionally healthy while responding to years of domestic violence calls, realize that people will continue to get hit and domestic partners will continue to kill and injure one another in spite of your best efforts at peacekeeping and bringing the accused to justice. That is the reality of life. You may lock up an abuser tonight, but you probably cannot keep him off the streets forever. Realize that the domestic violence criminal you jail today may post bail and murder his domestic partner tomorrow. That's not your fault. All you could do for the victim was your lawful best. If you've done that, you've ably and ethically carried out your assignment. Realize that and get ready to help the *next* victim. He or she is coming soon. Follow to the letter the domestic violence handling dictates of your jurisdiction's pertinent laws as well as your department's operational rules and procedures for responding to these kinds of calls. That way, you can preserve your emotional well-being right along with your life. It's worth doing because it works.

SUMMARY

While they may never be your favorite kind of call to handle, you realistically should expect to respond on a great many domestic violence intervention assignments during your tenure as a law enforcement officer. You also should anticipate that because of the dynamics involved, these calls will remain among the most potentially hazardous you will answer. By preparing yourself mentally and physically to handle them in safety and carefully planning your response ahead of time, you can reduce the hazards you face to a manageable level. By using a tactically sound approach and arrival, getting sufficient help and gathering in all your senses can tell you, the assignment can be made much safer. By remaining constantly alert, positioning yourself carefully and using careful scene control and arrest and control techniques you can defuse the danger that close quarters battle otherwise can bring.

In safely mastering the threats of the domestic violence intervention you best serve the needs of the victim and the community while you shield yourself from harm. That's officer survival with a community-oriented twist!

STREET SURVIVAL CHECKLIST FOR DOMESTIC VIOLENCE INTERVENTION

1. Respond inconspicuously and approach quietly. Preserve the element of surprise.
2. Stop, look and listen to ascertain what is going on before you commit yourself.
3. Do your best to get help on-scene before you intervene in a domestic violence situation.

4. Stay constantly alert during your approach and assessment. Keep looking for new threats or changes in the situation. Call additional help, if indicated.

5. Separate the principals, isolate them and attempt to remove any "uninvolved" parties from the immediate vicinity.

6. Keep watching for weapons, and keep careful track of your own weapons in relation to other people present on-scene.

7. Act decisively when you have the facts and take appropriate enforcement action under the protection of an alert cover officer.

8. Make a clean break. Exit the area promptly and watch your back.

Chapter Eleven

SAFE STRUCTURE SEARCHES

In the South, officers were searching a residence for two jail escapees. At about 1:15 P.M., a 24-year-old deputy opened a bedroom door and was immediately hit in the front of the head and below his body armor with several revolver rounds. Eventually a SWAT team recovered the dead officer's body and fired tear gas into the house, which caught fire. The two escapees' bodies were found in the debris.

In the Southwest, a member of a SWAT team was killed while helping serve a civil pickup order at the home of a man believed to be suicidal. At about 3:50 A.M. officers entered the residence. The victim officer, who was serving as the team's point man, was hit by at least seven of a dozen rifle rounds fired as he entered the home's kitchen area. He was struck in the head and chest by rounds that penetrated his body armor and by bullets that entered via the vest's arm hole area. The structure was later gassed and the subject surrendered.

In the southern U.S., two detectives went to a residence shortly before 7 A.M. in an attempt to serve an arrest warrant for burglary. The plainclothes officers were directed to a rear bedroom. While one officer was positioning himself next to a closet door, a male subject jumped out and shot the officer fatally in the head with a .38-caliber handgun. He wounded the second investigator before escaping out the bedroom window.

Veteran law enforcement officers will tell you that structure searches are more dangerous today than they used to be. Various factors are sometimes listed as causes for the heightened danger. Some feel that improved technology that more often gets officers to the scene of the trouble before the offender can flee has something to do with it. Others swear that the biggest and potentially the most dangerous factor lies in the sort of offender being contacted more frequently by peace officers today, an offender who is armed and willing to take on the cops from within the recesses of a darkened structure or

149

elsewhere. Whatever the cause or causes, the danger is real and as close as the next radio call to a silent burglar alarm at a local business or residence.

Structure searches for hidden offenders qualify as high-risk assignments for you, the law enforcement officer who probably will do a lot of them over the span of a career. But your career could be cut short if you permit even a moment's apathy or carelessness to come between you and the search of a building or other structure. It's already happened too many times, and for a variety of reasons.

AVOIDING THE ERRORS

Fatal structure search errors sometimes committed by otherwise competent law officers have included the following:
• Poor approach to the structure
• Poor entry tactics at the structure to be searched
• Absent or inadequate communication and coordination among members of the search team
• Inadequate manpower to conduct a safe search
• Searching alone
• Poor or no use of cover during the search
• Making dangerous assumptions before or during the search
• Searching too quickly
• Incomplete, inadequate or incompetent search techniques
• General apathy and carelessness displayed during the search operation.

There are, of course, other equally perilous errors that can be made by the officer involved in a structure search. But the ones listed here account for almost all of the casualties suffered by law enforcement personnel involved in structure search missions in recent years. There is really not much new about the kinds of errors being made. What *is* shocking is the frequency with which the same searching mistakes are still being committed by modern-day officers who *should* know better by virtue of their training and experience.

Knowing what the errors are is the first step towards avoiding them. The next step requires that you error-proof your building search procedures accordingly. Consider the following tips for solving some of the most-often identified deadly errors of structure searches:

Poor Approach to the Structure. Whether you are arriving by car at the location of a silent burglar alarm or approaching afoot at an address where you have discovered an unsecured premises while on foot patrol, *how* you get there can contribute to your safety—or lack thereof—on-scene. If you do arrive via a vehicle, park it around a corner or down the street to avoid giving away your arrival. Never drive right up and park in front where you are a sitting duck for a burglar with a gun. During your approach, watch for suspicious persons or vehicles in the area that might be involved. Do not pass by loitering people or parked vehicles until you have checked them out and satisfied yourself that they are uninvolved in the situation you are investigating.

As you approach the structure itself, use available cover to your advantage. Don't stand around in the open when good cover exists to protect you. Use cover properly as you make your initial survey of the scene. Again, avoid loitering in an area where a bad guy either inside the structure or hiding in the shadows could take a shot at you.

Poor Entry Tactics. Never do a building search alone. It's simply too dangerous if one or more offenders are inside. Once you do have help on-scene and are ready, the key for you is to make entry quickly as well as cautiously. Never, ever loiter in the "fatal funnel" that exists in the open doorway of the structure so that anyone inside knows exactly where to target his rounds to take you out. Consider having a third officer create a noise diversion on the side of the structure opposite where you and your partner are actually about to enter.

If your entry point is a door and it opens inward, throw it open forcefully to assure that no one is hiding behind it. If no gunfire results, you and your backup should move quickly through the portal, one at a time. (Agree in advance who moves first. It's embarrassing, not to mention very hazardous to your health if the pair of you collide in the doorway!) Move quickly to cover inside the structure as you scan the area for immediate threats. Verbally challenge from cover anyone you encounter. It's now up to them to convince you of the innocent nature of their presence. Stay alert for surprises.

Poor Communication and Coordination Among Members of the Search Team. All of your sworn helpers must know the plan of attack before the search begins. Get the word out in person or by radio. It's now that any questions need answered—before anyone goes in harm's way. You also need to maintain contact with your dispatcher. He or she may be able to update you with additional information as the search proceeds. If you are using multiple search teams due to the size of the structure, clear and effective communication becomes especially valuable. That way the movement of fleeing suspects can be broadcast and misidentification dangers headed off. Radio communication between officers inside and outside the building are also vital to prevent a searcher getting nailed when he pokes his head out of an exterior door during the operation. Surprises are the last thing you want right now. The perimeter watchers outside also need to know how the search is proceeding and where the police searchers are so that officers' movements noted inside do not get reported from the outside as suspects on the move.

Inadequate Manpower. Even if you have to wait awhile for sufficient aid to arrive, it never makes sense to start a structure search without sufficient law enforcement personnel and other resources (such as a police dog, if available) on-scene. Borrow personnel from a neighboring jurisdiction if you have to, but do not search "short." Assess your manpower needs as soon as you arrive on-scene, and get sufficient resources on the way early. A large or irregularly configured structure generally will require more people than a small, box-shaped building. Do not allow business proprietors or homeowners to search with you. You are responsible for their safety and their untrained participation probably poses more danger than benefit to you. They should wait outside until the structure is declared safe.

While the building's size and the availability of police personnel may dictate how many search teams you will need, you always will want to search with at least a two-person team, or several of them. This will allow the concept of contact and cover to be applied to a structure search scenario. Remember that you will want to have a couple of officers on the perimeter outside, too, to intercept offenders who may be fleeing the searchers inside. These officers also should be alert and well-versed in the proper use of cover, as perimeter officers have been killed by suspects bursting from a building being probed by other law enforcement personnel.

Searching Alone. It's worth saying one more time. Unless a structure is so small and open that you literally can see into every nook and cranny from the outside, do not undertake a structure search by yourself. You need the added safety of a covering officer while your attention is focused on looking for hidden offenders. He or she can help prevent an ambush attack or an assault from an unexpected quarter while you are otherwise occupied. Wait for help. Run the risk of having a crook escape rather than go after him with insufficient safety backup. There likely will be another time to grab him. There may not be if you act rashly while under the influence of cowboy courage.

Poor or No Use of Cover. Remember: concealment only interferes with vision; you want to be behind something that stops bullets, if necessary. Both during your approach to the target structure and while you are inside it, move from one good cover spot to another while your partner watches out for you. Then, you provide the same service for him. Cease worrying about cover only when you have ascertained that the structure is truly devoid of threats of any kind.

Making Dangerous Assumptions. Deadly assumptions can come in all varieties during a building search mission. The alarm is false. The person in the building is an employee working late. That noise you heard inside was the wind. The offenders were gone before you got there. All cornered burglars give up peacefully. Believing in any of these officer survival fairy tales could get you killed. Don't be too quick to decide that you are facing a situation that contains absolutely no potential for danger. You should assume only that you really *don't know* precisely what you are dealing with until you investigate further.

Searching Too Quickly. Yes, there probably are other calls on the radio requiring your attention. Yes, you are short on the street–again. But you solve none of these problems and may create new ones if you take insufficient time to do your search the right way. If you miss a hidden bad guy in your haste, you just might get hurt or killed as a consequence of your carelessness. At the very least, other officers will have to come back to repeat the search or take a crime report after the offender has fled. Resist the fateful temptation to "get it over with cause there's nobody here anyhow." That's combining dangerous assumptions with unnecessary haste. The result can be a personal disaster.

Incomplete, Inadequate or Incompetent Searches. If it is worth doing at all, it's worth doing the right way. You apply that maxim in your other law enforcement duties; it is no less pertinent to structure searches. Search the *whole* structure with your partner, then switch tasks and search it again. Look into every spot where a human being might be able to seek concealment. That includes cabinets, closets, crawlspaces, attics and other out-of-the-way places. Try to put yourself in an offender's shoes. Where would *you* hide from the law? One veteran burglar noted that he always tried to hide in a high spot, as he thought "cops never look up." Call upon all the resources at your command to do a thorough, complete job of your potentially hazardous hide-and-seek mission.

Apathy and Carelessness. You could get killed while probing a structure for hidden offenders. The sad truth is bolstered every year in this country by the additional deaths of peace officers engaged in searching operations gone awry. Nevertheless, some law enforcement officers still approach a search assignment as just another futile chase after ghosts. They put themselves into it half-heartedly. As a consequence, they expose themselves unnecessarily to death or injury on the job. By regarding each and every structure search as a potentially high-risk endeavor and adjusting your survival mindset accordingly, you can keep from joining this ill-advised group of officers. By staying alert and applying all you know about threat awareness, recognition and response, you can assure that you end a shift or a career in as good condition as you started it.

SEARCH SURVIVAL RULES

As you should have guessed by now, the second rule of surviving a search assignment is to carry out your searching duties with your senses finely-tuned for danger and your personal response gear set to react to any hazard you might encounter. The first rule of search survival requires that you learn as much as you can about the assignment you are confronting *before* you commit yourself and your assistants to the operation itself. Although you will never have ALL of the data you would prefer to have before you enter a structure, the key questions you should answer to the extent possible include the following:

• What is believed to be going on? Are you responding as a result of a dispatched call of a silent alarm, a report from a citizen or a personal observation made while on patrol? In other words, why are you going to do a structure search?

• Has a possible offender been seen? By whom? Is the reporting party available for interview? Has more than one subject been sighted? Where?

.• How current is your information? Has a possible offender just been sighted five minutes ago, or is the information an hour old?

• Besides a potential suspect, who else might be inside? Residents? Employees working late? A janitorial crew?

• Are there animals or other complications known to be present inside the structure to be searched? How will you deal with them?

• Are keys to the building available? Keys to interior doors that may be locked from the inside will be especially valuable to the searchers. Can you or your dispatcher find a person with a complete set of keys?

• How many possible entry and exit points are available? All will need covered by your perimeter officers. Which of these points will be the safest for you and your search partner(s) to enter?

• Exactly what appears amiss on-scene that leads you to believe you have a crime or other problem in-progress? Is there evidence of a forced door, broken window, damaged roof vent, or what? Are there out-of-place persons or vehicles in the vicinity? Why do you believe there may be suspects inside?

• If you've been to this location before, what did experience teach you? Where are the best hiding spots? Where are the alarm system trip points? How about special hazards and other complications?

• If you are responding to an alarm, what kind is it? A motion detector covering an interior hallway tells you something different than a window or door sensor that says the exterior perimeter may have been breached. Is it possible to narrow down the area of alarm activation to a specific part of the building? Your dispatcher's direct communication with a monitoring alarm company may be able to answer this query for you.

• What is the physical layout of the structure to be searched? How many floors are there? How about basements and equipment rooms? As a general rule, the larger and more complex the structure to be searched the more people you will need to do it right.

Every structure search will be at least somewhat different from the last or the next. Each will bring questions specific to the call and the premises. Answer them as best you can before you make entry, but, again, realize that you will not be able to satisfactorily answer *every* imaginable query before you need to act. Gather as much data as you realistically can, share it among all members of your on-scene team and proceed with caution from there. In doing so, you will want to keep in mind some "searching survival" guidelines for conducting your operation safely and effectively.

SEARCHING IN SAFETY

Be sure the exterior is covered. The outside of the target structure must have a human perimeter placed around it to intercept offenders who may flee from the search team inside the building. If exterior perimeter duty falls to you, you'll want a spot behind cover that permits you to view as much of the building as possible. Most likely, there will be at least one additional officer keeping an eye on the opposite side of the structure. You'll first need to assure that a crossfire situation does not exist should gunfire develop. You also must have clear radio communications with all other officers on-scene, both inside and outside the building. From your observation post you will be watching for anything or anyone suspicious. Anyone exiting the building should be verbally challenged from cover, but realize that there is always the possibility that an innocent party that no one knew about could have been inside. Act with caution but also with restraint. Remain in place on full alert until you receive word from searchers inside the structure that the place is now cleared and secure.

Practice excellent firearms safety and control. During a structure search you must balance the chance that you will have to use your firearm to defend yourself with the real danger of an unintentional discharge of the weapon. Unless you are searching as a member of a SWAT team or similar tactical unit, a long weapon (shotgun, rifle) is probably not the best choice for a close-quarters structure search. Instead, your handgun should be out and held firmly in your strong hand, pulled in close to your body so that it cannot easily be grabbed away in an offender's surprise assault. Your other hand should be free to hold your flashlight, open doors or ward off unexpected blows.

Your sidearm should be pointed ahead and downward just in front of you. Take care not to direct it at your feet or your backup officer. Your finger should be off the trigger and outside the trigger guard unless and until you perceive a threat that may require you to fire. By keeping your finger away from the trigger throughout the search you will prevent an accidental discharge that could be caused by an involuntary jerking of your hand muscles if you were startled, jarred or fell. Officers have even been known to pull the trigger with their strong hand while squeezing a door handle with the other. You want to avoid these dangers. A structure search is complicated enough without having to explain why you put a round through Mr. Brown's display case or Mrs. Smith's cat!

Move smart. Coordination between you and your search partner is vital if you are part of the team designated to probe the structure for suspects. Only one of you moves at a time while the other covers. Then the roles are reversed. Keep each other in sight throughout the building-clearing operation. This is not the time for any independent, free-lance searches. Teamwork is important because it helps keep you safe. If other search teams are operating within the structure, be sure that you know where they are through constant radio communication. You don't want to surprise one another.

If your search operation includes a police working dog, it is the K-9 handler's job to watch and "read" the dog while a second officer follows closely, covering the handler. To prevent a K-9 attack on a good guy, other police personnel should be either close to the dog and handler or out of the structure entirely. Realize, however, that while trained dogs are incredibly valuable tools they can miss things and people, just like you can. Maintain your high level of alertness while working with a dog and handler team and be prepared for a surprise. If you feel strongly that someone may be in the building but the dog turns up nothing, search the place again.

Use your senses. During your building search, listen for sounds that may give away a subject's location. Stop your search from time to time to do nothing but listen carefully. At the same time, remain conscious of the noise that *you* make. You do not want to telegraph your location through needless chatter with your partner (use handsigns, instead), jangling equipment, a noisy radio or galumping boots. Leave the giveaway noise to your adversary.

If you've come into a dark building from bright sunlight, wait inside and behind cover a few minutes for your eyes to adjust. Consider turning on all the lights in the place rather than trying to search by flashlight, but make extra careful use of cover when you do. If you can see the bad guy better, he'll also have a better chance to spot you. Look before you go to another room or section of the structure. Expose just enough of one eye to see the lay of the land ahead. If your quick peek reveals potential trouble, get yourself back behind cover and do not peek from exactly the same spot a second time. Keep an offender guessing as to where his next potential "target" will appear.

Use all the tools in your trick bag. There are a number of items that can help you conduct a structure search in safety. Police dogs and law enforcement aircraft, where available, are obvious choices. But there are plenty of less exotic tools for getting the job done well, too. Fire department ladders can aid you in getting access to the roof, for example.

Don't neglect the time-saving, safety-bolstering tools you easily can carry with you, however. Even if you're working the day shift, you should always have a high-powered handlight with you. After all, you never know when your unpredictable job is going to take you far out of the light. A small pocket mirror can help you see around corners before you expose any part of your anatomy there. A roll of masking tape can allow you to mark doors you've already checked. Chalk works well, too. Use your experience, imagination and initiative in putting together your own structure search tool box.

Clear rooms carefully. You could look at each room you encounter as a separate structure to be checked out for danger. Apply your structure-clearing basics to each one:

Peek before you commit your body.

Take plenty of time to search in detail.

Work with a partner and coordinate your movements.

Use cover wisely.

Be prepared for the unexpected.

Check out any spot in the room that could hide a person. That includes cabinets, storage lockers, under or inside vehicles, under furniture and beneath bedding or piled items. If you are probing a known criminal's home or workplace, be aware that some crooks actually have built hiding spots beneath the floor, behind walls and elsewhere to shield them when the cops come calling. Drug manufacturing labs can be especially prone to this sort of architecture.

Prepare for some "special" targets: closets, stairs and hallways. A closed closet door should be treated like any other closed door: with caution. Don't stand in front of it while it's being thrown open. Do a peek quick and low, using your flashlight to illuminate dark corners, if need be. Treat a closet space like a small room. Search with a covering partner anyplace a human body might be concealed. That includes atop shelves, behind clothing and under or behind stacked boxes.

While you should avoid elevators if at all possible (they put you in a confined targeting space), stairs present their own hazards. Although various complex maneuvers have been proffered for navigating stairways, often what works the simplest works the best—and the

safest. Move on stairways only under the covering watch of your partner, who is himself behind cover. When you reach a logical stopping
point, such as a stair landing, you become cover while your partner
moves past you to the next logical stopping point. The roles are then
reversed for as many times as required to clear all of the stairs in the
place. Move quietly, peek quick and low as necessary, watch for sudden threats and present as small a target as possible by moving in a
crouched or low position.

Hallways can be dangerous because they often limit available cover
opportunities while providing multiple doors from which assailants
can launch an attack. You can neutralize the added risks presented by
a long hallway by working carefully with your covering partner as you
both watch for the out-of-place: a door ajar, noises down the hall, moving shadows under a door, a light on that shouldn't be, and so on.
Don't walk down the middle of a hallway that has not yet been cleared
of threats. Stick close to the walls and near any recesses presented by
doorways. If a threat suddenly presents itself down the hall, you may
be able to kick in a door for the cover the opening provides once you
get inside. If absolutely no cover is available and you are suddenly
confronted by an armed threat, consider dropping prone on the floor
and issuing your command and control orders at gunpoint from that
position. It's by no means ideal, but it beats standing there flat-footed
while a crook sends hot lead at you. But again, don't hang out in hallways until you know the structure is devoid of threats.

Practice makes perfect. Not unlike most of your other on-the-job
skills, your building search tactics and techniques can get rusty if
they're not practiced on a regular basis. Particularly if you don't get a
chance to do structure searches for real all that often, take the opportunity to do some practice searches on "safe" turf using a make-believe
bad guy as roll call training or an in-service refresher. Naturally, no
live weapons are permitted on the premises during the exercise.
Critique your search results when you're done. The opinions of your
"bad guy" can be especially enlightening here. Find out if there were
points in the exercise when he felt he could have "had" you or your
partner if the operation had been for real. Then, work on your weak
spots to get better.

SUMMARY

Structure searches represent one more challenge to your safety as a survival-smart law enforcement officer. Fortunately, there is much you can do to slash the danger as you probe the unknown to bring an offender to justice. You reduce the danger quotient by gathering your data before you search, approaching and entering the structure carefully, working patiently with your partners and making excellent use of available cover. You never totally relax when you are in potentially hostile territory. You don't declare the area "clean" before it really is. And you never stop looking for the next threat, the as yet undiscovered hazard. When you're done with your search, you critique yourself, examine your tactics and start getting ready for the next one. That way you will always be ready when your search for trouble doesn't come up empty-handed.

STREET SURVIVAL CHECKLIST FOR SAFE STRUCTURE SEARCHES

1. Gather as much information as you can before you begin your search.
2. Never make entry or search alone. Have sufficient help on hand both outside and inside the structure.
3. Take your time to search in great detail; never rush your searching operation.
4. Search with a partner officer and coordinate your movements with him or her.
5. Make good use of solid cover both outside and inside the involved structure.
6. Maintain excellent communications with your dispatcher and all law enforcement personnel on-scene, both inside and outside the building.
7. Never relax too quickly. If you find one offender, secure and remove him and start searching for the next one.
8. Search as many times as you feel necessary to convince yourself that the place really is "clean." Don't quit too soon.

9. Make full use of all the searching equipment at your disposal: police working dogs, fire department ladders, law enforcement aircraft and powerful handlights.

10. When your search is done, critique yourself in an effort to do even better the next time.

Chapter Twelve

WHAT TO DO 'TIL SWAT ARRIVES

At about 10 P.M. a patrol officer responded to the second domestic violence complaint of the day at the same residence. The officer approached the home's garage on foot and found a 35-year-old man holding a female hostage at the point of a 12-gauge shotgun. The victim officer had drawn his service weapon when he was shot in the face and killed instantly. The killer later committed suicide while being pursued by police.

An eastern sheriff with 34 years of law enforcement experience was slain by a bank robber turned hostage-taker at about 9:15 A.M. The 57-year-old sheriff had approached the rear of a bank where a male robber was holding a husband and wife cleaning team hostage. While trying to use his car's P.A. system to communicate with the criminal the sheriff was struck in the abdomen with a fatal round from a 9mm semiautomatic handgun. Following hours of negotiations, a shootout resulted in which the woman hostage was killed and the male hostage and the offender wounded.

In the South, a 14-year veteran was killed while assisting another officer investigating a burglary. A neighbor had reportedly spotted a suspect hiding under a house. The subject was believed to be in possession of a shotgun and shells. The two officers were searching a large shed at about 12:30 P.M. when one officer was wounded in the shoulder with a blast from a 20-gauge shotgun. The second officer retreated, dropped to one knee and ordered the 15-year-old male suspect to drop the weapon and surrender. The officer was shot fatally in the throat. Other officers later wounded and captured the juvenile.

In recent years many law enforcement agencies have organized their own special response or SWAT teams. They possess the special equipment and training required to deal effectively with the barricaded offender or hostage-taking incident. Still, many of the nation's agencies are too small to support such a specialized unit and rely on either a larger, neighboring jurisdiction for a tactical assist or count on a

SWAT group put together from personnel of several different jurisdictions. In either case, it may be some time before a specially-trained unit can be at the scene of the trouble. Meanwhile, the first responding patrol units will be expected to contain the incident and at least begin a resolution of the crisis. That may well be where you get involved. Even if your agency does have a SWAT unit, you as a first responder may be expected to stabilize the situation until the tactical experts get there.

There are all sorts of potential barricades and hostage-takers out there. They include criminals interrupted in the act of committing a crime, drunks and emotionally disturbed persons, inmates seeking to escape, protestors and terrorists and "suicide by cop" candidates. A given offender may fit into several different categories. The point is that they are all potentially dangerous to you and others. Caution should be your byword.

A SWAT team can't do anything you can't do, given the time, equipment and training to get it done. With a basic understanding of the dynamics of barricades and hostage-takings you can reduce the volatility of the situation and perhaps even resolve it before the specialists can arrive. At the very least, the actions you take early on can help assure the safety of all involved until the situation winds down to a safe conclusion. The key for you is to have a purpose for the things you do. You also will need to execute successfully and cautiously the actions you take while awaiting the arrival of the tactical troops. Your safe and effective response should begin with some comprehensive intelligence gathering.

INITIAL RESPONSE

From the moment you receive the radio call of a possible barricade or hostage-taking incident in progress, there are a number of steps you can take to stabilize, isolate and eventually resolve the crisis. The idea is to do nothing to aggravate the problem while you start the ball rolling to "fix" it, or at least lay the groundwork for a team of specialists to do so. It all begins with finding out as much as you can about what you are confronting.

Gather the facts. Obviously you will be doing a number of things, all at the same time, as you work to solve the problems at hand.

Gathering information likely will proceed simultaneously with your efforts to secure the site, get more help and develop a tactical plan to solve the crisis. Information collection is a key function that will aid you in the performance of each of the other duties.

It is up to you and those assisting you to gather as much reliable data as you can in the time available. Your sources may be numerous, but likely will include the initial reporting party or complainant, witnesses, escaped hostages or victims and the friends, relatives and others associated with the involved persons. Your agency's records department and communications section may be able to help provide you with additional information regarding the involved location or people. In reality, your sources for facts should be limited only by your initiative and the time you have to work in. You can make the entire event less hazardous for everyone by seeking the answers to such queries as:

Who am I dealing with?

How many suspects and victims (or hostages) are involved?

How are they dressed? What do they look like?

What kinds of weapons are involved?

What does the bad guy want? Escape? Revenge? Or what?

How did the confrontation begin?

Are there injuries? What kind? How serious? To whom?

What is the interior and exterior layout of the involved location?

Are there vehicles involved? Descriptions?

How is the situation still changing? What's happening right now?

What other resources will I need to handle this?

What crimes are involved so far?

Is lethal force an option?

Has gunfire occurred already, or does it appear likely? Any known fatalities?

What don't I know about this that could prove deadly?

To avoid confusion later on, write down all of this information on a chart or tablet and draw up a diagram of the interior and exterior arrangement of the premises. All of this could prove invaluable to you and your help as the incident proceeds, particularly if a forced entry and rescue operation becomes necessary. (For some background here, take a look at this book's chapter on raids and warrant service [Ch. 14] as well as the one covering structure searches [Ch. 11] done correctly.) One word of caution: Note which of your "facts" are in reality unconfirmed reports or rumors. You do not want to be counting on the presence of one offender when several are lurking inside, for example.

Get enough help. You will require lots of assistance to properly secure the incident scene and eventually solve the problem. Depending upon the location and kind of incident taking place, you may require anywhere from five to a dozen or more helpers to accomplish even an initial stabilization of the situation. Get plenty of help on the way early—the first moments of a barricade or hostage-taking confrontation can be the most dangerous and you cannot afford to be caught short. Summon your first helpers via radio even before you arrive on-scene and call more help—including SWAT specialists—as you see the need. Don't be timid about summoning sufficient aid—you can return to service any surplus assistance once you determine that you really don't need it. Recognize that your need for manpower and other resources may change either up or down as things happen and the situation changes. Stay flexible and try not to get left short.

Seal off the problem. The process of isolating the offender and the danger he is causing for others is accomplished via good, tight perimeters. Perimeters, of course, require plenty of law enforcement officers. By sealing the troublemaker off from his surroundings you keep him from escaping at the same time you make him more emotionally dependent on the police negotiator. That way you also protect innocent others from wandering into his area of control to be injured or perhaps taken hostage. Pedestrians, onlookers, passing traffic and friends and family of the involved parties must all be kept out for their own safety and the ultimate success of the law enforcement operation. It's quite naturally easier for you if you do not have to deal with added people and distractions. You should keep those who may have involvement and thereby information close by, but you do not want them in the faces of your officers.

Frequently, both an inner and an outer perimeter will be required. Two to four officers may be needed to secure an inner perimeter just outside the suspect's area of control and possible line of fire. If the standoff is occurring in a home or small business, officers on opposing corners of the structure, placed so that they can view all exits while remaining behind solid cover and out of each other's line of fire, may be adequate. Larger and irregularly configured structures with lots of possible exit points will require more law enforcement officers, as will the known or suspected presence of multiple offenders. (It is vital that the bad guys *never* be permitted to outnumber you!) Be certain that, in addition to adequate cover, each officer on the perimeter maintains clear and continuous communication with every other officer involved in the operation. Everyone needs to know the threat and the plan devised to deal with it. Mistaken identity problems and crossfire dangers can be avoided that way.

Inner perimeter officers assure that no one goes in or out of the offender's hiding spot without your permission. Meanwhile, officers on the outer perimeter, which could well be a city block or more removed from the trouble spot, are responsible for seeing that foot and vehicle traffic is excluded from the danger zone. Once again, communication with all other law enforcement participants is important to help avoid costly mistakes and nasty surprises.

Officers on both perimeters will have the additional responsibility of evacuating or protecting in place innocents who might otherwise be in danger of being taken hostage or struck by a criminal's bullets. Protecting them may simply call for advising them to stay behind locked doors, down and away from windows. Or it may require evacuating them carefully through doors and windows beyond the offender's sight and gunfire. The options you choose will again depend upon your analysis of the situation you are facing and the degree of danger it presents to the surrounding community. Consider the kinds of weapons involved, too. An offender with a high-powered rifle and scope will pose greater problems than one equipped with a handgun. More distance and thicker cover will be mandated for you and those you are protecting.

Establish control. While your inner perimeter officers can serve as your "forward listening posts" for intelligence-gathering purposes, you will need a centralized point for control and decision-making. This will be the command post where sense is made of intelligence, tactics and plans devised and operations supervised and controlled. The person in overall charge of the entire operation—you, perhaps—should work at this post. Everyone should be clear on who is in charge and will be issuing directions from there. It is from the command post that data will flow in, be analyzed and shoot out again in the form of plans and orders.

You can use a patrol car with phone and radio as your command post if that's the best option you've got available. But the interior of a building, located perhaps around the corner and down the street from where the problem is occurring, may work even better. That way you should be better shielded from the weather and interfering crowds of

onlookers and uninvited others. Safety remains the primary concern
in selection for your control point, however. Comfort will be an added
bonus—chairs, lights, water and restrooms would be nice—but security
of the chosen site remains foremost. Be sure your command post has
it, even if it means stationing an officer outside.

RESOLVING THE CRISIS

You can anticipate that a hostage-taking or barricaded criminal incident will draw considerable attention from the passing curious as well
as the news media. You should plan on detailing officers to remain
with any gathering crowd and prevent them from penetrating your
safety perimeters or otherwise endangering themselves and your officers. In their intense efforts to ferret out the story and "get some great
pictures," reporters and their attendant camerapersons may pose extra
problems for you and require extra attention. If you have more than a
couple of these folks on-scene, you should seriously consider assigning
an officer to deal just with them and their need for information while
keeping them safely out of harm's way. The expenditure of precious
manpower may prove well worth the investment for the problems that
are thereby prevented.

Open communications. You should not wait for the specialists to
arrive and take over before you start talking with a now-isolated
offender. Hook up with him and start communicating right away. Use
the telephone (preferably) or shout around a corner if you have to, but
start talking as early as feasible. Expect some threats and posturing
from the suspect, but get the talking (or yelling!) underway anyhow.
It's that important.

This chapter concludes with some advice on how to negotiate with
an isolated offender. Review it carefully. Do not be too concerned
about "saying the wrong thing." Just let the offender vent and talk and
assure him that you are there to help resolve the standoff peacefully
for *everyone*, him included. It's not too early to get him thinking about
the reality that you are his ticket out of the danger he has put himself
into, even though he will have to give up to you to get that assurance
of safety.

Don't hesitate to *tell* the subject to surrender. It's what he is going to
have to do eventually, so don't hesitate to broach the subject early on.

It may help bring him back to reality. But nothing is going to happen if you don't try to talk to him. Two-way communication is a ticket to safety for everyone involved, you and the suspect included. Give it a shot.

If you must effect a rescue.... Forcibly entering a structure where an offender is barricaded with hostages very often results in *someone* getting hurt or killed. Do so only if it becomes impossible to do otherwise because the offender is seriously harming his hostages or otherwise is posing an escalating and imminent danger to the lives of others, such as by continuing to fire into a populated area. If you absolutely *must* mount a rescue operation, your primary choices are two. You can enter his area of control by stealth and attempt to surprise him by moving very quietly from one point of cover to another. Or you can assault his place of hiding by utilizing diversionary tactics, entry and room search techniques and force to confront the subject, thereby causing him to surrender or be neutralized by one degree or another of force.

Before forcing entry into a structure occupied by an armed offender, consider using chemical agents such as pepper gas or tear gas to drive him out. Be sure the chemical agents are dispensed according to the manufacturer's directions by personnel trained in their use. But before deciding to use these potentially hazardous products, consider the negative effects chemicals may have on any hostages present, particularly children and the elderly. The decision to employ any kind of chemical agent should not be taken lightly. Think: What other options are available?

If you do decide that a forced entry is your only option because of what a dangerous offender is doing or about to do, consider employing these sensible, lifesaving tips:

• Put your entry team together. A unit of three to four officers is a good bet, assuming you have the manpower available. Regardless of resources, you should never make an entry alone.

• Be sure everyone on the perimeter and every member of the entry team knows what's about to happen and the plan for resolving the standoff. Be certain everyone is equally clear on the rules limiting use of lethal force.

• Use plans, diagrams, your own observations, interviews with occupants and anything else at hand to learn the layout of the place you will be entering before you go in.

• Unless you are attempting a furtive entry, create a diversion on the side of the structure opposite from where you are actually going in. This can be accomplished by a pyrotechnic device ("flash-bang" grenade) or by simply breaking a window with a rock, for instance.

• Once you are inside, get away from the entry point quickly and move promptly to better cover. Stay alert for sudden threats.

• Move quickly and stay low. Only one member of the team should move at a time as the other member(s) provide cover. Coordinate your movements carefully.

• Stay ready to fire if threatened by a deadly weapon but realize that innocent persons may be present, too. Identify your target before firing.

• Take your time and search carefully and in detail. Don't overlook anyplace a human being might hide, including crawl spaces, attics, cabinets, bathrooms and closets. Try to place yourself in the offender's mind as he attempts to find a spot in which to seek cover and perhaps launch a surprise attack.

• Physically secure areas already searched so that an offender does not move in behind you or go to a floor you have already declared "clean." Guard these sanitized areas with officers, if necessary.

• Once you have located and controlled an offender, remove him and begin searching for any others–good guys or bad–who may be present. Clear the entire structure carefully. Realize that undiscovered innocents or hostages may be hiding within, so search with restraint as well as caution. Continue looking until everyone is accounted for.

Arrange a safe surrender. Hopefully, a forced entry won't be required. Once your subject has agreed to toss in the towel, your next job is to get him safely into custody without further harm befalling anyone. To accomplish this, all members of your law enforcement team as well as the subject himself must understand what is about to happen. This is not the time for unexpected moves or other surprises. This is especially vital for officers on the inner perimeter who might otherwise be startled into the wrong reaction. They need to know who will leave cover to secure and search the subject(s) and who will maintain armed surveillance of the suspects and the location until it has been cleared of other possible offenders.

The subject must be told where and how to exit. He should be advised to be unarmed when he surrenders and follow all police instructions exactly. To avoid his overreacting when he is confronted by arresting officers, tell him in advance what to expect. Also plan out the oral instructions he will be given, such as: "Step out with your hands on your head! Stop there! Turn slowly all the way around! Freeze facing away from us! Don't move again!" Add to the directions as circumstances dictate.

Your whole on-scene team must know to remain alert throughout the surrender process. It's not over yet. Officers have died at this point when an offender changed his mind about quitting or tried to commit "suicide by cop" and directed his gunfire at the arresting officers. Keep using good contact and cover tactics.

Transfer control of the incident, if required. Some barricades and hostage-taking incidents take many hours to resolve. That's alright, as time most often is on the side of the authorities. But a good deal of time passing may mean that you eventually have to relinquish control of the incident to SWAT or other specially-trained officers. If that is the case, be sure you convey all of the intelligence you have gathered to the officers who will relieve you. Diagrams must be interpreted and passed along. Safe and gradual relief must be obtained for your perimeter officers. (Be certain no one gets missed in the process.) It is important that your relief know all the locations that have been covered and where all the "players" in the incident are believed to be at the moment. All questions your relieving incident commander may have should be addressed at this time. To help things work even smoother, consider leaving a liaison (such as yourself) behind at the command post to facilitate the transition and contribute towards answering any new questions that arise later. Once more, good communications can mean increased safety as well as greater effectiveness for the law enforcement operation.

NEGOTIATING TECHNIQUES

As a negotiator, in most cases you have a simple fact of life working in your favor: It is just as much in the offender's interest as anyone else's to see to it that the confrontation ends without bloodshed. Unless he is truly crazy, suicidal or both, he will in time realize that he is not going to defeat the overwhelming, armed force surrounding him. The totally out-of-touch offender may not be able to grasp this, but most will, sooner or later. Meanwhile, it is to your advantage to keep him talking–and thinking about his predicament.

One of the negotiator's primary goals is to give nothing to the offender without receiving something in return. If he wants a cup of coffee, he must give up a hostage or a piece of information the negotiator desires, and so on. While today there are fewer absolutes in law enforcement negotiations than there were 20 years ago (experience has been a good teacher), a few near-absolutes remain. For instance:

• To avoid giving the offender an even stronger bargaining position with law enforcement, officers will not be exchanged for civilian hostages.

• No weapons or ammunition will be given to offenders.

• Prisons or jails will never release inmates as part of a negotiated agreement. (If they did, no corrections or detentions officer would ever again be safe from being taken hostage.)

• Drugs or alcohol will not be supplied to a barricaded perpetrator. The results of doing so are simply too unpredictable.

Negotiations represent the *talk* side of the tactics, time and talk triad for successfully resolving a hostage or barricade incident. Some officers make the mistake of sealing off the barricaded offender and then waiting for later-arriving specialists to open negotiations. It is important that you open communication with the perpetrator as soon as your tactics have isolated him and removed uninvolved others from his area of control. Expect to take a lot of verbal abuse as he unloads his anger and frustrations on you, the only representative of "the system" he can reach at the moment. Let him rave. By doing so he may be defusing himself at least a bit. It may make him easier for you to handle later, once he calms down some. Don't make threats of prison, death and mayhem; just listen for awhile.

If you are the negotiator, your intent should be to make the perpetrator feel as isolated and dependent on you as possible for his continued well-being. That means you may want to have your peers shut off his power and seize control of his incoming telephone calls via the phone company so that you are the only one he can communicate with. Your inner perimeter also should serve to isolate him from any hope of escape or relief. Indeed, you *are* his only ticket to safety, at least in his mind.

Generally speaking, mothers, wives and girlfriends should not be permitted to join negotiations with a barricaded offender unless you are *certain* that hearing from any of them will not further inflame your subject. The same goes for attorneys, news reporters and other hangers-on. He should be forced to deal with law enforcement and come to see the negotiator as his savior and advocate. If you are the designated negotiator, use your first name and attempt to learn his so you can use it a great deal in "connecting" with the subject. But no matter how brave you are, face-to-face negotiations with an armed offender are out of the question. Do it over the phone, over a bullhorn or around a corner while you are protected by a cover officer. Too much can go wrong too quickly during a toe-to-toe exchange. Getting yourself killed will not resolve the crisis.

The officer in overall command of the incident should not be the negotiator. First of all, he has too much else to do. In addition, it is important that the negotiator be able to blame someone when he must turn down requests from the perpetrator. In other words: "I'm sorry, but the boss (or the rules) won't allow it. Let's figure out another way I can help you." (Like by your surrendering!)

Don't forget to tell the subject that he must surrender as quickly as possible in order for everyone to stay safe. (Officers have actually talked to offenders for hours without once telling them to surrender. When finally instructed to do so, some have given up immediately!) Make the request frequently during negotiations. It must be made clear to the offender that his surrender is really the only way the episode can end well for everyone–including him. Let that thought sink in for awhile, than go back to it until he gets the message of the hopelessness of his position. You are, after all, doing him a favor. You just might be saving his life.

As you continue to listen to a barricaded offender, attempt to gather intelligence that could later be of lifesaving value should an entry team be forced to go in after the subject. Does he sound irrational, drunk or high? What other voices can you hear? Who else is with him? Who are the hostages, if any, and exactly where are they? Are they alright? (Careful here, if he figures out you're more concerned about the hostages than you are about him he may become a lot harder to handle.) Is he settling down or sounding more and more agitated? Is he making threats to kill or hurt hostages or others? What is he saying? What's taking place inside right now? Take everything he tells you with a grain of salt (if he's willing to take hostages, he's almost certainly willing to lie!) and pass it on to tactical officers who eventually may have to confront the offender. Meanwhile, keep him talking. There's a good chance that as long as he's talking he's not preoccupied with doing something more destructive.

To maintain your credibility and effectiveness as a negotiator, it's important that you not get caught in a lie. Do not make promises that an offender knows you can't keep. ("Come on out and we'll forget the murder!") And while it is vital that you keep him talking, you must avoid saying anything that encourages his fantasies of escaping and otherwise dodging responsibility for his actions. You should remind him that he must eventually surrender, and that you are his safe means to do that.

While you need to bring the subject back to reality as necessary, you should nonetheless try to sound genuinely empathetic to his gripes. ("Yeah, it sounds like you have had a rough time alright, but that's no reason to get yourself killed!") Meanwhile, ignore any deadlines he sets and set none of your own. Keep talking past any deadlines with threats attached that he may try to establish. Realize, too, that he may try to bluff you into thinking he has carried out his threat to harm someone. Hostage-takers have been known to fire shots into the floor and then claim to have killed a hostage. See a body before you believe it. But realize that if he does start to cause serious harm to a hostage he may well do the same to any others he has access to. It is probably time to go to a rescue entry option in an effort to save lives.

Throughout your contact with the offender, continue to assess his willingness to keep talking. Listen to what he has to say. If he is straying further and further from reality, a rescue attempt may become a more reasonable alternative. At the same time, be conscious of indicators that the process is working: he's sounding calmer, he's continuing to talk, his demands are lessening, he's treating hostages well and allowing his deadlines to pass without harming anyone, and so on.

Do not lose faith in the negotiation process even though considerable time may pass with no obvious sign of progress. Since time is most often on your side, let it run and give him an opportunity to calm down. Meanwhile, continue your efforts to defuse him by talking more slowly and quietly than he is. Continue to avoid threats of mayhem— he already knows that he's in a major fix. Be prepared for long gaps in the negotiation process, as he may need some time to sulk, rage or a combination of the two. The process may be working for you even though he is not responding to you directly. The offender may tire and start making critical mistakes. Hostages may take action on their own and escape. The effects of the well-known Stockholm Syndrome may come into play as the perpetrator begins to bond with his captives, at least to some extent. But beware: the Stockholm Syndrome can work against you, too. Hostages may actually lie to you in an attempt to "protect" the offender from the police. Or you may connect with the offender you have been talking to for the last hour to the extent that *you* subconsciously start to protect him. If you are doing the negotiating, it's a good idea to keep a peer at your side to offer ideas and let you know if the effects of the Stockholm Syndrome are showing on you.

Most barricades and hostage situations, once isolated and stabilized, eventually are resolved without further violence once the offender starts to settle down and comprehend his situation. You may need to remind your more action-oriented peers of this, along with the fact that many barricade and hostage incident casualties occur at the forced entry or rescue stage of the operation. You want to avoid resorting to the use of force option if you can.

Any hostage-taking or barricade incident will require every scrap of your initiative and common sense in resolving it, particularly if you are the one tasked with filling the role of negotiator. While each incident will be unlike any other, these guidelines should help you resolve a crisis without harm coming to anyone, yourself included. That, after all, is what defusing a hostage or barricade assignment is all about.

SUMMARY

There is a great deal you can do to assure the safe and successful resolution of a barricade or hostage-taking crisis, whether that crisis is solved before or after specially-trained helpers arrive. Operating under the guidelines of *tactics, time and talk,* you must call in necessary assistance, thoroughly isolate the offender's location and immediately commence gathering information concerning who and what is involved. You must evacuate or protect in place innocent persons in the area and conduct a continuing assessment of what you are facing and how best to respond to it. You must establish a command post and open communications with the offender. If possible, you should negotiate his immediate surrender and then plan for its safe implementation. If you are unable to end the crisis yourself, you must arrange for a smooth transition to the members of a tactical unit or SWAT team. When it's all over, talk with your peers about what worked and what didn't. Kick some ideas around. Learn from the experience and get better for the next time.

There is much you can do to win a barricade or hostage encounter. But it is also important to remember that factors totally beyond your control may cause the confrontation to end in violence. If the offender has decided in advance that the incident will end in his death, you ultimately may be unable to prevent that result. That's his choice, not yours. Realize ahead of time that a tragic outcome always remains a real possibility. All you can do is the best job you can. By utilizing your good survival know-how, your basic common sense and your excellent decision-making abilities you can greatly improve the survival odds for yourself, your peers and innocent others while you await specialized help. It *does* work!

STREET SURVIVAL CHECKLIST FOR WAITING FOR SWAT

1. Gather as much intelligence as possible on the barricade or hostage-taking incident you are facing.
2. Get sufficient help before you tackle the incident.
3. Isolate the problem site with good inner and outer perimeters.
4. Establish clear on-scene control and set up a command and control point.
5. Establish communications with the offender and begin seeking his surrender.
6. Be prepared to exercise a negotiator's skills to resolve the crisis. Utilize sound negotiating techniques, and do not give up something for nothing in return.
7. Be sure everyone knows the plan and maintain excellent team communications throughout the operation.
8. Arrange for the safe release of hostages and the surrender of the subject.
9. Debrief and critique afterwards to do an even better job the next time.
10. Never take personal responsibility for a violent outcome brought about by the offender. You must survive emotionally, too.

Chapter Thirteen

HIGH-SPEED DANGER

In the northern U.S., a police captain with 30 years of law enforcement experience was killed while engaged in a pursuit of robbery suspects. The captain in an unmarked car and an officer in a marked unit were pursuing when the suspects' vehicle stopped suddenly in a residential area. The two male adults exited immediately and began firing semiautomatic shoulder weapons. The suddenness of the attack prevented the captain from exiting his vehicle, and he was struck six times by .308-caliber bullets. The assailants, who were wearing body armor, escaped the other officer's gunfire but were later caught, convicted and sentenced to life without parole.

In the southeast, a 23-year-old patrolman was killed at a roadblock for a fleeing traffic violator. At about 12:53 A.M., the officer blocked the road with his car and remained inside the vehicle. Apparently realizing that the oncoming car was not going to stop, the one-year officer exited and ran to the front yard of a nearby residence. The offender allegedly drove in the same direction and his vehicle hit the officer and carried him on its hood for 200 feet. The officer died of multiple injuries.

In the West, a state trooper was murdered at about 8:30 P.M. while assisting a deputy sheriff in a high-speed vehicle pursuit of a subject who had left a gas station without paying. As officers attempted to bring the suspect's vehicle to a halt, shots were fired from a .22-caliber rifle. A round pierced the windshield of the trooper's car and struck him in the left eye. An 18-year-old male was subsequently charged with murder.

"I'm in pursuit."

It's a phrase guaranteed to start the adrenaline pumping in not only the officer who utters it, but in every other peace officer who hears the words while behind the wheel of a police vehicle. There can be no doubt about it: high-speed pursuits are more than a little exciting.

Perhaps for an additional set of reasons, high-speed pursuits also are very exciting events for law enforcement managers and risk management specialists. They know all too well that of all the things that can happen during a vehicle chase involving law enforcement officers, a good many of them are bad. The potential for injury or death to officers, other citizens and suspects is relatively high. The risk of significant property damage is even higher. Indeed, in a society gone litigation-crazy the high-speed chase would seem practically tailor-made to feed journalists' cravings for sensationalism and a cabal of attorneys' needs for a reliable meal ticket—all at law enforcement's expense.

To meet those threats and assure their officers' physical as well as legal survival, more and more law enforcement managers have tightened up the rules governing when and how a high-speed pursuit may be started or continued. In some areas, more restrictive laws have had the same effect. You as the officer behind the wheel and on the spot are increasingly being reminded that the law says that in many instances you *may* chase, not that you *must.*

Laws and administrators alike recognize that there are situations in which leaving a dangerous, violent felon on the street poses a greater danger to the public safety than pursuing his vehicle in traffic. It is in these situations that you may expect to begin pursuit. But it is in these same situations that you will be expected to pursue your quarry with due regard for your own safety as well as that of innocent others. Fortunately, there are plenty of things you can do to minimize your risks while you maximize your chances of running to ground a truly dangerous offender who is much-deserving of a state-financed "vacation." For you, the key lies in answering the right questions and following up with care and skill on the answers you develop.

QUESTIONS TO ANSWER

It is quickly becoming apparent what is about to take place. In response to your activating your car's emergency lights, the driver of the vehicle you are behind has kicked it into afterburner and began amassing what will amount to a whole litany of traffic offenses as the chase continues. In other words, a high-speed pursuit is now underway.

Before you decide on how fast, how long, how hard and even *if* to pursue him, you will need to know as much as possible about exactly what you are facing. You will need to know if the situation at hand fits your locale's laws and policies for engaging in a vehicle pursuit in the first place. You will need to know as much as you reasonably can about who and what you are dealing with so you can tailor your tactics accordingly. Realizing that you probably will never have *all* of the data you would like to possess, you can nevertheless make some sound decisions and devise some appropriate tactics for the situation by asking and answering questions like these:

What offenses are believed to be involved? Is it only traffic violations at this point? What you learn will help you decide whether the legal restrictions under which you operate will permit you to chase at all. Remember: Under the law, you can only use what you knew at the time you engaged in the pursuit to justify your actions. The fact that a dead body was found in the trunk *after* the fatal crash won't help you justify your tactics if all you knew at the time of the chase was that you were after a traffic violator who refused to pull over.

Who is being chased? Are you after a 13-year-old who took his folks' car without permission or an escaped convict who has just committed a string of violent felonies? The former may not need to be chased at all while the latter may merit an all-out effort to capture him. Act on the answers you develop to chart a reasonable course of action. Ask yourself: How would I want another peace officer to respond if *my* loved ones were in the path of this chase? Then, act on the informed decision you come up with.

What are the road and traffic conditions? To put it another way, how much additional danger is being created for the public (and you!) by allowing this pursuit to proceed? How fast are the vehicles moving? Naturally, it is possible for the hazard quotient to change as the pursuit continues. A pursuit that began in a quiet neighborhood or rural area may be leading into a heavily-congested area, or the other way around. A decision to chase or refrain from chasing is not irrevocable. Your decisions should be carefully reevaluated as the situation and conditions change. Obviously, a chase through largely-deserted streets at 3 A.M. is not identical in risk factors to one occurring on the expressway at high noon. Make your decisions about whether to keep chasing or pull out accordingly.

Are there known to be innocents in the vehicle being chased? One law enforcement agency engaged in a lengthy pursuit of a mentally-ill woman with two youngsters bouncing around in her car. Her identity was known. She could have been arrested later. The entire, dangerous exercise was probably unnecessary. Again, try to learn as much as you can about *who* you are chasing.

Are other alternatives available? As in the preceding case, sometimes the identity of the fleeing offender is known. It should be equally well-known that there will almost certainly be other, safer times to seize him or her. It really does not *have* to be accomplished at this very moment, perhaps following a bone-crushing crash. Work to exclude your ego from the decision-making process as you decide whether or not to persist in your high-speed endeavor. Because you're a good cop, you really *want* to catch him. But does it have to be accomplished instantly? Can it be done more safely at his home, work or elsewhere later on when he is without his cocoon of speeding steel? Think about it.

What limitations are you facing? Honestly evaluate your own abilities as a high-speed driver. Are the speeds and driving maneuvers getting way beyond what you are trained to handle in relative safety? Once again, strive to remove your ego from the equation. And how about your vehicle? Is it up to the task? You already know that many police vehicles are only slightly beefed-up passenger sedans with extra lights and a special paint job. You do not want to push your car or yourself beyond common sense expectations.

What makes it worth continuing the pursuit in spite of the risk of injury or worse? Perhaps the offenders you are after are so dangerous that you must stay after them in spite of the real and continuing danger of a high-speed pursuit. That's the tough decision that you and your supervisors will have to make in a hurry. It is also one that can change as the facts and conditions are altered.

The key question remains one that must be answered repeatedly throughout any high-speed pursuit: What is it about this situation that indicates the risks undertaken are worth it for the chance of capturing the pursued? As long as you can honestly state that the potential benefits of pursuit outweigh the potential for disaster, then pursue you may. But also remember: Knowing when to call a "tactical withdrawal" is a sure sign of a mature, competent, self-confident law enforcement professional. Ending a dangerously-escalating vehicular pursuit is an excellent example of the proper use of tactical withdrawal—and personal courage.

Having made the tough decision to commence or continue a vehicular pursuit, you obviously want to pursue the enterprise as safely and effectively as you can. While you can best learn these hands-on skills on a pursuit track under the tutelage of a qualified instructor, there are nonetheless some valuable principles and tactics for high-speed pursuit driving that you can pick up right here. Those guidelines for pursuit survival will be discussed next.

STAYING IN CONTROL

Every high-speed pursuit, not unlike every arrest or traffic stop, will be different from any other. Still, the dangers contained within every pursuit are similar enough to permit you to counter them with a set of sound officer safety tactics and procedures that are applicable *every* time, regardless of the particulars of the chase. Consider these common sense suggestions for pursuit survival:

Get ready ahead of time. Safe pursuit preparation begins before you hit the street. At the start of your shift, be sure your vehicle is up to the job. Inspect the tires for uneven wear, damage and proper inflation. Check the brakes and steering for problems. Are the lights and emergency equipment functioning properly? How about gas, oil and other fluid levels? Don't take out an unsafe vehicle that could fail you disastrously during a pursuit. Little, nagging defects have a nasty way of growing into big, dangerous ones under the stress of high-speed driving.

Also, be sure your lap and shoulder belts are working properly and *in use* before you go anyplace. Belts regularly save police lives, but only if they are used. Stow your equipment carefully. In a high-speed pursuit or crash, flashlights and briefcases can become dangerous missiles. Secure everything now while there's time; there won't be once the action starts.

Keep communicating. Get on the radio to alert your dispatcher and your peers the instant you sense that a pursuit is underway or imminent. Strive to retain a calm, clear voice as you tell the world what's going on. Give a clear description of where you are, the vehicle you are chasing, its plate number, the direction of travel, number of occupants and why you are pursuing. As the pursuit continues, keep up a running commentary of speeds and changes in location and direction of travel. Be ready to communicate with assisting units that may be coming into the area to assist you. Pass along information concerning any special hazards you are aware of, like weapons involved or the presence of multiple parties in the vehicle. Once another law enforcement unit joins the pursuit as a second car, consider having him take over the radio duties of "calling" the chase while you concentrate on the offender and tactics for bringing him safely into custody. Use the radio to give assignments to assisting officers to either block off cross-traffic ahead or assist you in an apprehension once the pursuit ends. Remember that the beginning of a foot chase may mark the ending of a vehicle chase, so plan and deploy accordingly.

Do not overpursue. You do not need to tag your subject's rear bumper or drive up on his trunk lid. You only have to follow and keep him in sight so you can achieve his eventual capture. Let *him* drive the fastest, find the dangers and make the mistakes while you follow his tracks. It's safety-smart as well as tactically sound. There is even some evidence that if you slow down he may do the same, as long as he is still able to stay ahead of you. It's certainly worth a try as opposed to pushing him harder and faster.

Watch your positioning. Do not participate in "felony stupid" driving, like pulling your speeding vehicle in front of or alongside the bad guy's car. Officers have died from gunshots or crash injuries doing just those things. Either puts you at a big tactical disadvantage. Stay to his vehicle's rear and bolster your safety margin.

Nix the radical driving maneuvers. The problem with bringing your rapidly moving vehicle intentionally into contact with another moving object (like a fleeing subject's car) is that you don't know for sure where either is going to end up following the collision. Very few officers are highly-trained in vehicle ramming, nudging or boxing-in techniques. Unless you are one of them, you should avoid utilizing your vehicle as a potentially deadly weapon. Realize that your decision to bring your moving vehicle into deliberate collision with another car may constitute the application of lethal force. Be sure your jurisdiction's laws and policies permit such a maneuver under the existing circumstances.

Gunfire is extremely risky. Obviously, firing at a moving vehicle can only be done if you are legally correct in applying deadly force to the fleeing offender. However, from a purely practical point of view it is worth noting that gunfire is seldom effective at disabling either a moving vehicle or the offender inside. Meanwhile, innocent others, including your fellow officers, may be endangered by errant rounds. Regardless of the gravity of the crimes involved, gunfire is often a poor option in the pursuit of a fleeing vehicle. Consider other options, like mats of road spikes, if possible.

Scan far ahead. Look as far down the road ahead of the pursuit as you possibly can for surprise dangers. Is a vehicle about to pull into your path? Watch for sudden threats from pedestrians and cross-street traffic, too. At night, never out-drive your headlights–there could be big danger lurking in the dark.

Practice restraint. You cannot afford to copy the driving practices of the offender you are chasing. Slow down to a near stop or stop for intersections where the traffic controls are against you. Keep *all* of your vehicle's audible and visual warning equipment operating *all* of the time during a pursuit. Resist the natural urge to drive just a little faster. Remain in command of yourself as well as your vehicle.

Continually reassess. You have not only the right but the obligation to terminate a vehicle pursuit the moment you determine that it has gotten out of hand and the dangers outweigh the potential benefits of continuing it. The good news is that there will almost always be another time to latch onto the offender–assuming you are still alive to do it. It is absolutely alright to call it quits for now to live to fight another day.

Practice good driving skills. As noted, you cannot master pursuit driving skills by reading a book or watching a videotape. Carefully-supervised, hands-on driving instruction is a must. All the same, a few principles of good pursuit driving are extremely relevant. For instance:

• Don't jab at the brake pedal or ride the brakes. Slow down, as required, instead. You do not want to overheat your brakes to the point that they could begin to fade on you.

• Thread your steering wheel through your hands, one hand to the other, rather than squeezing it to death. Avoid abrupt steering movements or jerking the wheel–either could cause you to lose control. Work towards smoothness in your steering efforts.

• Slow down *before* you enter a curve or turn, not after you are already into it. Start accelerating again once you have begun to leave it.

• If your vehicle's tires slip off the paved roadway and onto a soft shoulder, ease off on the accelerator and then steer gradually back onto the pavement while keeping a firm grip on the steering wheel. A radical maneuver here could prove disastrous. Take it easy.

• If you experience a tire failure at high-speed, keep a firm grip on the wheel and let up on the gas. Use the brakes sparingly as you steer straight ahead and come to a gradual stop. Once again, avoid an extreme, panic maneuver that could do you in.

Make plans. Have some idea as to who is going to do what when the pursued vehicle comes to a stop. Once more, clear and continuing communication between you and your assist units is critical. Use your radio to clarify who is to initiate contact and issue verbal commands and who is to provide cover at the end of the pursuit. From a safety standpoint, the last thing you need is an uncoordinated gaggle of officers running every which way and interfering with one another at the critical close of the operation. Good communications can help prevent that scenario from developing.

If you are fortunate enough to have a K-9 unit involved, be sure that everyone understands the role he or she is to play when the vehicles come to a stop. You don't want officers laying false trails by dashing around the area on foot before the dog gets involved. You also don't want to get nailed by a K-9 that launched from the police car that pulled in behind you just as you started to pursue on foot. Share the plan so that everyone stays safe!

AT THE END....

So, you've cautiously pursued him all over Hell's backyard for the last ten minutes, dodged cross-traffic, skirted major danger a half-dozen times and responded to the radioed instructions of three different supervisors. At last your quarry has wrecked or, even better, pulled over in an apparent effort to call it quits. All that remains to do is to sprint over to the now-stationary vehicle, extract the driver and snap on the cuffs. For all practical purposes, it's over. Right?

Wrong.

In the past, officers have died when, fueled by adrenaline and a desire to "finish it," they have marched up to a stopped pursuit suspect with little thought for good tactics or their own safety. In some cases, they have caught a bullet from an offender not quite ready to call it quits. In other instances, officers have launched into an immediate foot pursuit of a subject fleeing from a now-stopped vehicle without first checking the car for additional, hidden suspects. On occasion, the bypassed subjects have attacked from the rear after the officers have passed their hiding place in the vehicle. Indeed, the danger for you is *not* over just because the pursued vehicle is now at rest.

When a pursued suspect's vehicle stops for any reason, it is time for you to switch automatically into high-risk vehicle contact procedures. Keep in mind that if an individual is willing to create extreme danger for himself and others by fleeing in a vehicle in the first place, there is every reason to believe he may be willing to attack you as well, should the opportunity present itself. You must resist the powerful temptation to rush up to the vehicle. Instead, you and your backup(s) must stay behind cover, issue oral commands to the vehicle's occupants and remain alert for whatever happens next. Take your time. The situation could evolve into a foot pursuit or even a barricade incident should an armed subject refuse your orders that he exit the vehicle. Wait and see what happens so that you can anticipate and plan for new dangers and counter them with appropriate officer safety measures.

If a suspect or suspects remain in the stopped vehicle, be sure you have adequate help on hand and then order them out, one at a time, into a search position while you and your backup(s) remain behind good cover. Secure the subjects, then advance carefully on the "empty" vehicle under the cover of a backup officer and clear it. Naturally, the whole time you have been securing your extracted suspects a cover officer has been keeping the vehicle under constant visual surveillance. As you clear the vehicle, do not neglect to check the trunk, too.

If the subjects in the vehicle refuse to either exit or acknowledge your oral directions, stay behind cover and get enough help on-scene to set up a secure perimeter around the developing barricade situation. Beware of crossfire dangers as you position your helpers. If the stand-off persists, call in SWAT personnel as you would on any other barricade incident. Meanwhile, keep communicating from cover with the vehicle's occupants. Let them know that if prompt compliance with your orders is not forthcoming, "special" tactics may be employed and chemical agents introduced into the vehicle.

If your subjects elect to flee on foot at the close of a pursuit, tell your dispatcher and assisting units what is going on before you begin a foot chase. Do not go after multiple suspects alone; wait for help to join you. Once you are ready to pursue afoot, carefully check the stopped vehicle for hidden occupants before you dash past it. Treat it as if you *knew* it contained a hidden attacker: carefully and under the watchful eyes of a cover officer. Also, leave an officer with the suspects' vehicle (and your own) just in case a bad guy doubles back to try and resume the chase. It's happened before. Realize, too, that one or more subjects may have "gone to ground" very close by and are watching everything that goes on at the vehicle. They just might return if they think the odds have shifted in their favor, or if they are just plain desperate. Stay alert for danger at the vehicle itself.

There is one additional danger to your survival that may arise at the conclusion of a high-speed pursuit. This one poses a threat to your *job* survival more than your physical well-being, and it occurs as a result of the heightened emotions and inevitable adrenaline dump that accompany an exciting, perhaps terrifying vehicle pursuit.

In recent years television audiences have been treated to the spectacle of what can happen when charged-up officers confront still-resistive offenders at the conclusion of a vehicle pursuit. Sensational video images and charges of rampant brutality are all-too-frequently the results of these encounters. In the process, the apparently out of control officers are pilloried and all of law enforcement gets painted with the broad brush of unprofessional, thuggish, criminal conduct. You don't need it.

It does little good to "win" a pursuit on the street if you end up losing in a court of law or at a departmental disciplinary hearing because you acted–and overreacted–in the heat of the moment. It's worth practicing extreme self-restraint to assure that your pursuit "victory" is a total one.

Be aware of your emotions as a chase culminates. Use firm and controlling voice commands, but don't scream curses or racial epithets. Be aware of your burgeoning emotions every time you must lay hands on the subject or subjects involved in the chase. Remember the mandate to employ minimum force to overcome resistance and exercise good self-control. The law gives you the authority to apprehend and accuse–not punish.

The driver you have been chasing probably has just repeatedly endangered your own life along with a number of others. It's perfectly normal to want to extract a little personal retribution. But you cannot do it. If you sense that your emotions are still running at a fever pitch, attempt to minimize your contact with the offender until and unless you are certain you have regained a firm grasp on yourself. Allow another officer to transport and process your prisoner while you remain at the arrest site to do the paperwork and allow the emotional dust to settle. It may be the wisest course of action for everyone involved. It's another way of surviving the street.

SUMMARY

High-speed vehicle pursuits are very dangerous affairs. You should begin or continue one only as a last resort when you have gathered as much pertinent information as you can, analyzed what's to be gained and what's to be risked by chasing and made a conscious decision that pursuit is worth it. Once you decide to pursue, remain aware that you retain the right and the obligation to call a halt at any point at which you determine that the risks outweigh the potential gains. In other words, your decision to pursue is not an irrevocable one.

Pursue in control. Practice your high-speed driving maneuvers with a competent instructor and follow your jurisdiction's laws, rules and procedures for pursuit driving. Don't push the envelope when it comes to staying safe. Remain supremely alert throughout a pursuit for potentially disastrous surprises like a tire failure or unexpected side-road traffic or pedestrians. You don't want to get hurt yourself, nor do you want to be responsible for harm coming to other innocents who just happen to be sharing the road at the moment.

To better your chances of surviving a high-speed pursuit, avoid multiplying the danger by ramming or pulling in front of a pursued vehicle. At the conclusion of the chase, remember that the danger isn't over until the offender is safely jailed. Don't rush into an ambush by rushing a stopped vehicle. Stay in control of yourself and play it safe. Bring the bad guy out to *you*. Let *him* make all the errors.

High-speed pursuits are valid law enforcement tactics that must on occasion be used to bring very dangerous offenders to justice. See to it that when you engage in one you do so with careful decision-making skills bolstered by top-notch tactics designed to keep *everybody* as safe as possible.

STREET SURVIVAL CHECKLIST FOR
HIGH-SPEED DANGER

1. Know your jurisdiction's laws and your department's rules governing vehicular pursuits.

2. Know as much as possible about what you are chasing before you start or continue a pursuit.

3. Recognize your own limitations and those of your vehicle in any high-speed pursuit.

4. Throughout a pursuit, maintain excellent communications with your dispatcher and other field units.

5. Visually scan well ahead and be prepared for roadway surprises.

6. Pursue in control. Call it off if the driving conditions or speeds involved escalate the danger.

7. Don't get too close. You only have to follow, not tag his rear bumper.

8. Do not rush up to a stopped vehicle at the end of a pursuit. Follow high-risk vehicle contact procedures.

Chapter Fourteen

RAIDS AND WARRANT SERVICE

A narcotics officer was searching a residence as part of a six-man team armed with a search warrant in a southern city. As the 34-year- old officer moved past a closed bathroom door, a 68-year-old male subject suddenly stepped out and began firing a handgun. The officer was struck by four rounds and died from his wounds. Other officers returned fire and killed the attacker.

Again in the South, a patrolman was killed at approximately 11 P.M. while assisting other officers in serving a search warrant for drugs at the apartment of a suspected drug dealer. The officers were securing a subject in the living room when they were fired on from an adjacent hallway. During the ensuing exchange of gunfire the victim was struck fatally in the neck with a bullet from a .357-magnum revolver. Another officer and the 26-year-old assailant were wounded.

On the West Coast, a 31-year-old SWAT team member was killed at about 2:30 A.M. while helping execute a narcotics search warrant. After forcing entry to a residence, the victim officer moved down a dark hallway and entered a bedroom. He apparently did not see a male adult crouched in a corner. The subject fired one .357 round at the officer and missed. The subject and the officer then exchanged gunfire and both were killed.

Every day in this country law enforcement officers serve countless arrest and search warrants for offenses ranging from dog-at-large to murder. Each day other officers mount raids of structures and locations occupied by fences, drug dealers, illicit drug manufacturers, robbers, anti-government fanatics and crazies. The majority of the time these warrant service expeditions and raids go off more or less according to plan and no one is seriously injured. Quite frankly, raw luck sometimes plays a role in the outcome of some less-than-well-planned-and-executed operations. All too often, however, things go critically wrong and someone—perhaps a peace officer—dies in the process.

189

Sometimes the victims are law enforcement rookies. But more often they are veteran, well-trained SWAT and tactical team officers. Exactly what is going on here?

It's no secret that errors and oversights committed in warrant service or the execution of a raid can have fatal consequences. Sometimes it is hard to say what went wrong. More often, however, the causes of the tragedy are obvious. On occasion, more than one of these fatal errors is present in a single incident. The more common mistakes prone to result in disaster include the following:

• Preoperation planning and preparation were inadequate for the threat faced.

• Too few resources, especially officers, were committed to the operation.

• Positioning of personnel and the approach to the target site were botched.

• An unsafe entry, forced or otherwise, was attempted.

• Coordinated team movement and use of cover inside the structure were lacking.

• Offenders encountered were not properly secured and monitored.

• Officers were not uniformly alert and prepared for the unexpected.

In most instances, these fatal failures are found in either the preparation or execution stages of an operation. Sadly, sometimes they can be found in both.

A successful raid or warrant service operation depends upon your following a handful of proven-effective principles. These are identified as:

Maintain unity of command. One operation, one commander. It's as simple as that. Avoid overlapping areas of responsibility that can divide and confuse your personnel. Every officer involved should know who he or she is accountable to.

Keep it simple. The best military leaders know that uncomplicated, direct plans have the best chance of succeeding. Feints and diversions shouldn't be so complex that you confuse your own people. The time-honored concept of K.I.S.S. ("keep it simple, stupid") really does work!

Guarantee superior numbers and resources. Do not go up against the known presence of automatic weapons with handguns. Rely on your intelligence-gathering to tell you how many people you will be confronting. Match that number, then add some more officers as a safety margin. Never knowingly go in with fewer people than the opposition can muster. Be sure your mix of weapons is adequate for the threat you expect.

Surprise is vital. You must keep your adversaries off-balance while you avoid surprises yourself. Keep the bad guys guessing. Surprise them with a 5 A.M. arrival and transport your raiders in rental vans, for example. Plan your entry from a point they would not expect.

You need speed–sometimes. Slowing down during certain points in your operation (like entry, for instance) can prove very dangerous. Surprise and speed help bring offenders safely under your control because they reduce the criminals' opportunities to assault you, and that's good. Do not, however, give up caution for speed. You need both to stay safe.

Teamwork means survival. Team players don't just win. They are also more likely to stay alive. Be sure everyone knows the plan and has an opportunity to practice it, if feasible, before you do it for real. This is not the time for free-lance heroics on anyone's part.

Use cover properly. Before an operation begins, know where the solid cover is located both outside and inside the target premises. Then, utilize it as you approach the site and enter it. As in your other law enforcement activities, do not unnecessarily expose anything you want to keep attached!

Whether you are serving warrants or particpating in a raid, whether you are a member of a SWAT team, drug enforcement unit or a uniformed patrol officer assisting these specialists or going it without them, following several basic guidelines for survival will make your participation a lot safer. To do it right (translate that to mean "to do it safely"), there are tactics and procedures you must master. The first and one of the most important involves the collection of good information.

INTELLIGENCE GATHERING

The success or failure of a warrant or raid expedition could well hinge on the quality of information you have available upon which to base your tactical plans for a safe operation. Bad or inadequate information can lead to all sorts of surprises, most of them bad. Your sources of good information should be several: law enforcement records, various governmental data bases, informant statements, observations and personal knowledge of fellow officers as well as the results of careful surveillance, perhaps including both photos and videotapes of the location and parties involved. It's hard to have too much information available when you are about to go into a potentially risky encounter.

If time and circumstances permit, surveillance of your target over a span of several days is useful for identifying all of the players and vehicles that may be involved there. Lots of this data can come from neighbors—if you trust them to keep quiet about your pending operation. Otherwise, you probably will depend upon the detailed observations of your undercover surveillance officers. Just-before-the-raid reconnaissance by your plainclothes people is also a good idea, just in case last minute changes in the scenario have taken place.

Record the information you discover for dissemination to every member of the raid or warrant service team. But to learn these key answers, you must first ask a lot of questions. The queries will vary at least a bit from one situation to the next, but they should include at least the following questions:

The Suspects

Who are they? How many are there? What are their criminal records? Have they been known to violently resist arrest or attack law enforcement officers previously?

What do the offenders look like? Are their photos available? How are they dressed right now, if known? Are they currently under surveillance?

How are the suspects armed? What kinds of weapons—long guns, handguns or what—are involved? Can they be expected to have access to really heavy-duty stuff, like military ordnance or other explosives? How about booby traps?

What else do we know about the offenders? Are they likely to be drunk or high at the time of our operation? Are they mentally unstable or fanatics of whatever stripe? Are they professional criminals or perhaps equally-dangerous amateurs? And, most important, what *don't* we know about these people that could prove dangerous?

The Target Site

What sort of environment will your team be operating in? Is it a rural setting or a densely-populated downtown high-rise? Are the neighbors and passersby likely to be hostile to law enforcement? The answers you come up with could affect both your surveillance techniques and the number of personnel you will require to complete your task in relative safety.

What is the best site for staging—your own law enforcement facility or somewhere nearer the target? Be sure it's secure from nosy busybodies or bad guys.

How can you best approach the target itself? Is there good cover available or not? Are there likely to be lookouts or guard dogs, gates or high fences to be overcome?

On the structure itself, where are the doors, windows and other entry/escape points located? Is there an attic, crawl space, hidden rooms or another "problem" location? How and where can you gain access to each?

What is the artifical lighting situation if you plan a nighttime operation? Can you really approach unseen in the dark? Will there be an advantage for you in arriving during the hours of darkness, such as just before the sun comes up? (Veteran raiders will tell you that is probably the hour least likely to produce violent resistance from your offenders.)

Are there additional considerations, like young children or uninvolved adults on the premises, that you should be thinking about and planning for now? How about other added dangers, like explosive chemicals or munitions?

The Incident Itself

What sorts of crimes are known to have been committed? Are you dealing with felonies or something less?

What is believed to be going on *right now*? How is the situation changing, if that can be determined? Any chance the suspects are asleep or otherwise indisposed?

Are there undercover officers, informants or other potential hostages inside? Will they be there at the time the operation goes down? If so, exactly what do they look like and how are they to be handled?

What sort of contraband or other evidence are you seeking? Where is it most likely to be found?

How do your resources stack up against the bad guys'? You want to be certain that you don't go in either outnumbered or outgunned.

Once more, ask yourself: What don't I know about this incident that could hurt me or my people? Try to remedy any information lack, but realize that you will virtually *never* know everything you would like to know ahead of time. Don't allow a missing minor fact or two to freeze you into doing nothing at all.

Even as you gather information, assess each piece for its accuracy, currency and completeness. Record rumors as such, not as confirmed facts. Try to answer several queries concerning your data and its sources: Who or what is the source of the information? How old is it? If you are relying upon an informant's report, would he or she be likely to lie or exaggerate? What are his or her motives for cooperating with law enforcement?

Do a thorough information accuracy assessment now, before officers' lives are placed on the line. Don't overlook the possibility of good faith errors in facts reported by your own people. Wherever possible, it is nice to have duplicate sources or corroborative pieces of information. In other words, it's great that one source reported only one suspect on the premises. It's even better if two more sources independently reported the same thing. Even so, the smart operation leader makes the assumption that one or more undetected bad guys may be present, so far unseen. Resolve any unconfirmed reports or rumors on the side of officer safety. You must always "err" on the side of caution. If reports indicate the presence of a solo bad guy, be prepared to encounter more. It's the safest and overall best use of pre-operation intelligence-gathering.

OPERATIONAL PREPARATIONS

By this time your pre-operation reconnaissance and other information-gathering efforts should have given you some knowledge of who and what you are dealing with as well as at least some idea of the potential risk involved. It is now your duty to get everyone participating in *any* part of the operation together to go over what you have learned and formulate a safe and reliable plan of attack. The goal is to prevent injury to *anyone*, bad guys included. (It's simply *easier* that way.) At this meeting, held in a safe and secure environment such as your headquarters or stationhouse, each operation participant is informed of the plan, what he is to do, where he is to go and his over-all responsibilities. Pictures of offenders and a map or diagram of the target location will be supplied. If the operation is a large or complex one, copies of written instructions and the identities of the "players" will be provided. Particularly if several agencies are involved in the operation, the pre-raid briefing also will give everyone a chance to see what everyone else looks like to help prevent mistaken identity dangers later.

One officer should be in overall command of the operation. He or she should have the lead role in conducting the briefing and answering any and all questions posed by operation participants. By the close of the briefing, no one should have any doubts about the role he is to play in the upcoming operation.

Officer safety must take priority over everything else connected with the raid or warrant expedition. Each participant is responsible for his or her own safety and survival, but if the operation is a large one you should consider appointing a *safety officer* to oversee preparations intended to meet and defeat any dangers even remotely anticipated to present themselves. Among his other tasks, this officer will participate in operational planning, arrange for appropriate weapons and body armor and develop plans for officer down rescue and emergency medical aid requirements. This officer also should have veto power over any element of the plan that appears to him to be unnecessarily risky or ill-advised. It is up to him to then provide, if feasible, a safer means for attaining the same objectives.

The pre-operation briefing should include a review of use of force policies and procedures relevant to the threats you are confronting. If the raid is planned as a "no knock" affair, your people will need to know exactly what the pertinent laws and policies expect of them. Everyone must know ahead of time what he is and is not allowed to do on-scene. Naturally, the rules requiring probable cause, common sense and minimum use of force required to get the job done do not go into hiberation simply because this is a raid or warrant service expedition. You want to survive legally as well as physically if somebody gets hurt—or worse.

Plan for enough officers to exceed the expected number of offenders; then, add a couple more just for insurance against surprises. Also, be sure that your equipment and other resources are equal to (and, preferably, better than) those of your opponents. There should, for example, be adequate body armor and vehicles for everyone. There also should be adequate restraints for the number of arrestees you are expecting—and then some. An adequate supply of handlights also will be required for a nighttime operation. Don't overlook binoculars and night vision equipment if it is relevant to what you are doing. In addition, an adequate supply of working portable radios and some spare batteries is also necessary. As you plan, think about what *might* be needed for every likely scenario and try to have it handy ahead of time.

As noted, body armor for every operation participant is a must. Whether soft body armor or something heavier will be required will depend upon what you expect to encounter. Consider equipping at least the entry team with the heavier, SWAT-type armor if you anticipate armed opposition. But whatever type of soft body armor you wear, do not wear it *on top* of your clothing. Soft, flexible body armor is intended to be worn as underwear, not a topcoat. Unless you are wanting a bullet in the head, do not advertise that you are wearing it. Cover it up and help frustrate the intent of any bad guy who decides to shoot at you.

Naturally, every raid participant will be armed with a sidearm. From there the rest of your weaponry will depend upon the threat level you are anticipating from your intelligence-gathering. You'll want to do more than match your adversaries weapon for weapon; you'll want to outgun them. That may mean some members of your group need to be armed with shotguns or urban rifles. But not everyone should be. Even if the long guns are equipped with slings, some officers need to be free of the encumbrance to deal with resistive arrestees or help control prisoners. A mix of weaponry that leaves some officers with hands free is a good plan.

If you are seeking offenders who seem likely to barricade themselves, you will need to have the ability to respond with chemical agents, such as OC or pepper gas products. If that's the case, your team should include SWAT or tactical officers trained in the safe and proper deployment of nonlethal chemical munitions. It's one more eventuality to prepare for—just in case. Contingency planning for just about any scenario should be a big part of your pre-operation preparations. You can hope and pray that none of the more violent or complex scenarios come to pass. (Most probably, they won't.) But you absolutely must be prepared to deal with them safely and effectively if they do. And that gets right back to detailed planning and preparation.

Making your personnel and team assignments is a critical part of your pre-operation preparations. Several teams may be required to get the job done. The *perimeter team* will be responsible for sealing off the area while the operation goes down. It is their job to isolate the offenders' location so that no one goes in or leaves. While they keep the bad guys from escaping, they also prevent innocent motorists or pedestrians from straying into the danger zone. This group should consist of uniformed officers in marked law enforcement vehicles for ease of recognition. Naturally, they must be "wired in" via radio to the rest of the operation's participants.

The *arrest team* will make entry to the offenders' location–forcibly, if necessary–and seize the subjects of the raid or warrant serving operation. They should be thoroughly briefed on what to expect inside and outside the structure. They also must be skilled at moving as a team, using excellent cover tactics. Unless they are serving a "no knock" warrant, they must announce themselves loud and clear. ("Police! We have a warrant! Open the door now!") They must be prepared to respond if met by flight or gunfire. Beyond the expected equipment such as armor, weapons, prisoner restraints and flashlights, the team should have handy forcible entry tools such as sledgehammers and battering rams, just in case a forced entry becomes necessary.

The *backup or assist team* consisting of a handful of officers serves as the "ready reserve" for handling unanticipated contingencies, such as extra prisoners. They will assist the arrest team once entry is made and may take part in prisoner control, transport and processing. (These officers should have their own vehicles readily available.) They may become involved in searches for people or property and will work in concert with the entry or arrest team. They may help inventory and book evidence. Just in case the operation turns violent at the outset, the members of this team initially should be in position to provide suppressing gunfire and perform the rescue of a downed officer should a worst-case entry scenario develop. In other words, these officers should be flexible and skilled enough to do whatever is required to make the operation a safe success.

EXECUTING THE OPERATION

Your preliminary reconnaissance and information-gathering should have given you at least a fairly good idea of who and what you are up against. This information should have enabled you to devise plans for safely handling both anticipated and unexpected hazards. Now it's time to put your planning into execution. It starts with a safe approach and entry to the target.

Making a safe approach and entry. It is critical that you be prepared for any eventuality. That's why you should make your approach and entry as if you expected to be fired on or otherwise attacked at any moment, even if you do not really anticipate that kind of reception. Statistically, most officers who are killed on raids and warrant expeditions are slain at or near the point of entry, so this should be an area of extreme caution for you. Plan ahead of time who is going to move first, who is going to take the lead, who is going to boot the door, if required, and who is going to go where once the doorway is breached. You don't want to collide with one of your peers at such a critical moment.

As you approach and enter, move from one piece of good, solid cover to another. Do not tarry in the open and never remain in the "fatal funnel" present in every doorway you pass through. Get through quickly, move off to the side and seek the best available cover beyond. Once inside, one member of the team should move at a time while the others cover. Don't charge blindly into an area where you cannnot see potential threats. Take a quick peek first, then do a wraparound technique on the doorway that gets you out of the opening quickly.

A successful raid generally needs to begin with speed on the part of all participants. But remember that the need for speed never supercedes the requirement for caution and common sense during that most critical of operations: approach and entry of a potentially hostile site.

Conduct a careful search of the premises. Your search for people and/or evidence should be an organized, systematic and thorough one. Two-officer teams work well, as one team member can cover while the other moves and searches until the area has been totally secured for hidden subjects. Form as many two-officer teams as the size of the area to be searched requires. Teams can then trade places and search each other's areas to guarantee that nothing is missed. But keep in mind and remind your teammates that until you can guarantee all danger has been located and neutralized you are operating in potentially hostile territory where anything could happen. You don't want to get so caught up in your search for evidence, drugs, weapons or other contraband that you forget about the human dangers of the place. Keep practicing the principles of contact and cover as the searching operation continues.

Don't overlook the advantage of trained police dogs to assist you in seeking people or contraband if you have access to these animals, even if you have to borrow them and their handlers from another agency. Dogs can cut your time and manpower needs a great deal. Remember, however, that even a well-trained K-9 can miss items and people, just like you can. Don't automatically accept your canine companion's assessment that the area is devoid of threats or evidence. Consider researching it with human searchers if an area you thought would prove fruitful turns up absolutely nothing, at least according to the K-9. The dog (or his handler) just might be having an off day.

Consider taking still photos or videotape of your searching efforts. That way you can answer with solid evidence any claims that officers overreacted or unnecessarily damaged property during the operation. Full-sound videotape can also dispel any doubts about whether or not oral warnings were given before force of one degree or another had to be applied.

For still more advice on searching in safety, take a look at Chapter Eleven, "Safe Structure Searches."

Protect yourself from what your search turns up. Every person you contact at the site of your raid or warrant-serving operation should be checked for weapons and kept under close surveillance as long as you (and they) are on-scene. If you have an arrest warrant or probable cause to arrest them, they should be handcuffed promptly and secured separately from other parties on-scene. This may require putting them in a police vehicle under guard. Subjects who arrive at the raid site during the operation likewise should be checked for weapons and a decision made as quickly as possible on whether to detain them or send them on their way. Unless they have a compelling, legitimate reason to be there, you do not need any extra people wandering around while your operation is still in progress.

While it is a good idea to have the subject of the search on hand as a witness while a search warrant is being served, all prisoners should be removed from the scene as soon as practical. That way you remove distractions and extra bodies at the same time you reduce the likelihood of an escape attempt or a sudden assault from a disgruntled subject. Naturally, those arrested will have to be granted the ability to communicate with others following their arrest. But letting them make telephone calls from the arrest site is generally a bad idea. That's a good way for co-conspirators to learn of what you're doing in time to attack you, avoid you or destroy evidence. You are better off to let prisoners make their phone calls from the security of the booking desk.

Watch out for the "other" dangers, too. An offender's bullets are not the only things that can hurt you when you are conducting a raid or serving an arrest or search warrant. Other dangers may lurk, as well. If your preraid reconnaissance and other information-gathering have told you that there may be one or more vicious dogs present, arrange to have animal control officers with capture equipment on hand when the operation begins. If time or other constraints prevent your having specialized help present, remember that fire extinguishers and pepper sprays, accurately targeted, can discourage the nastiest junkyard dog. Detail an officer to monitor and deal with these beasts, should they attempt to intervene. Using gunfire to suppress them should be an absolute last resort, for reasons of humaneness as well as the need to preserve your element of surprise.

You should also watch out for trip wires and other indications of booby traps that may have been set by drug manufacturers, outlaw bikers or other cop-hating types at the location of your operation. A good rule of thumb for you here is "if you don't know for certain what it is and why it is there, leave it alone." Warn your peers of its presence, too. Suspected explosive devices should be left for the attentions of ordnance experts or bomb squad specialists. Attractive items that seem to be begging to be handled—like a bulging bank bag lying alone in a corner—also should be approached with much caution. A nasty surprise just might be waiting inside. Again, look for the unusual or out of place, like wires, strings or other attachments, before you freely handle such items. It may slow you down, but it literally never hurts to be cautious.

Illicit drug labs can be especially hazardous for the law enforcement raider. These can be found almost anywhere, from downtown warehouses and lofts to rural hovels and hardscrabble farms to rented motel rooms. All of them are potentially risky due to the ongoing chemical processes and active ingredients that may be involved in drug-making. These labs may be high-tech modern or represent the cheapest in low-tech, as exemplified by corroded, leaking barrels and nightmare plumbing and electrical hookups. Some of the chemicals involved may burn or explode on their own or through contact with other substances. The possible combinations of these skull and cross-bones items are many, but a sampling of the chemicals you may encounter includes freon, naptha, acetone, denatured alcohol, chloroform, ether, red phosphorous and fentanyl compounds. Getting even a little of some of them on your skin can lead to serious injury or death. With others, breathing their fumes or gases can have the same disastrous effects. Speed (methamphetamine) labs are notorious for their propensity to produce fatal flash fires and explosions, too. If you're careless, you could escape the fumes only to get fried to a crisp.

If you know in advance that you are going into a drug-making location, take an expert on the subject from the Drug Enforcement Administration (DEA) or another qualified specialist with you. He or she can help make the environment safe, even if "cooking" or manufacturing operations are underway when you arrive. If you stumble upon drug-making operations or the stored, chemical precursors or products of such by surprise, touch nothing, back out and await the arrival of drug-manufacturing specialists from law enforcement. Never take a suspect's word that he will make the scene "safe" for you!

If you get drug chemicals on your skin or clothing, brush or wipe them off immediately. Quickly shed contaminated garments and wash your eyes or skin with water for a full 15 minutes following a splash of liquid or a dusting of a powdered chemical. Collect and isolate contaminated clothing and shoes for safe disposal later. It would be advisable to treat the whole operational area as a hazmat site and secure expert help for the decontamination effort. You cannot afford to make the problem worse by spreading it, no matter how innocent your intentions.

You can help avoid contamination in the first place by following some rules of common sense hygiene. Do not smoke at a locale where drug chemicals or other contaminants are present. Don't eat or drink anything there. Touch things minimally and wash your hands frequently, if possible. Wear protective latex gloves the whole time you are on-scene. Meanwhile, you and your raid peers should keep watching yourselves and each other for any unusual sensations or symptoms, such as dizziness or nausea. Seek emergency medical attention at the first indication of anything out of the ordinary. Get a victim who apparently has been overcome by fumes into fresh air and be ready to start rescue breathing, if necessary.

Whether you come across them in a u-rent-it storage locker or in an isolated ranch house, drug labs and the materials associated with them pose a real danger to you. Use your common sense in their presence. Do not sniff, taste or handle unknown substances. (You certainly don't want to do any of the preceding if you *know* you are dealing with drugs or drug chemicals!) Rely on the specialized knowledge of trained assistance. Be alert to one more danger of the raid or warrant service expedition and act effectively to neutralize the hazards.

AFTER-ACTION DEBRIEFING

Once the operation's most intense moments are past and any bad guys are safely removed, you need to get all law enforcement participants together to discuss what went well and what could use some fine-tuning for next time. The overall incident supervisor should use this setting to elicit opinions on intelligence, tactics, resources and officer survival practices employed. If the process is to work, every officer must feel free to speak without ridicule or retribution later on. If honesty and openness are lacking, the whole "what worked and what didn't" process will be a failure.

A lot of important questions can be discussed during your after-action gathering. Were the tactics employed appropriate for the realities you encountered on-scene? Did the approach, entry and arrest plans work right in practice? What surprises were encountered? What pieces of equipment worked well and which items failed to perform as needed? Were intelligence-gathering operations up to the challenge? Could they be improved? Was there a breakdown in communication or supervision anywhere along the line that endangered law enforcement personnel and provided dangerous subjects with an opportunity to attack? Were your agency's safety rules and procedures followed? Don't hesitate to examine any area of the operation in your efforts to do it even better and safer the next time. But remember: Criticize things and tactics, not people. Personalities and personal likes and dislikes should not enter into your post-action discussions.

The after-action debriefing or critique does something more than identify what went well and what could use some improvement. The session is also a team-builder that provides a kind of psychological boost for the officers who participate. You all have just gone through an exciting and potentially dangerous undertaking together. Talking about your experiences and realizing that others felt what you felt is emotionally healthy for all of you. From such a session everyone is left with the correct impression that what he or she felt was "normal," and realizes that similar things were experienced simultaneously by fellow officers. In other words: Whatever is normal for *you* is normal. That's an important realization for surviving the stresses of raids and warrant service.

SUMMARY

Due in large part to the dangerous breed of offenders faced by today's peace officer, the serving of warrants and the execution of raids can be very hazardous undertakings indeed. In spite of the various reasons for which a warrant may be served or a raid conducted, for you the safety rules that will get you home in one piece remain similar from one assignment to the next. Prepare well in advance. Secure the information, equipment and personnel you will require to do it right. Plan and then execute a safe and well-covered approach and entry to the target premises. Once inside, maintain excellent communication and work in close coordination with your teammates. Stay sharp and search carefully and in detail. Expect the unexpected and be ready with a surprise of your own. Handle prisoners carefully, and never stop looking for the next threat, whether it comes in the form of a person or a weapon.

Serving warrants and conducting raids of all kinds will remain potentially dangerous operations for you and your comrades. By applying your good survival sense and sound decision-making skills to the tactics and techniques you learned here, you can make them much less so.

STREET SURVIVAL CHECKLIST FOR RAIDS
AND WARRANT SERVICE

1. Before you act, gather as much information as possible on who and what you are up against. '

2. Plan and practice your operation in detail.

3. Have sufficient equipment and manpower on hand before you begin the operation.

4. Plan for and execute a careful approach and entry to the premises.

5. Search systematically and carefully. Use cover wisely and coordinate your movements with your partners.

6. Practice top-notch prisoner control. Handcuff and search well. Maintain constant surveillance over subjects encountered during the operation.

7. Remember that things as well as people can hurt you. Watch out for booby traps, animals and hazardous chemicals and explosives.

8. Be prepared for surprises and the need to adjust your operational tactics to unexpected changes on-scene. Additional resources may be required.

9. Get your group together afterwards and critique the operation. The goal is to do it better and safer the next time.

Chapter Fifteen

HANDLING EMOTIONALLY DISTURBED PERSONS

A sheriff's deputy was killed at about 2 P.M. while working with three other officers in serving a mental evaluation order at a residence. When the officers knocked at the door, it immediately opened and a gunshot fired through the screen door wounded one of the deputies. A 30-year-old male then came out on the porch with a 12-gauge semiautomatic shotgun and engaged the officers in a gunfight. The 42-year-old deputy, who had sought cover near a police vehicle, was hit fatally. The subject was also killed.

At approximately 5:40 P.M. a 74-year-old sheriff's deputy was killed responding to a disturbance call at the residence of a former mental patient in the South. A struggle resulted in the yard of the residence and the subject struck the officer in the head with a seven-pound clothes iron. The deputy died of his injuries.

At about 1:30 P.M. the chief of a small city department in the southwestern U.S. responded to the home of an 84-year-old man with a history of mental problems. The man had requested that the chief come and observe the position of his furniture. The chief had exited his car and taken only a couple of steps when he was shot mortally in the chest with a .38-caliber revolver. The killer then committed suicide.

A mass murderer who keeps body parts from his deceased victims as grisly souvenirs of his crimes;

An extremely depressed housewife who has stopped taking her medications;

A barricaded gunman who sees his home surrounded by alien monsters instead of the police oifficers who are actually outside;

A teenaged youth intent on dying because of bad grades, but determined to force a police officer to be the cause of his death;

A paranoid, burned-out druggie with a half-baked brain who sees enemies everywhere, most especially behind a badge.

What do all of these people have in common? Generally speaking, each is a pathetic, troubled human being who, due to physiological, psychological or other problems, does not see the world in the same way it is perceived by most people. Instead, the environment may be seen by these mentally-cornered individuals as a highly-dangerous, confused and perhaps violent place. If their reactions and responses to the way they perceive their world are bizarre and dysfunctional enough, these souls are often referred to as mentally ill or emotionally disturbed.

One more thing that these individuals share in common is that in just the right (or wrong) set of circumstances, each could pose a real danger to you, the law enforcement officer who may be called on to deal with them and the difficulties they cause for others. Thus you, the law enforcement professional, are expected to deal effectively yet compassionately with emotionally disturbed persons (EDPs) who may desperately need your help but who may, at the same time, represent a major threat to your safety. What, in Heaven's name, are you to do?

THE SIGNS

Recognizing what you are dealing with is the first step towards accomplishing the safe and effective handling of an emotionally disturbed subject. Some mentally ill persons will represent little challenge by way of recognition: the ranting jumper on the roof ledge, the nude man marching down Main Street shouting Bible passages, the "odd" elderly woman with 87 cats. But other, equally troubled EDPs will not telegraph their presence nearly as obviously. Your skills of observation and problem analysis may be much more severely tested when you arrive at the scene of a vehicle accident, only to learn an EDP was its cause, or go on-scene at an "assist the fire department" call, and determine that a wild pyromaniac is at the heart of the problem.

Detecting the presence of an EDP may depend upon ferreting out exactly what is out of the ordinary about the scene you are observing. How is the person you are focusing on reacting to the environment and those around him? Is he unreasonably angry or otherwise agitated without just cause? Is what he is saying outrageous or nonsensical?

How about his facial expressions? Is he scowling, clenching his teeth or displaying extreme terror? Is he apparently perceiving some threat or other stimulus that no one else is aware of? Any sort of grossly inappropriate behvior—like going naked in public—also could indicate that you may be dealing with an emotionally disturbed person. Take it all in and decide if an emotionally disturbed person may be the cause of the incident you have been summoned to investigate.

Keep in mind, however, that there may be another logical explanation for the odd behavior of the subject you have under close scrutiny besides mental illness. He may be drunk or high on drugs. He may have a dangerous mixture of the two coursing through his system. Or he may be displaying the effects of a head injury or illness. It may take a medical professional to say for sure. Getting your subject safely into protective custody and in front of someone qualified to determine what the problem is often will be your best bet for unraveling the mystery of your strangely-acting person.

A mental health professional has terms for describing some of the behaviors you may have detected in the person you are holding. The person who insists he is in Dallas on Thursday when you know for a fact that it's Denver and Sunday may be described as *disoriented*. The woman who says she's the Queen of England when she is actually a cleaning lady in Queens, New York may be said to be *delusional*. The young man who sees and hears persons or things that simply are not present likely will be seen as *hallucinating*. And any person who engages in strange behavior such as howling, growling or rocking back and forth endlessly might be labelled as *acting out*. However they may be described by the professionals, any and all of these bizarre behaviors should signal to you that you may be working with an emotionally disturbed person. Respond with caution.

THE DANGERS

The very last thing you want to do is underestimate the potential for life-threatening danger that is present any time you encounter an emotionally disturbed person. Your code of ethics tells you that you must be compassionate and just in working with a mental subject. Your good common sense and well-placed concern for officer safety should tell you with equal force that you must remain alert at all times when you are around an emotionally troubled human being. There are simply too many things that can happen—all of them bad—if you let down your guard for even a moment.

Over the years, law enforcement officers have perished at the hands of mental subjects in just about every conceivable scenario. Law officers have been lured into ambushes by mental subjects enraged by an earlier ticket or arrest, often as not from a different officer. They have been killed by EDPs who thought they were being accosted by communists or nazis or demons. They have been murdered by deranged people who were hearing voices that commanded them to kill. They have been slain by offenders so out of touch with reality that they were undeterred by control holds, chemical sprays and even bullets.

Not infrequently, peace officers are killed after losing control of their weapons to EDPs. Perhaps lured into a false sense of security because they believe they are confronting no more than an oddly-acting character—a nut case—they neglect to employ their normally effective safety practices and get careless. They fail to watch a subject's hands, miss danger flags, let him move in too close. Then, following a subject's bullrush or a furtive, quick grab, they find themselves in the grip of a surprisingly strong, numbed-to-pain offender. Sometimes, a lost weapon and a lost life are the terrible end results. The same, tragic scene has been played out time after time. Most tragic of all, it almost certainly will be played out again.

There is practically no end to the list of reasons why an emotionally disturbed person represents a very real threat to you. If he is truly out of touch with reality, he will have no reservations about hurting you because he does not fear retribution from either you or the criminal justice system. If he is thinking of suicide, he could very well care less if he takes you or anyone else with him. If mental illness has blocked the pain messages that his nerve endings are sending his brain, your control hold, impact weapon or even sidearm may not stop his attack right away. Indeed, the EDP is very much a danger to you.

The very worst way in which to regard an EDP is as a "character," "odd duck" or "harmless nutcase." It's vital that you keep in mind the term *unpredictable* as the best descriptor of an emotionally disturbed person. You must accept the fact that it is impossible to predict what a given EDP is going to do in a given set of circumstances. The same, well-known EDP you have contacted a half-dozen times without trouble may go for your throat this time, with no cause or reason apparent. Newspapers occasionally report accounts of the town character that everybody had snickered at but never really feared. Then, one day, the "town character" walks into a fast-food joint and proceeds to mow people down with gunfire. Same town. Same character. But now the "character" has become a mass murderer. It's quite possible that no one will ever know what pushed him over the edge.

Never, ever regard an emotionally disturbed person as "just a nut." That failed viewpoint could do much more than reveal you as someone without empathy. It could set you up to get killed.

Staying safe while effectively handling the variety of problems posed by EDPs requires that you steadfastly follow a set of time-proven guidelines for intervening in safety with a mentally troubled and perhaps dangerous person. Those survival guideposts will be the next topic for discussion.

DEFUSING THE DANGER

Collect information. A sudden, unexpected confrontation with an EDP who is acting in a threatening manner will force you to respond with only the information brought promptly to you by your own observations. You'll be required to seek additional background only *after* he is secured and the situation controlled. In many instances, however, you will have the time to talk to people and seek other information sources *before* you act. Whatever the case, try to talk with family, friends and witnesses to an EDP's disruptive actions. Who is he? Is he known to have prior mental health problems? Is he on medication and, if so, has he stopped taking it? What precipitated the current incident? Is there someone who is known to be particularly effective at communicating with him when he is in this state? Anything and everything you can learn might help.

How threatening is the EDP's behavior? How much help are you going to need in controlling him and the situation? What use of force options, such as defensive sprays, are available and appropriate for the existing conditions? Keep gathering information to answer these questions and more. Then, with the intelligence you have gleaned, plan a safe response for a potentially risky confrontation.

Remain alert. You are aware that no EDP is "guaranteed harmless" and that it is impossible to predict with accuracy what any mentally troubled individual is going to do next–like assault you. You also know that a constant level of high alert is your best defense against the myriad dangers that EDPs can bring with them. Take no chances. Make no assumptions beyond the one that says *all* EDPs are potentially dangerous. Recognize that the badly afflicted person who is laughing hysterically one moment could well go for your gun with seemingly superhuman strength in the next. What will keep him or her from succeeding in a sneak attack is your constant vigilance with every EDP or suspicious subject you contact. Keep your backup alert, too.

Stay on the lookout for surprises and sudden changes in your subject. His reactions to you or others present could change dramatically and violently for no obvious reason. Watch for indicators (clenching fists, a twitching jaw muscle, gritted teeth) that an attack may be imminent. Be prepared to resort to a chemical defense aerosol or other weapon, as required to protect yourself. It's alright to *tell* an EDP that you see him escalating and want him to calm down before you have to respond forcefully to his behavior. It's worked before and it's worth a try. He just may retain enough sense and self-control to obey you. Nothing is lost if he doesn't and you have to go on to your next force option.

Making no assumptions and taking nothing for granted mean that an EDP's promise to you that he will or won't do something is meaningless. Not handcuffing an EDP because he promises to behave is a quick way to become a casualty. Don't do it. Take for granted only that persistent caution on your part is the best way to survive a lengthy career of encounters with emotionally disturbed persons.

Maintain a buffer. Keeping a reactionary gap between yourself and the subject you are dealing with is never more critical than when you are working around a mentally troubled individual. Remain conscious of the location of your weapons in relation to the person you are interacting with and be certain you keep them well beyond his reach. Keep your gun side turned away from him at all times. If you must finally approach to take him into custody, do so from his rear with him off-balance and a backup officer in a covering position. Throughout the contact, stay sharp for the sudden appearance of a weapon, makeshift or otherwise. Some pretty crazy people have come up with some pretty ingenious (and deadly) weapons.

Be empathetic but maintain control. You *must* be patient, kind and empathetic. You absolutely must *not* become a victim of an EDP. By relying upon sound survival tactics and your good safety sense, you can do both at the same time.

Speak in a normal tone of voice when you converse with an EDP. Do not talk "down" to him or her as if you were addressing a child. Listen attentively to what he has to say. Be fair and do not lie. Do not reinforce his delusions by agreeing with him when he clearly is perceiving things that simply are not present. Be supportive and non-threatening, but also mean what you say and do what you say you are going to do. You can be empathetic and firm at the same time. Remember that you may have to work with the same individual again, and even an EDP may recall how he was treated at your last meeting.

Stay patient with an EDP who may be verbally abusing you. Repeat your questions and instructions, if necessary, without losing your patience or your temper. It may simply take your subject's disturbed mind longer than normal to interpret and act on your directions. Meanwhile, stay on your guard in case it is the EDP who becomes impatient or outraged and threatens you. If you *are* menaced, utilize the minimum amount of physical force you can to overcome resistance and protect the both of you. Remain in control of yourself and your emotions as you act effectively to control the EDP, too.

Believe all threats. While, as noted, you cannot afford to believe an EDP's promises, you *must* take seriously any and all threats he makes against you until they are proven to be empty ones. He may be hallucinating and out of touch with reality, but he may nevertheless have every intention of making good on his promise when he tells you that he's going to rip your guts out. Safety says you must believe that he's going to try, and protect yourself accordingly via survival tactics and techniques. Your countermeasures will vary from one EDP encounter to the next, but might include calling for more assistance, resorting to a chemical defense weapon, backing off temporarily or all of the preceding. The EDP's threats are not unlike all the others you receive in your sometimes difficult job: they are to be believed and defended against until proven unfounded.

Use proper subject control measures. Every emotionally disturbed subject who comes into your custody for any reason must be handcuffed and then searched for your protection and his. This means hands cuffed to his rear with the handcuffs double-locked and checked for a snug (but not circulation-stopping) fit. Multiple searches must be done until you are comfortable that your subject has nothing with which he could hurt himself or others. Belts, shoelaces, dress ties and all sharp or pointed objects must be secured beyond the EDP's reach. Ditto for fire-starting devices and anything else at all that might double as a makeshift weapon for attack or self-destruction. Search as many times as you must to remove all doubt that the EDP has been completely "disarmed." At the same time, recall that an EDP's personal weapons–teeth, head, feet–can bring you grave injury or death, too. Stay very careful.

Seek professional assistance. The suspected mental subject you have taken into protective custody or arrested for a crime should be checked out by a psychiatrist or other medical or mental health professional as soon as possible. The problem may turn out to be drug or injury related, and emergency treatment may be required to save a life. Meanwhile, do not take chances with your own "legal survival." Do not put an apparent EDP into the lockup without further investigation into what may be going on with him or her. Jail or the alcohol detox unit may be the worst possible place for a true EDP. Get a professional's opinion and find out. Seeking some informed advice just might prevent complications for the both of you. It should cost you no more than a little of your time and could well save you both time and bother in the long run. From a humanitarian point of view, it is also the *right* thing to do.

SUICIDAL SUBJECTS

Of all the mentally troubled and emotionally disturbed persons you will be called upon to deal with in your law enforcement role, none will be more challenging and potentially more dangerous to you than the individual Hell-bent upon self-destruction. The suicidal subject poses extreme danger not only to himself but to those around him who may seek to interrupt and prevent his life-ending efforts. He (or she) poses a major threat to *you*, the professional, emergency intervention specialist.

Although there may be as many as 25,000 suicides each year in this country, recognizing the suicidal individual *before* he or she commits a final, desperate act is sometimes not an easy task for mental health professionals and those close to the victim, let alone the peace officer called in at the last moment to intervene and perhaps preserve a life. Nonetheless, there are indicators that you may be able to learn from relatives, friends or coworkers of the potential suicide that might help you intervene effectively and in time even as you protect yourself in the process. Your observations and, if feasible, your questioning of the involved subject can provide you with much valuable information for both successful intervention and officer safety. Thus armed, you can better shield yourself from someone's self-destructive as well as aggressive behavior while you simultaneously work to help save him from himself. Recognition of the danger signs should be your first line of defense.

A suicidal individual often makes threats of self-destruction before he acts. All such statements should be taken seriously. By making them out loud, consciously or subconsciously he may be asking someone to keep him from doing what he is thinking about doing. The individual pondering self-destruction may show little interest in anyone or anything. He may make comments about the futility of life and even talk about means of self-destruction and their relative merits. He may state that he blames himself for all of his own or his family's difficulties, real or exaggerated.

The budding suicide often will display extreme depression and may neglect the basics of personal hygiene and grooming. He may abuse alcohol, drugs or a combination of the two and go on binges that last for days. He may begin giving away prized possessions and do other things to set his affairs in order, such as writing or changing a will. Any past, unsuccessful attempts at suicide will place the subject into an especially high-risk category. If he appears to have commenced actual preparations for self-destruction, such as buying a gun or hoarding pills, the potential for an actual suicide attempt is even greater.

The potential suicide may have recently gone through one or more major life crises, such as the death of a loved one, breakup of a marriage or relationship, loss of a job or discovery that he or she is seriously ill. These events may have resulted in obvious, deep depression. At the same time, a sudden and obvious lift in spirits in a previously depressed and self-destructive individual could be an indicator that he or she is relieved at having finally made the decision to "end it all." A serious attempt at self-destruction could be imminent now that the subject has arrived at a "solution" for all of his woes.

As every veteran officer knows, most, some or none of these warning indicators may precede an attempt at self-destruction. The presence of any of them should cause you to exercise caution in your approach and handling of the person evidencing them. At the same time, you should be aware that an individual may act to destroy himself or make you do it for him with virtually *no advance warning* of his intentions. It is this last individual—the "suicide by cop" candidate—who merits your special attention and precautionary handling.

While an exact count is difficult to come by, more than a few people force law enforcement officers to help them commit suicide every year. Lacking the "courage" or ability to end their own lives, these individuals, often armed, threaten officers with death in order to force the peacekeepers to respond with lethal force. On occasion, they actually kill or attempt to kill officers to force the officers' peers to then kill *them.* Frequently, these subjects precede their attempt at "suicide by cop" by telling the officers they are confronting what their intentions are. "I want you to kill me," "You'll have to kill me" and "I'm going to make you kill me" are among the phrases heard. Any person who makes these or similar remarks to you must be assumed to be extremely dangerous until and unless proven otherwise. Respond with extreme caution. Your safety is clearly at risk. Realize that the individual who does not display an obvious weapon to accompany the threats is not necessarily less dangerous than one who does. Particularly if he has no ready access to the means to kill himself, he may be planning on taking *your* gun to do it with.

While there is no guaranteed formula for successful suicide intervention, there are certainly things you can do to protect yourself as you seek to defuse the suicidal crisis and perhaps save a life. Take your time in working with the suicidal person. Avoid judgmental remarks and listen to what he has to say. Appear interested in his dilemma. Don't get *too* close, but show through your words and demeanor that you want to help. Try to keep him talking and be prepared to switch subjects as well as tactics if he appears to be escalating towards a self-destructive event. Don't threaten, yell or bluff the subject. Speak with a calm, even, authoritative voice and tell the truth. Do not make promises that cannot be honored ("I won't handcuff you"). Don't argue with the subject or try to play psychiatrist. Never, ever dare him to carry out his threat or challenge his courage to do so.

Your own safety must be foremost in your thoughts and tactics anytime you are in close proximity to a self-destructive subject. Watch his hands for weapons, actual or improvised. Keep a healthy reactionary gap of at least six to ten feet between the two of you while you are conversing. If possible, consider keeping a physical barrier, such as a piece of furniture, in that gap so that he'll have to overcome it to get to you. Be ready with a defensive aerosol or impact weapon if he appears about to rush you. Of course, if your suicidal subject is known or believed to be armed you will want to avoid any up-close-and-personal, face-to-face discussions. Do your talking from behind solid cover with your sidearm at the ready.

You should not confront a mentally disturbed person at all without having a cover officer present. If one is not on-scene when the confrontation begins, call for help immediately while you keep your physical distance from the subject. Get too close too soon and you could end up dead before help can arrive. Meanwhile, do nothing to crowd your subject or otherwise force a confrontation.

It's been said before, but it's important enough to reemphasize: Be especially conscious of the location of your firearm in relation to your subject. Inasmuch as he may be planning to use it to end his own life (and possibly yours), keep your holstered weapon side turned away from him and well out of his reach. Unless you have need for your weapon to be in your hand, keep it snapped securely in your holster and covered by your arm. Meanwhile, try to leave yourself an escape route in case you must avoid a sudden attack or quickly back off from a threatening subject until help can arrive. Also, never get between a potential suicide and his apparent means of self-destruction, such as a bridge railing or rooftop edge. If he is really serious about dying, he may not mind pulling you over with him. Stay back and live.

All emotionally disturbed subjects, including suicidal ones, must be properly handcuffed and searched when they are taken into custody or transported. Hands must be cuffed behind the back and searches must be repeated as many times as necessary to convince you that the individual retains nothing with which he could hurt himself or others. With the suicidal subject that means belts, shoelaces and perhaps even clothing must be removed. For his own safety, he may have to be given a "paper suit" to wear to preclude his hanging himself with cloth items. Lockup or treatment personnel must be warned of the subject's suicidal threats so that he can be monitored carefully. Professional medical or mental health attention must be sought right away. Your self-destructive subject may belong in a medical facility as opposed to a jail lockup. That decision calls for professional mental health or medical advice.

When dealing with the suicidal individual you must look to your own mental and emotional health in addition to your physical survival. Remember that you did not place the suicidal subject or EDP into his current state. You may not be able to save him from himself. Indeed, there is evidence that it may be impossible for *anyone* to save a truly suicidal person if he has actually, already decided to terminate his life. All you can do for him is your best while you protect yourself from his unpredictable actions. He has made a decision for himself and acted on it. Now you must decide to save yourself so you can help someone else another day.

SUMMARY

Emotionally disturbed or mentally ill people are often tragic individuals who need your help at least as much as the other "clients" you work with every day. They deserve your empathy, but they also merit your attention to the basic tenets of officer safety simply because some of these same people will most certainly kill you in a heartbeat should the opportunity arise. To survive your encounter with an emotionally disturbed person, gather all the data you can about him or her. Learn the symptoms of mental illnesses and monitor your subject for their presence. Know that EDPs are extremely unpredictable and may do totally irrational things, even to the point of critically harming themselves or someone else–like you, for instance. That's why suicidal subjects represent a particularly great threat to you as a peace officer.

Get plenty of help and maintain a safety buffer or reactionary gap between yourself and an EDP. Keep track of your weapons and keep them well away from the mental subject. Believe an EDP who says he will hurt you. Be patient but firm in your dealings with him and take for granted nothing you do not know for a certainty. Properly secure and search any EDP who comes into your custody. Then, seek prompt, professional help for your emotionally disturbed and potentially dangerous subject. It is the most beneficial, humane thing you can do for everyone involved.

SAFETY CHECKLIST FOR HANDLING
EMOTIONALLY DISTURBED PERSONS

1. Where possible, gather as much information as you can on the emotionally disturbed person you'll be handling *before* you make contact.

2. Emotionally disturbed persons are not to be considered "harmless nuts." They represent a potential threat to your safety.

3. Never handle an emotionally disturbed subject alone. Call in as much help as you think you will need.

4. In dealing with a mentally disturbed person, be as nonthreatening and truthful as you can possibly be.

5. Be conscious at all times of your weapons and their positioning relative to your subject; he probably is.

6. Be aware of the extreme danger to you posed by a suicidal individual. "Suicide by cop" remains a real possibility.

7. Leave yourself a retreat or escape route when dealing with an emotionally disturbed person.

8. Handcuff and search for protection (yours and his) any mentally disturbed person you take into custody.

Chapter Sixteen

OFF-DUTY SURVIVAL

An off-duty officer with a northern, big city department was at a bar dancing when a fight broke out between two women at around 1:15 A.M. The officer identified himself as a policeman and was intervening between the two when a male subject produced a 9mm handgun and shot the officer fatally in the chest.

In the Northeast, a 34-year-old investigator with the state police was shopping with his wife in a supermarket when he observed a robbery in progress at the store. The 11-year veteran, who was unarmed, attempted to disarm and subdue the robber. The two men fell through a plate glass window while struggling. The subject then fired a single round from a sawed-off shotgun into the officer's chest, killing him.

In the West, an off-duty officer was Christmas shopping with his wife in a mall when he learned of a robbery in progress at a shoe store. The officer asked his wife to go call the police and took cover behind a parked van outside the store. As the escaping adult gang member ran towards the vehicle, the officer left cover, identified himself as the police and ordered the male to halt. The subject turned, went into a crouched position and fired two rounds from a .38-caliber revolver. The officer was hit twice but returned fire. Both men received fatal wounds.

Off-duty law enforcement officers, in uniform and out, capture countless offenders and rescue numerous victims from further harm every year. Annually, crimes are solved and citizens protected by officers who see their calling as something more than a 40-hour week of predictable duties. Not infrequently these off-duty enforcement activities bring officers into contact with violently resisting offenders. On occasion, they include the exchange of deadly gunfire. Law enforcement officers acting in the line of duty while actually off-the-clock win far more of these confrontations than not. But all too often, off-duty officers who courageously have responded to crimes in progress have ended up injured or dead for their selfless efforts. The odds arrayed against them have proven too great to be overcome, and tragedy has been the result.

As a safety-conscious law enforcement officer, you already know that you can confront sudden and extreme danger at *any* time, on-duty or off. That's the nature of the business you are in. Off-duty, danger can arrive literally in your own backyard in the middle of the night. Or it can appear without warning while you are on a shopping expedition with your family in the middle of a suburban mall at high noon. Danger is like that: it frequently fails to telegraph in advance that it is coming. When it does arrive, you may be least able to confront it safely and effectively while you are in an off-duty status, perhaps mentally as well as physically.

Because you are the kind of person you are (that's one of the reasons you went into law enforcement, isn't it?) you are apt to feel a strong drive to act decisively to "set right" an off-duty crime or incident. While some of the off-duty scenarios you may face may involve nothing more serious than graffiti vandals or an obnoxious drunk, others may include offenders who will hurt or kill you if the opportunity presents itself. It is in this element of unpredictability where lies a considerable degree of risk for you if you elect to act officially.

The key for you is to know when a situation poses such a threat to the safety and survival of yourself and others that you *must* do something more than call 911. Coming across a felonious assault in progress could well fit this category of events calling for *some* kind of a personal response. On the other hand, your common sense should tell you that risking your own well-being to confront alone a pack of rowdy drunks or vandals probably is not a very good idea. Neither would most traffic or petty offenses require your immediate, off-duty intercession. Here, your most logical and responsible course of action likely would be to serve as an excellent observer and summon the on-duty law enforcers. After all, you do not exactly help the situation if you add to the list of victims by becoming one yourself. Likewise, you make things much worse if you force an unnecessary confrontation that ends in gunfire or other added danger to innocents.

It quickly becomes clear that in an off-duty confrontation it is vital for you to assess the odds for and against you before you leap into the fray. Doing that will require that you take an honest look at the added risks and limitations your off-duty status may bring to the crisis at hand.

YOUR LIABILITIES

When you decide to take enforcement action while off the clock you will be acting without some of the advantages you enjoy when you are in an on-duty status. That does not mean that those added difficulties cannot be overcome by sound tactics and extreme caution on your part. It simply means that these additional liabilities must be weighed in your decision-making about whether to intervene or not and must be considered in your planning and actions should you decide to act officially. The limitations and liabilities you will need to think about could include the following:

Equipment considerations. First of all, are you armed for your off-duty encounter? Is it the same high-capacity handgun you carry on-duty or is it a snub-nosed, watered down version of your duty weapon? Certainly any firearm is better than none at all, but will it serve you well if shooting starts?

Off-duty officers have been killed while challenging visibly armed offenders although unarmed themselves. Tragically, that kind of sacrifice amounts to tombstone courage, plain and simple. Even if a subject is not visibly armed, you as an off-duty officer must assume that he could produce a weapon without warning. That means you should never act officially yourself unless you are adequately armed to respond effectively to the sudden appearance of a deadly weapon.

If you are off-duty, are you in possession of an extra magazine for your semi-auto or extra rounds for your wheel gun? However unlikely it may appear, an "extra rounds" off-duty confrontation remains a possibility.

How about your other off-duty equipment preparations? Unless you are truly paranoid, it's doubtful that you're wearing soft body armor. It's absence puts you at obvious increased risk if gunplay erupts. How about handcuffs or similar restraint devices? How are you going to secure your off-duty capture after you arrest him, if you must do so without on-duty aid? You obviously *can* win and survive without a vest or cuffs, but their conspicuous absence is something to think about before you jump into an off-duty encounter with possibly dangerous offenders.

Backup help. Being able to rely upon the strength of numbers is one of your biggest assets as a law enforcement officer. The quick availability of trained, backup manpower makes your otherwise too-risky job survivable. While summoning on-duty help before you act remains one of the cardinal rules for engaging in off-duty police action, the real possibility neverthless exists that circumstances will prevent your calling it before you must act, perhaps to save a life. Or you may have to act before help can arrive, again because of the criticality of the situation.

Acting solo will, of course, put you at increased risk that a crook or crooks will take you on. When you are on-duty, you avoid making "lone ranger" arrests whenever possible. This basic safety rule should not go out the window when you are on your own time and, perhaps, especially vulnerable.

Communications. Your portable, two-way radio is a life-saver. You know that. Do you have it with you off-duty? If so, great. If not, does this lack put you in added danger to the degree that you need to reconsider your plans for intervening? Think about it. Perhaps the presence of a cellular phone or a bystander willing to call for help for you can help even the odds. But do realize that you are surrendering a big advantage when you act without a strong communications lifeline to on-duty assistance.

Identification. When you flash a badge, show a gun and/or start issuing orders, will everyone know that you are one of the good guys and submit to your authority accordingly? Particularly if you are out of uniform, your unexpected display just might bring about panic, disobedience and even outright opposition. Obviously, you should never venture out armed unless you are also in possession of your law enforcement badge and credentials. But even if you are so equipped your surprise intervention could result in totally unpredictable responses from those around you. Are you ready for that eventuality?

The enemy. You already know that events may force you to act without help if you act at all. How about the opposition you will be facing? How many offenders will you be going up against? Are they armed? How? Are they evidently drunk, high or otherwise emotionally worked up? The number or condition of your opponents may amount to such an increased threat that you must decide to phone in the problem rather than jump into it yourself. That's one more area of liability to consider *before* you commit yourself to taking law enforcement action while off-duty. It's not one to be taken lightly.

ASSESS AND DECIDE

Your assessment of the situation you have encountered and your decision to intervene or simply witness it must of necessity be accomplished quickly and under less than ideal conditions. To add to your possible problems, the situation could change radically after your initial assessment. The shouting match between two drunks has changed with the appearance of a knife in the hands of one of the belligerents. Or, to the contrary, a shoving and cursing bout between a man and woman in a parking lot has now dissolved into some making-up billing and cooing between the lovebirds. What to do? Assess and reassess, if need be, before you commit. Try to do so unnoticed and from a safe vantage point.

Your assessment of whether or not you should get involved as an off-duty peacekeeper always should include a mental review on your part of what seems most likely to happen if you call for a law enforcement response rather than get personally involved in the action. In other words, what would be the likely outcome of your decision to leap into the fray—or refrain from doing so? If your careful but quick analysis tells you that someone most likely would *not* die or be seriously injured by your avoiding direct, personal intervention, common sense may dictate that observing and reporting to the on-duty law enforcers probably would be the most logical and responsible course of action. On the other hand, your witnessing a robbery victim being bludgeoned or an individual being sexually assaulted would no doubt mandate a direct response if you were at all positioned and equipped to intercede. The difference in the scenarios, of course, centers around the potential for actual or greater harm to occur as a result of your action or inaction.

Your assessment of any potential, off-duty confrontation should include a weighing of your strengths and weaknesses compared to those of the opposition. How are they armed? How are *you* armed? How many of them are there? Are you sure you have detected them all? How about backups or getaway drivers who may be outside your line of sight? Do *you* have any help immediately at hand? What kind?

There are, of course, other factors to analyze and consider. Where is the problem occurring? Are there others present who would be endangered by gunfire, should it develop as a consequence of your intervention? How about victims or bystanders who could become hostages should you force a confrontation? Is there a good chance your intentions might be misunderstood and an attack launched against *you* by the good guys? All of these things must be considered *before* you intervene as an off-duty rescuer.

What are your chances of coming out on top if you decide to jump in? Are you severely outnumbered and outgunned? Are quick reinforcements from on-duty officers unlikely? Think carefully. Do not act impulsively in your admirable desire to help. Your restraint could save lives—your own included. If you do intervene, continue your assessment of the threats you are facing as the situation unfolds. Stay alert for the appearance of participants—victims and suspects alike—whose presence you did not initially notice. Remember that on-duty officers could arrive and intervene at any time, called or not. If they do, you do not want to look like part of the problem.

INTERVENING IN SAFETY

So, you have completed your initial assessment of what you are confronting and decided on personal intervention as your reasoned and required response. Now what? Actually, intervening in relative safety while off-duty requires that you break your careful response into several, distinct actions. Consider the following guidelines for handling a potentially hazardous off-duty confrontation:

Call for help. Once you decide to intervene, before you do *anything* else get help on the way by calling for on-duty reinforcements. If you do not have immediate access to a police radio, dial 911 from the nearest telephone and tell the operator who you are, where you are and what is going on there. Stay on the line until the call-taker has all the data he or she needs to send the troops. Meanwhile, advise the 911 operator of any hazards or potential problems the responding officers need to be aware of in order to handle the incident in safety. Although you will never have *all* the answers you'd like, try to provide information regarding:

Your plans to intervene or wait for help to arrive

What you plan to do if you cannot wait

Your appearance, what you're wearing and where you will be

Number and descriptions of known suspects

Apparent crimes involved

Weapons believed involved

Presence of a possible lookout or getaway vehicle

Number, location and condition of victims, if known

Any other special dangers you are aware of.

If you are unable to place the call yourself, try to send more than one responsible-looking passerby to do it for you. You probably will not have the time to brief them with all of the information you would have been able to relay to the operator personally, but at least stress to them the importance of advising 911 of what is going on, where it is happening and the fact that an off-duty peace officer is on-scene. Don't be too surprised if the first person you try and hand this notification task to declines to help; keep at it until you find individuals with sufficient backbone to get involved.

Scan and plan. Do not give away your presence before you have to. Try to remain insignificant and unnoticed to the crooks you are monitoring. Stay back and take in all that your senses can tell you about the situation and the players involved in it. Is it really what it appears to be? (One off-duty cop was about to draw his weapon and go after some robbers of a fast-food joint when he discovered his "robbers" were high school drama students involved in taping a "real-life" crime scene for class!)

Scan carefully for the presence of backups and getaway vehicles placed by the offenders. You do not want to put these behind you when you act. Look for uninvolved bystanders or others who may be about to stumble into an in-progress crime. Warn them away, if you can do so in safety for them and without giving away your presence to the crooks.

As you size up the scene and the situation, decide how to approach without being noticed, if intervention remains your plan. If the incident is occurring inside an establishment, try to avoid an always-risky confrontation inside, whenever innocents are present. If violent conflict is going to occur, it is better that the offenders come outside to you and (hopefully) your on-duty helpers. In the meantime, do not do anything to rush a confrontation unless someone is actually being harmed right in front of you. Even then, do not rush into a confrontation you are unlikely to win.

Plan how and when you will confront your opponents if you *must* do so before on-duty help can arrive and take over. Think about cover and concealment. Keep watching for complications—like additional people appearing on-scene. Lay plans for meeting any added threats. Naturally, you will not have all the time that you would prefer for observing and plotting your response. But don't go into action at all until you have at least an idea of what you are trying to do and how you are going to go about accomplishing it. To act on emotions and good intentions but without a plan of action is asking for disaster. Don't do it.

Seek cover and surprise. Go into your best "stealth" mode for attack. Don't even appear interested in what's going on around you until you are ready to take decisive action. Approach your adversaries from the rear. If you have even the slightest suspicion that they are armed, remain behind good cover with your weapon at the ready and do not get too close. (Once more: *do not challenge armed offenders if you are unarmed yourself!*) If they break to run when you orally challenge them, let them flee for the time being. Do not leave good cover and thereby set yourself up as a great target. Just as when you are on-duty, stick with the strength of solid cover. It could well save your life.

Issue commands. Again, if you think that your opponents are armed, stay behind cover with your handgun drawn and give your orders from there. Wherever you are speaking from, begin by announcing your authority in clear, direct terms: "Police! Freeze in that position! Do it now!" You can then add additional instructions depending on the situation at hand and the response you receive. Display credentials *if* it is safe and convenient for you to do so. But keep your gun hand empty unless your weapon is in it.

Realize that you may need to repeat your directions more than once. The sudden appearance of someone in street clothes shouting instructions, perhaps while displaying a weapon, may at least temporarily baffle suspects and victims alike. Stay focused without over-reacting or losing your cool. Use a forceful tone that announces loud and clear that you expect compliance. Stay away from threats and cursing. Neither will help the situation at all and either just might turn otherwise compliant people against you.

Stay alert. Expect the unexpected. Be ready for new threats to appear, including the arrival of on-duty officers who do not yet know you're the good guy. Know that a victim or witness suddenly could go into "overload" and do something irrational, like running screaming from the scene. Be aware of this possibility and do not allow such an event to distract you from the threats you are watching. If necessary, issue new, verbal "reminders" to your suspects to keep them aware of who is in charge. Stay sharp. Realize that the situation may change as offenders discover you are apparently alone. Their courage may return and they just might decide to test you. Stay ready for anything, including the possibility that a use of lethal force scenario could develop. Continue to look to your cover needs and keep watching for the next threat to materialize. Keep doing that until help is on hand and the incident is totally under control.

Don't rush in. If at all possible, do not move in close to your suspects while you are alone. If you feel they might be armed, stay behind cover. Maintain a reactionary gap of at least six feet—more, if feasible. Do not rush in to handcuff, assuming you have cuffs with you, if it's possible to wait for your on-duty peers to do it. Your moving in close could be just the opening an offender is looking for, particularly now that he has deduced you appear to be off-duty and unassisted. Keep your distance, even if it means tolerating a one-fingered salute from a fleeing offender. Engaging in a foot pursuit or a wrestling match with one or more punks while you are off-duty is not a really smart way to fill your idle hours. The disadvantages and resultant risks are simply too great.

Effect a smooth handoff. It's not over until the offenders are transferred safely from your custody to that of your on-duty helpers. Cooperate fully with the instructions of the arriving cavalry, even if they initially respond to you with less than complete affection. Like you, they will want to know exactly what's going on before they start building lifelong friendships. Expect them to want a great deal of information—as you would. And realize that they *may* temporarily disarm you while they sort things out. That's reasonable. Hopefully, they read officer safety books, too!

Also, be prepared to stick around to give statements and help with the arrest paperwork, if you are asked to do so. After all, you wouldn't much like it if an off-duty colleague dumped a bucket of prisoners in your lap and vanished without so much as an "adios!" Be sure that you graciously extend your thanks to your on-duty partners for the timely assistance. Then, be sure you're ready to return the favor if you are asked, one day.

OFF-DUTY WORK AND MISTAKEN IDENTITY DANGERS

If you work as a private security officer when you are off-duty or supplement your income by laboring at "extra duty" work for your agency at ball games, celebrations and similar events, you once again increase your exposure to potential danger. You can, of course, cut your risks by refusing to work extra in places where the working conditions or nature of the job itself place you in increased danger. Working alone as a bouncer or doorman in a rough bar could serve as a classic example of this sort of a bad news assignment. Avoid it. You don't need the money or the excitement *that* badly. Also, avoid working off-duty anyplace where backup is hard to obtain and where communication with on-duty help is difficult, at best. Too many things could go fatally wrong in an environment like that.

Wherever you decide to work security or extra-duty law enforcement, be sure the non-police employees working around you know how and when to summon on-duty help for you. Have a plan of action for the premises, and clue your civilian co-workers in on what you expect of them in an emergency. Advance planning for a hazardous confrontation can be especially critical if you work security in a financial institution or similar establishment where your uniformed presence is supposed to serve as a deterrent against robbery. Have some hand signals or voice codes in place ahead of time so that you and your co-workers can seek help from each other should danger threaten without tipping off the bad guys about your intentions. Be sure your civilian cohorts know the circumstances in which you want them to do nothing, and when you expect them to hit a silent alarm or telephone for help. But no matter how much you trust your nonpolice helpers, try to always have two-way radio communication at your fingertips anytime you work an off-duty assignment.

Remember that all the bad things that can happen to you while you're working a regular shift can befall you when you are handling an off-duty job. That means you must avoid the same fatal errors and practice the same survival techniques you so effectively employ when you are walking a beat, steering your "mobile observation platform" about the precinct or checking a cell block in the lockup. No bad habits are permitted. A while back in the western U.S., a uniformed, off-duty officer was seated comfortably behind his desk inside a suburban bank when two armed robbers walked in. Each robber shot the officer fatally before he could defend himself. The message for you here: The bad guys won't cut you any slack just because you are working in an off-duty or extra-duty capacity. You cannot afford to let down your guard and cut them any, either.

While it is bad enough to get hurt by the criminals, it could be downright embarrassing (if not fatal) to get nailed by your peers. Misidentification dangers, as noted previously, are very real when you carry a weapon off-duty. Trouble can occur even if you are not in the process of taking enforcement action. (One officer was mortified when his sidearm, which he had unwisely given to his spouse to tote in her handbag, was accidentally dumped on the counter at the supermarket checkout stand. Once people stopped diving for cover, he was able to lamely explain the situation.) Whether your on-duty colleagues have arrived because you asked someone to call them to help you or because somebody called in after seeing your weapon peeking from under your jacket, the danger is real when on and off-duty officers confront one another unexpectedly. The hazards can be especially keen if you as the off-duty peacekeeper are out of your familiar jurisdiction or work for an agency so large that everyone does not know everybody else by sight.

During any "confrontation" with on-duty officers, the most important thing for you to remember is to do absolutely nothing that those officers could perceive as disobedience or a threat. Follow their instructions to the letter, even if it means letting a crook you are holding get away. Don't argue. Shout out your name and the identity of the agency you represent, but do not expect immediate recognition from the on-duty professionals. (Would you, as an on-duty officer, instantly believe a stranger, perhaps one with a gun in hand, who said he was a cop?) Again, follow instructions carefully. Do not protest, curse or threaten. Do not reach for credentials unless you are first given permission to do so. Then, move very slowly and deliberately to retrieve them. This is not the time for sudden moves or an argumentative personality.

If you have your weapon in your hand at the moment of confrontation, freeze stone-still in that position until you are told what to do with the gun. Identify yourself orally. Never, ever turn towards your challenger with your weapon raised. Doing so is a great way to die needlessly. Try identifying yourself again, but keep obeying commands and do nothing quick, surprising or otherwise threatening. Your life could depend upon your calm, measured response to this unusual threat scenario. There will be plenty of time to "discuss" things later. Right now you must act carefully to prevent a mistake from escalating into a tragedy.

Another potentially touchy situation could arise if you are pulled over by an officer while you are operating your personal vehicle. When you have stopped your car, do not leap out and go running back to the patrol car. (What would you do as an on-duty officer upon spotting such a performance?) Stay put. Place your hands on the steering wheel and wait for the officer to give instructions or contact you. If the two of you do not know one another, identify yourself and your agency when the officer reaches you and let him or her know if you have a weapon on you or in the vehicle. Again, follow directions completely even if it means you must endure some "precautionary measures" while the identity issue gets squared away. And again, do or say absolutely nothing in the meantime that might be seen as threatening noncompliance. Expect to be required to prove who and what you are. Remain gracious while you are doing so. This is not the place for arguments and bad feelings.

If, while off-duty, you come across an officer whom you feel may need some help, be very careful in how you approach him to offer it. He is not ungrateful, but if he's smart, he will be cautious in accepting your aid until he's pretty sure you're on his side. (You, hopefully, would do the same.) If you happen to be in your personal vehicle at the time and your on-duty peer is conducting his business on or near a roadway, be sure you park off of the road so that your vehicle does not block his car's emergency lights or otherwise create a traffic hazard. Approach slowly with both of your hands in open view. When you are within earshot, identify yourself as a peace officer and ask if you can assist. If he replies in the negative, feel free to be on your way. If he says yes but does not immediately give instructions, ask what you can do and then follow his directions. Do not, however, do anything at any time that distracts him from watching the situation he is involved with. Once more, you do not want to create a problem greater than the one you were trying to help solve. Rely upon your good judgment and common sense in deciding *when* to stop and proffer aid and in deciding *what* to do once you decide to help.

SUMMARY

Have no doubts about it. When you choose to engage in enforcement action of any sort while you are off the job, you have decided to take part in a known-dangerous scenario that results in police deaths and injuries every year. You may, in the end, win the confrontation and serve the cause of justice. You may even be called a hero. But realize that when you do elect to act officially, even though you are off-duty, you are likely acting without the critical benefit of communication, adequate equipment and backup support. If your careful assessment of the situation convinces you that you must personally intervene anyway, act with a clear plan and be prepared for the added dangers, such as misidentification, you may face. Use surprise and cover to your advantage and turn the job over to the on-duty peacekeepers as quickly as possible. Meanwhile, do nothing that would suggest to a witness, victim or fellow officer that *you* constitute a threat. Act with informed caution and restraint all the way around and stay safe. It's the best way to survive to go back *on*-duty.

STREET SURVIVAL CHECKLIST FOR OFF-DUTY CONFRONTATIONS

1. Use good judgment in the enforcement actions you elect to get involved in while off-duty. Your best and safest response may be to serve as an excellent witness.
2. Assess art off-duty situation carefully before you commit yourself to action. Do not leap into a hopeless confrontation.
3. If there is any way at all to do so, call for on-duty law enforcement help before you act.
4. Recognize the disadvantages you may face if you choose to take enforcement action while off-duty.
5. If you must intervene, do so with a plan of action in mind.
6. Always keep looking for unexpected dangers and new threats.

7. Realize that you could be misidentified as a bad guy by victims and officers alike.

8. Choose your off-duty jobs with a thought for safety. Make some advance plans for getting help in an off-duty crisis.

9. Tactically withdraw from an off-duty confrontation if you are in over your head.

Chapter Seventeen

TERRORISTIC THREATS

In the Midwest, a highway patrol trooper was shot to death after effecting a traffic stop. Unknown to the officer, who was Black, the vehicle contained a wanted, far-right wing fugitive with avowed racist beliefs. The killer's van was found to contain weapons, a large supply of ammunition and explosives.

In 1993, federal agents were attempting to serve arrest and search warrants at a Texas compound occupied by a heavily-armed, fanatical religious cult when a gunfight broke out. Four agents died and many more were wounded; six cult members also died in the firefight. When the ensuing 51-day standoff with authorities ended in a fire and explosion that killed another 79 cult members, including several children, the incident became a rallying point for far-right, antigovernment zealots, some of whom advocated retaliatory violence against the federal government.

On April 19, 1995, domestic terrorists detonated a large vehicle bomb outside a federal building in Oklahoma City, Oklahoma. The 168 persons killed in the blast included 12 federal law enforcement officers.

Terrorists and terrorism are not new to American law enforcement. But although their violent and illegal activities have been around for a long time, their appearances and professed causes have changed quite a lot over the years. A quarter century ago, American terrorists were, for the most part, antiestablishment types who scuttled about making bombs, shouting "off with the pigs!" and occasionally shooting at police officers. Most were White, although there were some Black, Native American and Hispanic extremists with their own violent agendas.

Today's terrorists are even Whiter than their predecessors, but rather than inhabiting the far-left end of the political spectrum, many are now off the far-right end of the scale. They are equally antigov-

233

ernment, although for a largely new set of reasons. And they still see law enforcement officers as agents of an enemy occupation force who must, on occasion, be slaughtered for the greater good.

To the peace officers who must deal with these in-earnest but badly misguided extremists, the political stripe of the violent, terroristic criminal makes very little difference. These officers realize that the bombs or bullets of one can kill you just as dead as the instruments of the other. Instead, the survival-smart officer concentrates on implementing the anti-terrorist tactics and techniques that will keep him safe no matter what the political or other agenda of his attacker.

Safety, of course, comes with knowledge of the threat being faced. And that calls for recognition of the faces of the potential enemy.

WHO ARE THEY?

In a very few words, the terrorist of today can be just about anyone with a grievance, cause or belief so strong that he is willing to kill others and perhaps even die himself to achieve his "goal," whatever that goal may happen to be. The mind of a terrorist can be particularly hard to understand because he very likely does not view the world like the rest of us. He and his kind hope to influence public opinion and government policy by committing acts that are so threatening and terrifying—translate that to mean bloody—that beliefs in the status quo or normal way of doing business is altered, perhaps radically. The terrorist wants to convince his audience—and he is very much playing to an audience—that he and his companions are so powerful that government and its agents are helpless and unable to stop them from carrying out their objectives.

That helps explain terrorists' eagerness to attack law enforcement officers and facilities. The message intended for public consumption is that if government cannot even protect itself against the terrorist's bullets or bombs, how can it protect its citizens? Perhaps it's time to come over to the terrorists' way of thinking for your own good, or so the thinking is supposed to go, at least according to the terrorists' textbook.

Modern day terrorists run the length and breadth of the political spectrum. They include both foreign and domestic threats to the safety of the nation's citizens. The agents of terroristic, fanatical foreign governments, such as the so-called religious fundamentalists who detonated explosives in New York's World Trade Center in 1993, represent an especially dangerous threat. Some of these zealots have demonstrated the willingness to commit suicide attacks in furtherance of their attacks against America, the "Great Satan." Some of these people are still out there today and the law enforcement officer must remain conscious of the potential dangers they represent, now and into the foreseeable future.

At the same time, many of the nation's terroristic threats today are home-grown. Some of their handiwork was seen in 1995's catastrophic bombing attack on the federal building in Oklahoma City. But it would be a mistake to view all of the country's domestic terrorists as being somehow united either logistically or in beliefs and goals. While some groups and individuals share the same general philosophy and dogma as do others, there is oftentimes not only disagreement but plain hostility among various factions. Some not only cannot agree on how, exactly, their desired ends are to be accomplished; they cannot even agree on what the ends *are*. Some of the disagreements can even be attributed to personal feuds and fallings out over who was to be in charge of a particular organization or subgroup. It should come as no surprise to the world-wise law enforcement professional that individuals who cannot get along with the rest of the world oftentimes cannot get along with each other, either. Nonetheless, the domestic terrorist's internal bickerings and generally antisocial tendencies can make it even harder for law enforcement to track his activities when he periodically abandons one group of zealots to join or form another, perhaps as a competitor.

America's domestic terrorists include a few of the old-fashioned race haters who preach racial supremacy and prejudice and direct violence against members of targeted minority or ethnic populations. As distasteful as their rhetoric may be, it is not a crime for these people to advocate the position that one race or group is superior or inferior to another. The racial supremacist—White, Black or otherwise—only becomes a legitimate problem for law enforcement when he begins to advocate or execute criminal acts against the targets of his hatred. It is worth noting that in addition to the race haters of the past, some of the so-called "skinheads"—today's half-hearted version of the Hitler Youth—may be counted among the violence-prone race and ethnic haters of the world.

The government haters are also out there today. The extremists among these groups go far beyond grousing about taxes and government giveaway programs. These people go to the point of advocating the overthrow of the government and violent attacks against its agents, including law enforcement officers. The extremist antigovernment survivalist types and some of the loosely-titled, self-appointed "militia" movements of today may represent the most heavily-armed and potentially dangerous threats to American peace officers today. Once more, it's not a crime to hate, even if the objects of your hatred happen to include your government and its agents, some of whom just happen to be law enforcement officers. But when that hatred encompasses the willingness to launch attacks against government employees and property, fanaticism has crossed the line into criminal conduct.

Some of today's far-right fringe groups make no bones about their willingness to attack physically those who oppose them, including those they see as the law enforcement agents of ZOG, the illegal, unconstitutional Zionist Occupational Government fictionalized by the extremist right. Statements attributed to the members of some of these groups include specific threats to murder law enforcement officers. With even a handful of fringe "thinkers" out there espousing such views, only the brain-dead law enforcement officer would not be interested in remaining alert to the activities of these people and their organizations.

The lines separating some of the various violence-advocating extremist groups may be constantly fading and shifting, making it extremely hard to differentiate among them. Some race-haters, for example, also can be members of extremist, fundamentalist religious groups who advocate violence against government officials and others, such as homosexuals and those viewed as "different." A few of these individuals have given the Old West's image of a "leader" with a Bible in one hand and a gun in the other a new and considerably less wholesome meaning. In recent years, a small number of these extreme fundamentalists have posed a danger to law enforcement after attracting virtual cults of followers in which some members arm themselves heavily and engage in compound living arrangements intended to keep outsiders—particularly agents of the government—at bay.

But not every potential terrorist who represents a threat to law enforcement personnel dons camouflage clothing, wears a gun on his hip and slings another over his shoulder and runs around in the woods spouting anti-government venom. Indeed, some of these people look and sound and act a lot like you—up to a point. It's when their "hot" buttons get pushed that they become at least a potential threat to others: most certainly to their perceived opponents, but also, perhaps, to you if you happen to interfere with the carrying out of their violent, destructive intentions.

Included in this latter group of potential threats to you are such as the eco-terrorists, the animal rights extremists and the fringe anti-abortion crusaders. There are others. Any or all of these people may hold beliefs with which you strongly agree. The difference between them and you is that you as a law-abiding citizen will not engage in patently illegal and perhaps life-threatening behavior to make a point or further a cause, no matter how well-intentioned the goal. The mainstream members of such groups are almost universal in disavowing the crimes engaged in by their far-out supporters. These offenses may include vandalism, arson, intimidation, sabotage and even murder.

Clearly, the truly fanatical, out-of-touch supporters of causes of one kind or another represent potential danger to the peace officers who encounter them, even if the officer was not the intended target of their depredations. You might, for instance, be placed at risk if you interrupted what was initially intended as a crime against property. By accidentally encountering an incendiary or explosive device planted by one of these terrorists you could end up just as totally destroyed as the intended target. You might want to think about that if you encounter a suspicious package or device during your preliminary investigation of a break-in at an animal experimentation facility or abortion clinic. "Well-intentioned" terrorism can kill or maim you just as effectively as the infernal device carried by an anti-American suicide bomber from another country. And it amounts to terrorism all the same.

The face of terrorism sometimes does not remain static for long. It is safe to assume that terroristic groups and goals will change at least somewhat as the causes and issues that excite people also change with the times. Some groups will go quiet, shrink or wither and die as political and social issues fade. New groups with at least the potential for violence will form—some with members of older, faded groups among their membership—as new causes arise. It is vital that you, the law enforcement officer who may be called on to deal with their future threats, remain current on both who's out there and how they are going about their strange business.

HOW DO THEY OPERATE?

As has been the case forever, terrorism requires human participants who can be lead to take part in acts of violence against innocent others in order to achieve some identifiable "greater purpose." Terrorism still requires weapons of destruction, ranging from firearms to letter bombs to mammoth, vehicle-carried explosive devices. Beyond that, however, terrorism has been "modernized" at least somewhat to take advantage of technology in the Information Age.

Terrorism still relies on charismatic speakers and writers who make at least occasional sense and put words to what some of their intended audience may already be thinking. In some cases, today's front men (and women) for the extremist and violence-prone groups are better educated and much slicker than their predecessors. It may be, for instance, hard to argue with the speaker's goal of "doing away with welfare." It's only later that the listener discovers that the leader intends to end welfare by killing off a good many of its recipients.

It is in the means of communicating its message that terrorism has changed its m.o. today. Some of the more far-out, violence-advocating groups are seeking to ride the "cutting edge" by utilizing computer information services and networks to spread propaganda, sell their hateful or antigovernment materials, seek donations from sympathizers, recruit new members and communicate with one another. Some will refer the network browser to the electronic addresses of other, like-minded extremist groups and individuals. In addition, some groups have added professional quality video tapes to the old standby of printed hate literature to further their race-hating or antigovernment agendas. Audio tapes are also available—for a price. Broadcasts on commerical or short-wave radio also may carry the violence-encouraging messages of some of these extremist groups.

Some of today's extremist, violence-preaching organizations count ex- and even current law enforcement officers among their members. They want more. Since current officers can furnish information from police computer data bases and files as well as news of pending law enforcement operations, this peace officer participation, no matter how small or passive, can pose a potential threat to you, the "governmental agent" and avowed enemy of the more far-out among these extremists. And that's bad news indeed.

It may be hard not to sympathize just a little with the well-dressed, well-spoken zealot who looks a lot like you and says he's anticrime and anticriminal and advocates dumping the whole lot of liberal, left-leaning politicians who seem bent on driving the working American to Hell. But you need to listen a little harder and longer to find out exactly *who* the speaker identifies as his enemies, and exactly how he plans to deal with them. You may find that *you* appear somewhere on his "enemies" list if you do not agree with him on every facet of extremist dogma. You might even learn that he plans to whittle that list down in a particularly final fashion "when the time comes."

Pay particular attention to the zealot who wants to get really close to you. Your new pal may have ulterior motives in mind. Regard the information you get from him with suspicion. It may amount to an organized effort at planting disinformation with law enforcement. Then, remember who and what you are sworn to represent and protect, and keep your distance. That, too, is part of officer survival.

Realize that the terrorists who pose a danger to law enforcement are not necessarily the venom-spewing media stars who bring attention to themselves by spouting their violent rhetoric for colorful sound bites on the evening news shows. Indeed, these attention-starved performers may well not be the people who represent a physical threat to you when you cross paths on a late-night traffic stop or check of a rural campsite. Terrorists who are very serious about their plans for destruction are more likely to shun publicity, work alone or in small groups and say nothing when you catch them "dirty," perhaps with quantities of weapons or explosives. Do not regard their lack of "flash" as a trustworthy indicator that they do not pose a real threat to you. They do.

DEALING WITH THE THREAT

As an American peace officer, your safety is threatened by terrorists, foreign and domestic. While terrorism should by no means be your *greatest* worry as you go about your peacekeeping tasks, you should nevertheless be aware that the terrorist's threat is real whether you work in the big city, a suburban community or rural America. But as with every other threat you may encounter on the job, the personal risks can be minimized by your application of a few, sound officer safety and survival practices. Consider the following as a starting point for your terrorist survival regimen.

Know the Opposition. Stay abreast of law enforcement intelligence pertinent to your geographic location concerning which violence-prone extremist groups may be active in your area. Police professional publications often can provide you with some background information on identities and activities of the more well-known groups and causes. Even staying up to date with the TV news and newspapers often can tell you a lot about who's out there and what they are upset about.

Do not neglect your "current events" knowledge. What are the issues of the day and who has said what that sounds potentially threatening? Is there well-organized opposition? Are they believed to be armed and are they known to practice or advocate violence? Perhaps most importantly, do these groups or individuals reside or have meeting or training facilities in your jurisdiction? Information can mean safety. You cannot have too much of either where potential terrorists are concerned. Naturally, complaining about the state of the world in general and the government in particular does not constitute a crime. We all do it. Advocating or carrying out violence to "solve" the complaints *does* constitute unlawful behavior. Stay current and increase your safety margin.

Recognize the Terrorist on "Routine" Crime Scenes. Terrorists don't restrict their unlawful activities to blowing things up and assassinating their enemies. Terrorists and would-be terrorists sometimes get drunk, beat their girlfriends and get into beefs with their neighbors, too. In some cases, they may steal cars or commit armed robberies to finance their terroristic operations. They also may engage in thefts and burglaries to supply themselves with weapons, explosives, communication gear and other items. Watch for evidence (publications, automatic weapons, oral statements, etc.) that the person you are in contact with may be more than a "plain vanilla" crook, and guard yourself accordingly.

Look for the Warning Signs. In all of your contacts, keep your senses attuned for an indication that you may be involved with one or more members of a terroristic group, or at least one of their sympathizers. Look for things like:

• Unexplained, unusual or illegal weapons or ammunition. Unusual quantities of ammunition or any explosive components at all also could signal danger. Further inquiry would be advisable.

• Immediate and intense hostility to you as a "government agent." Lots of people do not particularly love law enforcement officers, but extreme and very verbal opposition could tell you of extra trouble ahead. Don't hesitate to get assistance. Then, really *listen* to what is being said. He may tell you more than he intends about just why he doesn't like you, and what he plans to do about it. Don't unnecessarily provoke him, but do let him talk. You could learn a lot of value.

• Hate literature or anti-government propaganda, perhaps present in quantity in a home, business or vehicle you may encounter. Putting your far-out opinions into mass circulation is not, of course, a crime. Advocating violence very well may be.

• A "bunker" mentality evident in a subject you have contacted. He could be merely mentally unstable, or he may be a member of an extremist group willing to visit violence on its perceived enemies. (He could be both.) Again, listen to what he has to say. Encourage him to talk, but realize you are unlikely to win a debate with him. Just listen.

• Refusal to display a license plate or a driver's license. Neither makes him a terrorist, but some violence-prone, far right-wing groups do deny government's authority to require either of these. Have a backup present when dealing with these individuals. In a traffic stop situation, bumper stickers or signs on the vehicle may give you early warning of a potential problem ahead, too.

Remember: dissent from prevailing opinions and "politically correct" views do not make anyone a terrorist. Carrying dissent into planned or actual criminal acts is a whole different matter.

Expect "Unusual" Tactics. A dyed-in-the-wool terrorist whom you contact may not respond to you like an "ordinary" criminal. He may be wearing body armor. He may be particularly heavily armed. He may be in possession of explosive devices, including military ordnance—like hand grenades. He may demonstrate knowledge of police or military tactics and attempt to apply them in confronting you. He may, in a few words, be an especially dangerous threat to take on alone. Get help on the way fast if you have any inkling you are dealing with a member or members of a terroristic group.

Also be aware that the true-blue terrorist may display a very different mindset from most of the lawbreakers you encounter. He may have done more than practice maneuvers in the bush. He also may have determined that, like you, he is going to win any encounter with an opposing force. To him, that force may be any of the agents of a government he sees as corrupt and evil. He may even be willing to die for a cause he believes in. And that makes him a very dangerous threat indeed. Do not take chances in handling the danger he represents.

Practice Good Survival Skills. The same, basic safety practices that serve you well in handling other threats to your continued well-being will work on the terrorist, too. Watch for the danger signs, make no unsafe assumptions, get necessary assistance and rely on the tactics and techniques you have trained in and practiced as you confront a terroristic threat of any sort. Don't get sloppy or allow bad habits and shortcuts to get you into trouble. Stay sharp and observant as you expect the unexpected. You just may meet it.

TERRORISTIC BOMBINGS

Bombs seem to be the favorite weapon of terrorists the world over. America's home-grown and foreign-origin terrorists do not appear to pose an exception to the rule. Chapter Three discusses some precautions you must take in dealing with possible explosive devices belonging to *any* criminal, whether plain crook or wild-eyed zealot. The key is for you to remain alert to the *potential* of a terrorist's explosives attack at any time and place, no matter how unlikely. You already know that law enforcement facilities and vehicles make attractive targets for would-be terrorists of all stripes. Realize that individual law enforcement officers can become targets of hate groups, too. In exchange for arresting or even ticketing a violence-willing fanatic you could find yourself the recipient of a threatening letter—or a letter bomb. It's happened before.

Bombings attributed to terroristic groups and individuals are clearly on the upswing in the United States today. There is no reason to believe that the trend will not continue into the immediate future. While federal law enforcement officers and offices have caught the brunt of the terrorist's ire of late, state and local officers should take little comfort in the fact. The average terrorist's mind would appear to discriminate very little among the authority figures of his focused hatred. It is no secret that some of the most extreme voices of domestic terrorism have called for the "neutralizing" of all agents of law enforcement. Bombs remain a potential and popular means to that end.

SUMMARY

If you are a law enforcement officer serving anywhere in America today, you are at risk, however small that risk may be, from terrorists and terrorism. The terrorists, foreign or domestic, remain small in number, as do the extremist organizations that attract them. On average, you certainly have a much better chance of being hurt by a "plain vanilla" robber or burglar than a race-hater or anti-government fanatic. But the danger exists, all the same. The threat is real.

You cancel or control the dangers of terrorism by practicing virtually the same officer safety tactics and techniques you rely on to shield you from the other hazards of your potentially risky profession. Practice them religiously and without exception. If your antagonist turns out to be nothing worse than a loud-mouthed fanatic, you've lost nothing from your application of extra caution. If he (or she) turns out to be something much more dangerous, you may well have saved your own life.

STREET SURVIVAL CHECKLIST FOR TERRORISTIC THREATS

1. Know which terrorist groups or individual members, domestic or otherwise, may be active in your area.
2. Realize that you may encounter a heavily-armed member of a terrorist group involved in a "regular" crime, such as a traffic offense, shoplifting or check kiting.
3. Stay current on the tactics and operations of known terrorist groups, such as entrapment bombings, sniper attacks or ambushes.
4. Watch for the warning signs that you may be dealing with a terrorist organization or individual: bulk quantities of violence-inspiring hate literature, unexplained and unusual amounts of heavy weapons or ammunition, or a "bunker" mentality accompanied by verbal threats.
5. Expect the possibility of unusual tactics from a terroristic individual or group, such as the wearing of body armor or the possession of explosives.
6. Recognize that an extremist may attempt to curry favor with you or even seek to get you to join his organization.

Chapter Eighteen

SURVIVING THE "OTHER DANGERS" OF THE JOB

In the West, a 33-year-old patrolman was killed by a narcotics offense suspect. The officer and his partner attempted to contact the man at a hotel room. A female opened the door and the subject was observed lying on a bed. The man, instructed by the victim officer to show his hands, produced a .380-caliber handgun and shot the officer in the head. The man fled after wounding the second officer in an exchange of gunfire. He later shot himself to death after being surrounded and wounded by a SWAT team.

A 20-year veteran West Coast officer was killed at about 2:30 A.M. after he stopped his marked car to assist a man seen working on a vehicle. The officer obtained the subject's driver's license and was examining it when the man produced a 9mm handgun from under his car seat. The officer, spotting the weapon, grabbed the man but was shot fatally in the head and chest. The assailant, arrested later, was found to be wanted for armed robbery and shooting at an officer in another city.

Two officers died in an incident that began around 7 A.M. in a northern city. The first officer died after requesting identification from an adult male he found sleeping in a car in a church parking lot. The officer was shot multiple times with a .38-caliber handgun as he was returning to his vehicle to run a "wants" check. The man then approached the fallen officer, shot him in the head and took his sidearm. Several hours later, a K-9 handler and his dog were shot to death while tracking the murderer through a wooded area. They were slain with the first officer's .40-caliber semiautomatic handgun. Captured later, the 26-year-old killer was determined to be an armed services veteran schooled in military tactics and the use of firearms.

It is tragic enough when a law enforcement officer dies at the hands of a cold-blooded criminal. The calamity seems somehow worse when an officer dies because of his own carelessness or reckless behavior. In too many cases, however, that is exactly what happens: a law enforcement practitioner dies or is seriously injured *accidentally* because of his or her own behavior. There are additional dangers out there, too. Failing to maintain physical and mental health can kill. So can acting courageously but inadvisedly at the scene of a fire or hazardous materials incident. Acting responsibly and surviving those "other dangers" of the job is vital to the continuing safety of every law enforcement officer. That's what this chapter is all about.

ACCIDENT CASUALTIES

In the example year of 1994, the FBI Uniform Crime Reports Section advised that 62 officers lost their lives due to accidents that occurred while they were performing their official duties. The big killers, as usual, were automobile, motorcycle and aircraft accidents, which claimed the lives of 50 law enforcement officers. Another seven were accidentally hit by vehicles. Two officers were fatally shot by accident and three were killed in other kinds of mishaps, including falls and drownings.

Over the ten-year period of 1985-1994, some 673 officers were killed in on-duty accidents of all kinds. A review of the particulars of these accidents confirms what common sense should have already told you: in more than a few cases, just a moment's inattention resulted in tragedy for the law enforcement employee guilty of the transgression. A typical example is seen in the officer who was trying to do too many additional things (use the radio, use the mobile data terminal, write on a pad, etc.) while driving a police vehicle, perhaps at moderate to high speed. Another classic tragedy is seen in the not-uncommon story of the police person who was cleaning a firearm with only half of his or her brain engaged. Too often, the results are as predictable as they are bloody.

Think safety even when bad guys are not in the immediate picture. Keep your undivided attention on what you are doing the *whole* time that you are involved with things that could harm you. It's the very best way to stay out of the emergency room—or the morgue.

Since so many officers come to accidental harm from motor vehicles on an annual basis, it's clear that additional attention needs to be devoted to safety education in this area of the law enforcement officer's activities. Police academies and inservice courses alike need to do more. In the meantime, you may want to consider the following tips for staying safe while utilizing one of the most important but potentially the most dangerous tools of your profession:

• Do a thorough safety pre-trip of your vehicle before you hit the street. Be sure the lights, horn, brakes and emergency equipment are working properly. Check the tires for proper inflation and uneven or excessive wear. Don't take out a defective vehicle. Deadline it for repair.

• Always wear your lap and shoulder belts while the vehicle is in motion. Not only do they help protect you (with a deployed air bag) in a collision, they also may help reduce driving fatigue by helping you stay properly positioned behind the wheel. They also can keep you in place during the extreme driving maneuvers than can arise without warning during a tour of duty.

• Don't drive if you are sleepy, ill or taking medication that can make you drowsy. It's simply too dangerous.

• Get in the habit of talking to your passenger or partner without taking your eyes off of the road to look at him. Any distraction from your primary duty of the moment could prove disastrous.

• Reduce your speed accordingly for bad weather and poor driving conditions, such as rain, snow or fog. At night , slow down and do not overdrive the "seeing" distance of your headlights.

• Use extra caution while backing. A lot of patrol car accidents occur while the vehicle is moving in reverse.

• During an emergency run, do not pass another emergency vehicle that is in motion unless you have radio contact with that vehicle's driver and your action is anticipated.

• Look well down the road for potential hazards. Slow up and prepare to stop or evade if pedestrians, intersecting traffic or oddly-behaving vehicles are noted.

• Particularly if you are alone and working a very quiet tour, get out of your vehicle and walk around from time to time. (It's a great way to check buildings or make community policing contacts.) These mini-breaks from driving can greatly increase your level of alertness when you do get back on the road.

• Try to stay out of another driver's blind spots. If you cannot see his face, either directly or via his mirrors, he may not be able to see you, either.

• As noted, do not get distracted by what you are doing inside a moving vehicle besides driving. Don't get too focused on a "police problem" outside, either. Bring the car to a safe stop first and then look to your heart's content.

• Follow all of your jurisdiction's laws and your agency's rules for making an emergency or Code 3 run. You help no one and only aggravate the situation if you crash instead of getting there. Keep your emergency equipment operating. Slow to a near-stop or pause before "busting" an intersection where traffic signals are against you. Watch and wait for all traffic to yield. And never follow another emergency vehicle closely through an intersection. Motorists may still be watching the lead vehicle and move right into your path without ever detecting your presence.

• If a crash is imminent, attempt to steer your vehicle to avoid a headon collision or one that results in your being hit in the driver's door. Although there is no "good" place to be struck, towards the right rear side of your car is probably preferable to some other possibilities if you are alone in the vehicle. Obviously, however, the key is to drive defensively so that you are not hit at all!

PHYSICAL AND MENTAL HEALTH

This book's early pages discussed the importance of good physical and mental preparations for the difficult job of law enforcement. The mandate to take excellent care of yourself in all ways remains with you until retirement, and beyond. In addition to exercising, eating right and getting enough rest, you also must avoid the bad habits and harmful practices that can sometimes creep up after years on the job. If you are a veteran officer, you have seen at firsthand the human wreckage that can result from the abuse of alcohol and other drugs, including prescription medications. As a peace officer, you cannot afford to become like some of the pathetic figures you deal with day after day. For you, there can be no such thing as "recreational" drug use. For you, *any* use of *any* drug, including marijuana and cocaine, will do more than endanger your physical health. It also will render you susceptible to blackmail and seriously challenge your moral authority to continue in a law enforcement career. In other words, a moment's indiscretion can terminate a promising career. Job survival, like street survival, is too important to be risked by even occasional "no brains" conduct on your part.

You maintain your good mental and emotional health by *thinking* as well as *acting* responsibly. Taking personal responsibility for your continued mental health requires that you recognize and accept your very human limitations. You cannot personally solve every crime and right every wrong. There will still be victims and victimizers after you are long gone. What you can (and must) do is promise yourself to give your all and do the best you can on every call and contact, for every "customer" the job brings your way. That's all, but that's plenty.

You are your own best evaluator of your mental and emotional health. Monitor yourself for indications that you may be getting stressed out. Being over-stressed cannot only affect your physical health, it can detract from your focus on safety. *That* can affect your continued good health, too, not to mention that of those around you. Watch for such possible indicators of building personal trouble as:

1. Deep depression
2. Abrupt, radical mood swings
3. Inability to sleep; sleeping much more than normal
4. Constant tiredness; zero energy or interest
5. Abuse of sick leave
6. Abuse of alcohol or other drugs
7. Obsessive worry and constant anxiety
8. New tendency towards being accident prone
9. Dramatic increase in citizen complaints
10. Repeated nightmares
11. Repeated flashbacks to a traumatic event
12. Severe startle reactions
13. General listlessness; not caring about anything at all
14. Difficulty in concentrating or problem solving
15. Steady deterioration in work habits.

The presence of one or several of these caution flags could mean nothing—or serious emotional and mental problems straight ahead. It's up to you to do some thoughtful self-evaluation. What's going on? Have you recently been subjected to an emotionally traumatic incident, such as seeing death *too* closely? Or might you be feeling the cummulative effects of months or years of lower-level stress? Whatever the case, you may be able to help yourself via some personally-administered emotional first aid. Talk to others about what you are feeling. (Talk a lot!) Stay active and busy. Get enough sleep, if you can. Exercise to the point of getting really tired. Eat healthy, even if you're not hungry at meal times. Talk some more. Don't indulge in self-destructive behavior, like alcohol abuse. Be patient—you *will* feel better eventually. And talk some more. You are not going crazy. You are a *normal* human being reacting to *abnormal* circumstances. (It is not, for instance, *normal* for the average person to be regularly exposed to the risks and other conditions of your job.)

Give yourself some time. If you are still not feeling better after days have passed, get some professional help from a police psychologist or counselor. It's perfectly alright to do so. You would seek help if your belly was hurting badly and failed to respond to your own corrective efforts after a time. It's no different when the pain is in your head. You are too valuable to be lost to law enforcement. Do whatever you need to in order to make it better.

Staying alive and healthy on and off the job calls for you to take care of your physical and mental health. You'll have more energy. You'll be sharper. You'll probably have a better attitude about life in general. You'll work safer. You'll feel better overall. You'll produce a better work product. You may even experience an improved sex life! Whatever the case, taking care of yourself in *all* ways is one more part of surviving the challenges of the street.

FIRE RESCUES

You as a law enforcement practitioner are not equipped to engage in fire rescue operations. You have neither the protective clothing nor the self-contained breathing apparatus required to carry out a fire rescue in anything even resembling relative safety. Add to that your lack of the specialized fire rescue training that firefighters undergo and you have a situation ready-made for tragedy should you choose to enter a fiercely burning structure or vehicle without doing some really intense decision-making *first.*

The problem is that you as a professional feel obligated to do *something* when confronted by a conflagration and a bystander's cries of "There's someone inside!" You may feel duty-bound to act heroically.

Before you do, however, there are a few things you should think carefully about.

If you have arrived at the fire scene ahead of firefighters, you may be able to provide the best help simply by gathering information for the professionals. Be a top-notch observer. Find out everything you can from those already on-scene. Are there people believed trapped inside? How many and where, exactly, are they believed to be? Do the occupants have the ability to escape, that is, are they handicapped or otherwise unable to flee? How good is this information? Are they adults or children? Are there other things inside, like explosives or dangerous chemicals, that arriving firefighters should be warned of? Gather your data and pass it along promptly.

You may learn from bystanders or family members only that there *may* be people still inside. Again, how reliable is the information? Double check. Never, never enter a burning structure simply to do an exploratory search for *possible* trapped parties. It's too dangerous, particularly if firefighters are only moments away. Remain outside, try to keep others from entering and tell the professionals what you have learned.

Even if you know there are people still inside, do not enter a burning structure if your good common sense tells you that their chances for survival are virtually nil. This may be obvious to you from the intensity of the smoke, heat and flames or the proximity of the possible victims to the blaze. Adding yourself to the tally of victims helps no one.

If you are considering making entry into a fire and smoke-filled structure, realize that there are ways for you to die there besides being burned to death. Indeed, smoke, fumes and gases claim more victims than burns. One especially nasty danger for you is a condition known as a *backdraft*. It can develop when a fire, unable to get enough oxygen to burn freely, smolders inside a closed structure while smoke and fumes build up. Inside pressures may build to the point that doors and windows rattle and the roof or sides of the structure appear to pulse or "breathe." Smoke may seep out of cracks in the building and you may be able to detect a deep red glow instead of flames on the inside.

You must not enter a structure when a backdraft is developing. If you should open a door or smash a window, fire could erupt throughout the structure with explosive force, perhaps killing you in the process. Wait for the professionals on this one—it's safer for everyone.

Once you are inside a burning structure, you could face another critical threat to survival. It's called *flashover*, and it develops when virtually everything inside the place gets hot enough to ignite simultaneously. This condition in which fire erupts everywhere may be proceeded by warning signs of intense heat, free-burning fire and unburned articles starting to smoke. If you are inside or about to enter and observe these symptoms of pending disaster, get away quickly while there is still time to save yourself.

As noted, entering a burning structure without the proper equipment, training and support is not a great idea. But if you decide that the situation compels you to enter anyhow to attempt a rescue of human beings whom you *know* are present inside, consider the following suggestions that may improve your survival odds:

• Always let your dispatcher know that you are making entry–and where (ground level, north door). Take your portable radio with you. Tell any bystanders where you're going and what you are attempting to do. Ask them to pass this information on to arriving firefighters if you have not exited by that time.

• Before you open a door or window from the outside, first check it for heat with the back of your hand. Do not enter or even open a door or window if it has a hot surface–it's too dangerous. Look for another possible entry point. If you are convinced that it's not too hot to enter and that a backdraft situation is not present, step to the side as you open a door or smash a window. You don't want to get caught in the venting of heat, smoke and gases. If you do smash a glass, keep your hands and arms above the impact point to avoid injury from falling shards.

• If you do decide you can safely enter, once inside stay close to the floor, where it should be a little cooler and the smoke may be less thick. Be sure you have your flashlight with you. It may help you find your way or signal to others if you become lost or trapped inside. Note any "landmarks" to help you find your way back out. Keep an eye out for other exit possibilities.

• If you are faint, coughing or choking as soon as you enter, or if you note that the smoke and heat are almost unbearable, realize that conditions are unlikely to get better further inside. Crawl out before you pass out.

• Call out to any trapped victims to help you pinpoint their location. If you know a trapped child's name, use it. If you are engaged in a blind search for a child victim, know that frightened children may attempt to hide from a fire, and may seek shelter in a closet or under a bed. Try these places, if you can get to them. Do not linger too long in any one area; keep moving and get out as quickly as possible.

• Stay on the floor. If you find an unconscious victim, drag him along the floor by his legs, arms or clothing to get out of the building. Do not stand up and try to carry him—the heat and gases may get you.

• Remember that deadly carbon monoxide has been building up in your bloodstream the whole time you have been inside. Given time, it will render you unconscious and then kill you. If you cannot immediately exit the structure, smash a window and at least get your head and that of your victim out into fresh air as you await more help to extricate you both.

• Once you are able to turn your rescued victim over to medical care, remember to seek the same for yourself. Get some first aid oxygen on-scene and seriously consider going for an ambulance ride to get checked out at a hospital. Your actions may have had more internal repercussions than you suspect. Play it safe and find out if treatment is needed.

Know, too, that trying to perform a rescue at the scene of a vehicle fire could hurt or even kill you. Even if no dangerous "freight" or other dangerous contents are known to be on board, the gases produced by burning plastic, upholstery and other materials found in a vehicle's interior can prove fatal. Stay well away from any vehicle fully engulfed in flames—you also have exploding fuel tanks and tires to worry about. Bumpers on the newer vehicles are backed with "shock absorbers" that can explode outwards in a fire. If you do decide to try to remove victims from a vehicle that is less than fully involved in fire, do your rescuing from the *outside*. Smash a window or pry on a stuck door with gloved hands and pull any trapped victims you can reach through the opening you have made, but stay out of the vehicle itself, if you can. Airbags may deploy forcefully and without warning inside the passenger compartment and cause injury in a fire. Again, leave firefighting duties to the professionals.

Never forget: no one expects you to surrender your life in an ill-advised fire rescue effort. Use your good common sense and decision-making ability. Know that your chances of entering a fiercely burning building or vehicle and emerging unharmed are not good. Faced with that scenario, stay out and stay alive.

HAZMAT INCIDENTS

Today's world is full of potentially deadly chemicals and other materials. Most of them pose a danger to anyone attempting a hazardous materials rescue in an environment in which these threats have been set loose. Once again, that rescuer could be you. Your involvement in a hazardous materials incident could come when you arrive at the scene of a truck transport accident where fuel or other combustibles are venting into the atmosphere or streaming down the roadway. It could come when you happen upon a leaking or burning railroad tank car while you are on patrol. It could occur when you face a scene of two dozen youngsters vomiting or unconscious at a municipal swimming pool where a chlorine tank has ruptured. Or it could come in a few hundred other ways. The point is, you feel *expected* to do *something* to help ease the crisis. The catch is to do what you can without becoming a victim yourself. So, what do you do?

Your first steps as a first responder are to call as much help as you think you might need (don't forget fire and medical), assess the situation you are facing and start gathering as much relevant information as you can, as quickly as you can. Someone on-scene who is connected with the involved material (a truck driver, train conductor, freight dock supervisor, plant operator, etc.) should be your best source of data, should he be accessible to you. If not, in a transportation accident seek out shipping papers that should be carried in the truck or locomotive cab, if you can safely reach them. (Never endanger yourself in a search for paperwork.) If you can get them, these manifests will often identify dangerous materials carried as well as provide basic precautionary information about them and their handling.

Look for signs or placards on the vehicle or materials container that also may tell you what you are confronting. Hazardous materials frequently are labelled with United Nations or I.D. numbers keyed to an *Emergency Response Guidebook* published and updated by the U.S. Department of Transportation. (The books are available from the Office of Hazardous Materials Transportation, U.S. Department of Transportation, Washington, D.C. 20590.) If you can get the name or I.D. number of the hazardous material you are dealing with, you should find it cross-referenced in the handbook as to the dangers you are facing and what precautionary measures you should take.

If you are able to learn what materials you are dealing with, you can then take advantage of another hazmat resource. CHEMTREC, a 24-hour information hotline for emergency responders staffed by representatives of the Chemical Manufacturers Association, can provide you with additional precautionary advice for safely responding to an incident. CHEMTREC can be reached at 1-800-424-9300. In order to get the most use out of this service to help protect yourself and others, when you call (someone with direct, on-scene knowledge should make the connection), be prepared to tell the CHEMTREC operator:
• Your name, agency and callback telephone number
• Nature of the incident
• I.D. or U.N. number of the involved products, if known
• Name of the manufacturer or shipper
• Container or transport type (box, tank car, tractor trailer rig, pipeline, aircraft, etc.)
• Rail car or truck number, if known
• Carrier name (Ex: Joe's Truck Line)
• Consignee name
• Local weather conditions
• What is happening currently (fire, explosion, vapor cloud, liquid leak, etc.)

Pass along what you have learned to your assist units and begin actions to defuse the danger without putting additional people in harm's way. As in the case of a fire rescue, do not deliberately place yourself in an environment where you do not have the proper equipment and training to survive. Leave the rescuing to those equipped and prepared to handle it.

In addition to any specific instructions and precautionary information you may receive, consider the following, general guidelines for protecting yourself and others on the scene of a hazmat incident:
• Approach the scene from upwind. If you are dealing with a spilled liquid, park your car uphill from it. Don't drive or walk through spilled product.
• Move everyone away from the scene and isolate it. Get as much assistance as you need to help you. Follow the D.O.T. handbook's guidelines for evacuation distances. Realize that a change in the weather conditions or the scale of the incident itself may require you to enlarge the evacuation area.

• Do not assume that clouds of gases or smoke are harmless just because they do not have a powerful smell or sicken you immediately. Avoid them until you are told by experts that they are "safe."

• With help, formulate a plan of attack to resolve the danger. Keep gathering information and share it with assisting officers and agencies. Appoint an overall incident commander with supporting personnel, including hazmat experts.

• Do not try to handle the actual cleanup of the spill by yourself. That, too, is a job for specially trained and equipped people.

• Do not expose yourself to smoke coming from a fire involving known or suspected hazardous materials. Do not attempt to fight a fire yourself if it has neared or reached a container or other area containing hazardous materials. Get yourself and everyone else away.

• Do not put water on a fire involving unknown chemicals. You could end up with a fatal explosion if you pour water on such burning materials as sodium, potassium or lithium. Watch for "Keep Water Away" warnings on containers or shipping papers.

• Avoid smoking, eating or drinking in the area of a hazmat incident. Any of these amounts to a great way to get dangerous contaminants into your body. Get well away and wash up thoroughly, first.

• If you think that your clothing may have been contaminated at the scene of a hazardous materials incident, remove all of your outer garments and your leather gear as soon as possible. Leave these items to be "packaged" at the scene—don't take contamination home with you. Don't forget to shed shoes and socks, some of the most often-contaminated items. Then wash yourself down thoroughly and monitor yourself for any injuries or ill effects. Seek treatment right away if anything out of the ordinary develops.

• Remember that biological agents and radioactive materials also can be involved in a hazmat incident. They can be lethal, too. Watch for placards or warning signs indicating their presence. Realize that there probably will be nothing to "see" of the danger. Isolate a big area around these special hazards and call in specialized help.

A particularly dangerous fire-hazmat situation you may confront in your law enforcement duties is known as a BLEVE. That's short for boiling liquid expanding vapor explosion, a catastrophe than can result in a fireball as big as hundreds of feet in diameter that destroys everything in its path. BLEVEs have killed or injured scores of firefighters and other rescuers over the years, and they remain a threat today.

A BLEVE can occur anytime a fire or extreme heat causes the failure of a tank or other vessel containing liquified gas, such as propane, under pressure. The resulting, flaming explosion can throw fire and debris for several city blocks if a large container is involved. Even a BLEVE of a propane container of the size used with backyard barbeque grills can kill or maim you if you are close enough when it detonates.

The best solution for the dangers caused by BLEVEs? In a word, *distance.* Get yourself and others well away from the scene of a leak or fire in a gas storage container, particularly where liquified gas under pressure is known to be involved. Once again, leave the leak-stopping, firefighting and rescuing to the professionals. Your primary duties are to gather information, communicate, evacuate and otherwise protect the public and yourself. Peace officers have died in hazmat incidents. You do not want to be the next victim.

WATER RESCUES

Several thousand people drown every year in this country. Many others would die in a similar fashion if not for the timely intervention of rescuers. As a law enforcement officer you could be called upon at any time to perform a water rescue. How you respond will have a great deal to do with whether or not the victim and you *both* stay alive. It is not rare for a would-be rescuer to lose his or her own life in an ill-advised water rescue attempt.

Water rescues can prove very hazardous for some of the same reasons that got the original victim in trouble: undercurrents, fast-moving water, underwater obstacles and panic. In his panic, a victim may well pull his rescuer under. A drowning candidate sometimes gets into trouble because he overestimates his ability as a swimmer. So might a rescuer. A victim sometimes invites disaster by diving into unfamiliar waters, striking his head underwater and going unconscious. So might an unwary rescuer. In addition, a swimmer on occasion suffers severe muscle cramps, becomes exhausted from his self-rescue efforts or edges into the effects of hypothermia from frigid waters. All of these problems could befall a well-meaning but unprepared rescuer, too. It is worth stating yet again: You help no one and only aggravate the situation if you become a victim yourself. But how do you avoid victim status while carrying out your sworn promise to help those in distress?

First, follow the "prime directive" of water rescues: *whenever possible throw, don't go*. Stay out of the water and extend something for the victim to grab onto while you keep yourself firmly attached to dry land. Use whatever is at hand and is long enough for the circumstances: a nightstick, tree branch, oar, swimming pool skimmer, garden hose, or whatever. Use your free hand to stay firmly anchored so that you do not go into deep water yourself. Reel in your "catch" until you can grab him firmly. You might consider lying flat on your stomach on the ground at this point so that you do not lose your balance and get pulled in.

If you have to wade towards a victim in trouble to get close enough to help him, remove any heavy items of clothing or equipment that may pull you down if you get in over your head. That includes boots and heavy jackets and utility belts. Check the footing ahead of you by feeling for the bottom with an outstretched foot before you shift your balance in that direction. If it is possible, it remains vital for you to hold onto something attached to the shore for safety's sake.

If you can't reach a water victim from dry land, consider shoving a flotation device of some sort towards him. That could include anything from a rowboat to a plank. That should give him something to hold onto until more help can arrive. And speaking of help: Do not start any water rescue effort until you have told your dispatcher what you are up to and gotten help on the way. Emergency medical help is a must. Even if your rescue effort is successful, your victim likely will need checked out for injuries, hypothermia or water ingestion. You might, also.

Swimming rescues of water victims are a dangerous business and should only be attempted by those properly equipped (that means a life jacket, for instance) and trained in carrying them out, perhaps against the violent stuggles of a terrified victim. Do not attempt a swimming rescue in rapidly-moving water or water over your head unless you are an accomplished water rescuer. Even then, enter the water yourself only after other, out-of-the-water rescue measures— extending an item, pushing out a flotation device, etc.–have failed. Swimming rescues can be risky even for highly-trained water rescuers who are excellent swimmers.

If you still *must* make a swimming rescue effort, know that you probably are dealing with a panicked, struggling victim who may grasp and claw at you or try and climb atop your body, pushing you under in the process. Your safest approach may be from behind a struggling victim where you can grab him by the clothing or hair and pull him along face-up behind you as you head for drier territory. In the process you try to stay out of his flailing grasp.

But remember: In the long run, you may be the most help to emergency responders properly equipped to handle a drowning by staying on dry land and gathering information instead of plunging into unknown danger yourself. You can also help a great deal by locating witnesses who can state exactly where a victim went down or was last seen. Passed along to professionals, this information can greatly narrow the underwater area that must be searched. A quickly-successful search may locate an underwater victim who can still be saved via prompt resuscitation efforts.

One more variety of water rescue deserves mention for the special danger it may entail for the rescuer. If you work in a climate where bodies of water freeze and thaw at some time during the cold weather months, you may one day be first on a scene where someone has fallen through the ice and is floundering in frigid water. This is clearly a life-threatening situation demanding intervention, but once again you do not want to compound the problem by needing rescued yourself. Once more, call for properly-equipped help before you do anything else. Enlist some already on-scene assistance, if available. Firefighters sometimes extend ladders lying flat on the ice for victims to grab. Since it's unlikely you will have one readily available, you will have to rely on whatever reaching device that might be at hand to extend to a fallen-through subject. A branch, oar, rope or whatever else is handy may have to suffice. If you *must* go out on the ice to extend something to a victim, don't walk but crawl out on your stomach, lying as flat as possible to spread your weight. Move slowly, and try to pull your party onto the ice with you as you inch backwards. Back off if the ice begins to break under you. Once you get a victim to safe ground, followup with emergency medical aid for hypothermia and other possible problems for you both. But where ice rescues are concerned, remain mindful that the same principle holds true as with any other sort of rescue from a watery environment: Throw, don't go, if at all possible. It's much safer that way.

SUMMARY

There are more than a few risky aspects of your job. There are also a lot more ways to come to harm than from a gunman's bullets. Fortunately, you can overcome these additional dangers just as effectively as you meet the criminal offender's threats. What it takes to do so is paying careful attention to your environment and the risks it may contain at any given moment. Operate your police vehicle with caution and awareness for what is happening around you. Take good care of yourself, physically, mentally and emotionally. Realize that you can be killed or injured by a moment's carelessness around equipment, ranging from your car to your firearms. Realize, too, that performing a rescue at the scene of a fire, water, hazmat or other incident can prove injurious or even fatal to you if you elect to act without the necessary planning, equipment, training and competent assistance. Think about that before you commit to action. If you do elect to intervene, do it with a plan and a set of objectives that helps minimize your exposure to danger. By responding to these "other" hazards of your job as carefully as you react to the offender-caused dangers of the street you reduce your risk-taking even as you responsibly serve your community.

STREET SURVIVAL CHECKLIST FOR THE "OTHER DANGERS" OF YOUR JOB

1. Practice good defensive driving skills at all times. Pay attention to what you are doing on the road. Motor vehicle accidents kill many officers every year.
2. Practice safe weapon handling procedures. Consider *all* weapons to be loaded *all* of the time.
3. Take excellent care of yourself physically, mentally and emotionally. Do not allow self-destructive behaviors of *any* kind to sneak into your life. *Talk* about what's bothering you.
4. Do not attempt a fire, water or hazmat rescue when your good judgment tells you that there is a very poor chance for success or personal survival. You only aggravate the situation if you become a victim yourself.

5. Do not enter any highly-risky environment just to do an exploratory search for "possible" victims. Have clearcut objectives in sight before you commit yourself.

6. Do not enter a dangerous environment at all when there are other means for accomplishing the rescue. Example: throwing a line to someone in the water is better than plunging in over your head.

7. Unless you have all of the equipment required for a rescue in a potentially deadly environment, you may be able to contribute the most by summoning properly-equipped rescuers and gathering pertinent information to be relayed upon their arrival. In other words, do not overreach your abilities.

Chapter Nineteen

MANAGEMENT'S ROLE IN OFFICER SAFETY

In a southern city, a 31-year-old patrolman was killed by a 15-year-old curfew violator. The officer had transported the youth as well as a 13-year-old male to the area of their homes so he could contact their parents. The officer removed the handcuffs from each boy and was checking the back seat of his cruiser when the 15-year-old got behind him and shot the officer in the back of the head with a .22-caliber handgun he had hidden on his person. The subject then took the downed officer's service weapon before fleeing.

In the South, a 26-year-old patrolman stopped a suspicious vehicle without notifying his dispatcher of his actions or location. Approaching the car, the officer ordered the male driver out. The subject immediately began firing a 9mm handgun from inside the vehicle, striking the officer with several rounds. Before falling, the officer returned fire and wounded his attacker. The subject then approached the fallen officer and shot him in the head. Responding help found both men dead.

Once again in the South, a sheriff's deputy was killed in a 3:45 A.M. traffic stop. The officer had stopped a car stolen during an armed robbery in another state. A trooper sent as a backup found the deputy dead from nine wounds from a 9mm handgun taken from an officer murdered earlier in a nearby state. In that killing, a patrolman was shot to death inside a convenience store after walking in on a robbery in progress that also resulted in the murder of a woman clerk. The 23-year-old assailant later shot two more people before killing himself.

Few would argue that the primary responsibility for a law enforcement officer's survival rests inescapably with the officer himself. Ultimately, that key responsibility cannot be shifted elsewhere. At the same time, the agency employing the officer as well as its managers cannot escape sharing in accountability for the organizational environment in which law enforcement officers confront danger on a daily basis. The department and its leaders can do a great deal to encourage and build an atmosphere of *expected* safe practices in which officers can work. On the other hand, that same organization can adopt a largely disinterested "official" posture towards the safety practices or lack thereof engaged in by its people. Not surprisingly, that agency posture will almost certainly be reflected in the casualty rates among first-line law enforcement personnel.

DEPARTMENT ATMOSPHERE

A law enforcement agency helps its officers survive the dangers of the street when it establishes, updates and enforces policies, procedures and rules that spell out expectations about safe practices. The agency may, for example, have and enforce the reasonable requirement that all street officers must wear body armor on the job, or that all disturbance calls require no less than two officers be dispatched to handle the problem. Policies may specify how and how often firearms, police vehicles and other equipment must be inspected.

Establishing an agency-wide *expectation* for safety requires that leaders from the sheriff or chief down through the watch commanders to the street sergeants emphasize safety in their own activities–and expect the same of their employees. It is not enough that the boss *says* that he or she expects subordinates to operate in a safety-smart manner. The leader must role-model safety in his or her own, daily actions.

It's no secret that a careful analysis of the anecdotes and statistics published annually in the FBI's *Law Enforcement Officers Killed and Assaulted* reports reveals the same, basic officer errors and shortcomings resulting in carnage year after year. It is those very same problems that the agency cannot afford to tolerate without repair. An agency-wide atmosphere of carelessness and neglect permitted to exist by the leadership will almost surely result in eventual tragedy for the officers allowed to participate in it. When that tragedy happens, the leaders who allowed the sorry state of affairs to continue will share the heavy burden of explaining "Why?"

By the same token, a safety-first atmosphere lead by management and reinforced by peer pressure from first-line officers and supervisors will reduce the likelihood of basic officer safety and survival errors culminating in disaster. In such a safety-conscious environment, the officers themselves will set the tone for the street and perhaps even "unofficially" censure unsafe behavior by their colleagues. With the possible exception of supervisory personnel, peer pressure probably is the most powerful force of all for assuring that peace officers work and think safely. This piece of the officer survival picture absolutely must be in place or the whole thing will collapse in unsafe behavior with its attendant, potentially disastrous consequences.

FIRST-LINE SUPERVISION

Safe, effective sergeants and other first-line supervisors lead by example. They *know* what to do to defuse or mitigate a hazardous situation, and they set a good example for their troops via their own, safe behavior. Effective supervisors also perform spot checks and inspections of their officers' field work in order to praise and reward appropriately safe behavior and identify for correction unsafe practices and poor survival habits. The supervisor's obligations remain the same whether he is dealing with the fresh-from-the-academy rookie or the grizzled old salt. Granted, calling the latter's attention to his errors and then getting him to fix them generally will be the tougher of the tasks, but it must nevertheless be carried out effectively. The annual reports of officers killed carry too many examples of murdered *veteran* cops for anything less to work. The veteran's service stripes do not shield him from well-intentioned correction—or a cop killer's bullets.

The wise first-line supervisor uses both counselling and additional training for officers he identifies as safety-deficient in one aspect or several. Negative discipline must be applied for the unsafe employee who simply can't (or, more likely, won't) alter unsafe behaviors. It's not a pleasant task, but it is one the effective supervisor is duty-bound to perform without fear or favor. He just may save a cop's life in the process.

The honorable and effective supervisor must deal promptly and effectively with a particularly dangerous employee who, if left unchecked, can accomplish the sad end of himself as well as innocent peers. This character is the "cowboy" or "cowgirl" officer. This testosterone-overdosed individual may be trying to prove something to someone, perhaps himself. He routinely disregards established safety procedures, deliberately goes on hazardous calls without waiting for a backup and, perhaps, starts fights when an escalation to physical force is not the most logical option. He waves off assist units, ridicules officers who ask for help and in general behaves with foolhardy bravado.

If left uncorrected the "cowboy" cop can have a negative effect on impressionable rookies who are looking for a role model to emulate. The consequences can be disastrous for these yet-immature young officers. It is the first-line leader's responsibility to see to it that the out-of-control officer's unsafe behavior is reigned in promptly. Hopefully, the errant employee can be counselled as to the error of his ways and turned into a safe performer. If not, the first-line boss is obligated to recommend separation from the agency for an individual whose continued employment spells danger. The misfit's actions, if allowed to continue, are *that* dangerous to those who must work with him as well as to the citizens they serve.

The first-line supervisor must be trained by his organization to remain alert for the signs that one of his employees may be emotionally burned-out or mentally fatigued by the stresses of the job. This is particularly true following an employee's participation in a critical incident, such as an officer-involved shooting or a close, personal brush with serious injury or death. The sharp supervisor picks up these warning indicators of trouble ahead by maintaining an open, give-and-take relationship with each of his or her subordinates. Simply *talking* with his or her people on a regular basis is the key. The organization plays its role here by providing easy access to professional assistance or peer group counselling for employees in need of emotional support. The first-line supervisor must be able to refer his people for these services on a confidential basis and without resorting to a major exercise involving the law enforcement bureaucracy. As in so many areas, *easier* really is *better* for all concerned.

If a need for specialized help is not present, the smart supervisor just offers a patient, noncritical ear for the incident-stressed employee who wants to talk. An empathetic listener may be all a frustrated employee requires to return to a sense of being in control once more. Making that opportunity available is *always* worth the effort for supervisor and supervised alike.

TRAINING RESPONSIBILITIES

It is well-accepted that solid, proven officer safety tactics and techniques must be taught by competent, interested instructors in the law enforcement basic academy. Recruits must be drilled and tested on these survival guidelines until they become second nature. But survival training must not end upon graduation. Tactics and techniques change as new threats develop and old ones take on slightly new faces. Officers also can forget, get careless and develop bad habits if abandoned to their own devices. Continuing, mandatory inservice training for all enforcement personnel is a must if initially-safe officers are to maintain their survival edge throughout a career. This means that teachings and instructors must be kept up-to-date on the newest threats—and how to counter them. To help maintain a safety-sharp atmosphere throughout the law enforcement organization, annual survival schooling should include at least the following inservice classes:
- firearms safety and proficiency
- driving skills, including pursuit driving
- use of force law and policy
- arrest/control and defensive tactics
- vehicle contacts refresher.

Wherever possible, classroom work must be accompanied by hands-on, practiced exercises involving simulations of real-life threat scenarios. Law enforcement people are practical individuals who learn best when they are given the opportunity to apply lecture-based instruction in a realistic but controlled setting under the guidance of competent, patient teachers. Building search exercises, for example, are very well-suited to the practical application of "book knowledge" concerning officer safety.

One specialized area of training cries out for the very best an agency can do in the interest of officer safety. The field training of rookie officers fresh from the academy is vital to the success or failure of these new, sworn employees. It is here that lifelong good safety habits are learned—or not.

What is learned about safety in the classroom will be lost without constant reinforcement by an interested, careful field trainer who teaches by example at least as much as by telling. He is constantly on the lookout for unsafe behavior by his charge and corrects it prompt-

ly. The good FTO is a patient counselor and problem-solver. He is
innovative in applying his own experiences to help the trainee fix his
or her safety lapses. While training "his" new officer in the myriad
duties of his new profession, the sharp FTO never forgets one of the
primary tasks of his specialized, vital assignment: producing a new
officer who will carry out his various, complex and sometimes hazardous tasks with an unblinking eye on safety when no one is looking
over his shoulder and coaching him anymore.

The talented field training officer knows that he is being watched
(and emulated) by his trainee all the time. He also knows that this
means he cannot permit himself even a moment's lapse in his safety-
conscious behavior. As a result, the FTO thinks, talks and acts in safety. He maintains his personal safety equipment flawlessly and
demands the same of his trainee. He does not cut corners on safety tactics or techniques, nor does he tolerate safety laziness from his "pup."
He admits his own safety errors to his charge when he makes them,
and shows how they can be corrected. The ethical FTO knows that the
"Don't do as I do; do as I say do" approach to teaching safety is *never*
acceptable for him. He walks the walk as well as talks the talk when it
comes to field survival. The quick and easy way is out for him if it
means compromising safety, and he performs his work accordingly. If
he finds that he can no longer do it that way, he asks to be relieved of
his FTO assignment.

The realistic field trainer also knows that, in spite of his most earnest
efforts, on occasion a trainee may not be able to meet the safety expectations of the organization. Through no fault of the FTO or his
employer, the novice officer is just unable or unwilling to grasp the
value of officer safety and apply it appropriately to his new job.
However uncomfortable it may make him, the FTO is mandated to
recommend termination from employment of the rookie who poses a
potential threat to the safety of himself or others. The FTO is in the
best position in the law enforcement organization to know if the
trainee is making it in the area of officer safety. He is also best positioned to know if repeated counsellng and remedial training have
failed.

It is alright that the FTO feels disappointed and perhaps sad that
someone he probably has grown to like will not be continuing as a law
enforcement employee. But he should take comfort in knowing that
by his timely intervention he may literally be saving the life of that

same, unsafe trainee. By "doing the right thing," he also just may be preserving the life of a fellow officer, a citizen or even *himself.* It's a goal worth the considerable effort required to accomplish it.

EQUIPMENT RESPONSIBILITIES

Simply and directly put, the law enforcement agency and its leaders are responsible for furnishing front-line employees with the very best safety equipment money (and the agency budget) can provide. That holds true even if it means scrimping somewhere else in the annual budget battle with sometimes-just-don't-get-it politicians and bureaucrats.

True, a $5.95 flashlight purchased in bulk at the local discount store will furnish enough light to read a driver's license. But it may not do the trick one night in a dark warehouse or in an open field when spotting and illuminating the bad guy may mean the literal difference between life and death for a front-line law enforcer. At such a moment, the $100-plus, 30,000 candlepower handlight may pay off big-time in survival dividends. "Little" things like that are not lost on the troops. Neither should they be overlooked by management.

At the same time, the smart police leader realizes that the catalog item with the heftiest price tag and the glitziest whistles and bells is not guaranteed to be the most effective life-saving tool for the people in the trenches. Very low bid items should, of course, also be suspect. The sharp manager will involve front-line officers and supervisors in testing and choosing the agency's safety-related equipment. Included on the list for field testing by the troops should be vehicle light bars, body armor, restraint devices, vehicles, belt-carried items and firearms. The buy-in of these officers should be sought at purchase time and their opinions given careful consideration. These people are, after all, in the very best possible spot to see and know what works best and what falls short in the real world of officer survival.

With the obligation to secure the right equipment for the street goes the requirement that police leaders must assure that their people are properly and continuously trained with those tools in the right way. The most effective tool is little more than a paperweight in the hands of an unskilled employee. Equipment acquisition, maintenance and training are inescapably linked in the officer survival structure. The responsible law enforcement manager will see to it that each piece is in place.

"POLITICAL" RESPONSIBILITIES

The public in general and the news media in particular are extremely interested in and, not infrequently, critical of what law enforcement officers do and how they do it. This is especially true in the area of use of force, lethal or otherwise. The questions are well-known to the veteran police manager: Why do *all* arrestees have to be handcuffed? How about kids? Or women? Why did the officer pull a gun on a youngster (who just happened to have one himself)? Why is it necessary to send "the whole force" to a "simple family fight"? The list of queries can go on and on.

The law enforcement agency's brass must seize every opportunity to educate the public as to what the police *really* do, and why. This is especially true in the realm of measures taken to assure officer safety during contacts with the general public. Much of this information can be made available through proactive approaches to the news media as well as via prompt and open responses to reporters' questions about the agency and its activities. It also can be distributed via all kinds of speaking presentations before civic groups, political gatherings and legislative bodies. The "word" also gets spread, perhaps even more effectively, in one-on-one exchanges with influential citizens and community leaders. All of these means of communication the responsible leader will encourage without being asked.

By virtue of his or her position in the community, the law enforcement leader can educate the public about *what* officers do to protect themselves and *why* they must do it. Those same leaders must then defend their officers, as appropriate, when they offend sensibilities while carrying out practices that have safety and survival as their core reasons for existing. The officer who knows he will be backed up by his organization when he performs according to good faith, established safety tactics and procedures is likely to work in a safe manner. The officer who feels he will be abandoned when he does it the right way but in so doing generates a citizen complaint may well perform hesitantly, perhaps to his fatal detriment.

SUMMARY

A survival-smart patrol officer never stops looking for one more threat. An equally safety-conscious law enforcement manager never ceases looking for more ways and means to keep his or her officers alive on the job. The effective leader ensures safety by encouraging and nurturing an organizational environment where *all* hands, regardless of rank or assignment, are *expected* to practice as well as preach safety. That manager will require safety-conscious performance by first-line supervisors who are given the authority as well as the responsibility to assure safe practices by front-line employees. Likewise, the safety-smart leader will think and expect officer survival as a major consideration in all of the agency's operations involving training, equipment acquisition and public information and community liaison functions.

By helping control the job risks faced by his people, the law enforcement leader aids them in *working safer* while he simultaneously bolsters their personal satisfaction with a job well-done. It is a task worth doing well.

STREET SURVIVAL CHECKLIST FOR LAW ENFORCEMENT MANAGEMENT

1. Encourage an organizational environment where safety is valued, expected, taught and practiced.
2. Require that the all-important first-line supervisors of the agency model, inspect, reward and correct for safety.
3. Assure that inservice as well as entry-level training covers proven, effective officer safety tactics and techniques.
4. Assure that the agency's equipment is properly used and is the best available for the safety purposes for which it is intended.
5. Managers must serve as personal advocates for officer safety and must role-model safety in their own actions, attitudes and words.
6. Managers must without exception support, explain and, if necessary, defend the proper, good faith safety practices of their employees.
7. If you are (or aspire to be) a first-line supervisor, you have an added obligation to help bring about the safe performance of the

officers placed in your care. There is no more important job in law enforcement.

ADDITIONAL OFFICER SURVIVAL READING

Adams, Ronald J., Thomas McTernan & Charles Remsberg. *Street survival.* Northbrook, IL: Calibre Press, 1980.

Albrecht, Steven, & John Morrison. *Contact and cover.* Springfield, IL: Charles C Thomas Publisher, 1992.

Brodie, Thomas G., *Bombs and bombings.* Springfield, IL: Charles C Thomas Publisher, 1995.

Brooks, Pierce R. "*Officer down, code three.*" Northbrook, IL: Motorola Teleprograms, 1975.

Cane, Andries C. *Basic arrest and prisoner control tactics.* Springfield, IL: Charles C Thomas Publisher, 1989.

Cheek, John C. & Tony Lesce. *Plainclothes and off-duty officer survival.* Springfield, IL: Charles C Thomas Publisher, 1988.

Clede, B. *Police handgun manual: how to get street-smart survival habits.* Harrisburg, PA: Stackpole Books, 1985.

Davis, James M. *Raids.* Springfield, IL: Charles C Thomas Publisher, 1982.

Downey, Robert J. & Jordan T. Roth. *Weapon retention techniques for officer survival.* Springfield, IL: Charles C Thomas Publisher, 1981.

Garner, Gerald W. *High-risk patrol.* Springfield, IL: Charles C Thomas Publisher, 1990.

Garner, Gerald W. *The police role in alcohol-related crises.* Springfield, IL: Charles C Thomas Publisher, 1979.

Johan, Sara Lee. *Domestic abusers.* Springfield, IL: Charles C Thomas Publisher, 1994.

Jones, Clarence E. *After the smoke clears—surviving the police shooting.* Springfield, IL: Charles C Thomas Publisher, 1989.

Kalinich, David B. & Terry Pitcher. *Surviving in corrections.* Springfield, IL: Charles C Thomas Publisher, 1984.

Meyer, C. Kenneth, Thomas C. Magendanz, Steven H. Feimer, Samuel G. Chapman & William J. Pammer, Jr. *Ambush-related assaults on police.* Springfield, IL: Charles C Thomas Publisher, 1986.

Mullins, Wayman C. *Terrorist organizations in the united states.* Springfield, IL: Charles C Thomas Publisher, 1988.

Reintzell, John F. T*he police officer's guide to survival, health and fitness.* Springfield, IL: Charles C Thomas Publisher, 1990.

Remsberg, Charles. *The tactical edge.* Northbrook, IL: Calibre Press, 1986.

The best of the police marksman, Connie Dees, editor. Montgomery, AL: The Police Marksman Association, 1994.

INDEX

V

Violator, 71
Violence, domestic, 139-140, 146-147
Vision, peripheral, 73

W

Warning signs, terroristic, 240-241
Warrants, 189-191, 203
Weapon retention, 8, 34, 92-93, 133
Weapons, 67, 106
  edged, 38-39
  pointed, 38-39
"Winner's attitude," 16-17
Withdrawal, tactical, 37, 72-73
Work, off-duty, 228-230
Wounds, head, 98-99

Z

ZOG, 236